The Future of Labour Law

Edited by
AILEEN McCOLGAN

CASSELL

First published 1996 by
Pinter, *A Cassell imprint*
Wellington House, 125 Strand, London WC2R 0BB, England
215 Park Avenue South, New York, New York 10003, USA

British Library Cataloguing in Publication Data
A catalogue record for this book is available from the British Library.
ISBN 1-85567-405-X.

Library of Congress Cataloging-in-Publication Data
The future of labour law/edited by Aileen McColgan.
      p.   cm.
    Includes bibliographical references and index.
    ISBN 1-85567-405-X
    1. Labor laws and legislation–Great Britain. 2. Industrial relations–Great Britain. 3. Law reform–Great Britain.
    KD3009.A2F87 1996
    344.41'01–dc20
    [344.1041]   95-52249
                                                                     CIP

Typeset by BookEns Ltd, Royston, Herts.
Printed and bound in Great Britain by Biddles Ltd,
Guildford and King's Lynn

Contents

iv   *Contents*

The Contributors

Matthias Beck, Lecturer in Economics, University of St Andrews
Damian Brown, Barrister, Gray's Inn
K. D. Ewing, Professor of Public Law, King's College, University of London
Michael Ford, Tutor in Law, Birkbeck College, Barrister
John Foster, General Secretary, National Union of Journalists
Steve Gibbons, Researcher in employment law
John Hendy QC, Chair, Institute of Employment Rights and Vice-President, International Centre for Trade Union Rights
Richard Hyman, Professor of Industrial Relations, University of Warwick
John Kelly, Senior Lecturer in Industrial Relations, London School of Economics
Aileen McColgan, Lecturer in Law, King's College, University of London
Sonia McKay, Researcher in employment law
Sue Maynard Campbell, Solicitor, Chair, Association of Disabled Professionals
Jonathan Michie, Institute of Management Studies, University of Cambridge
Gwyneth Pitt, Professor of Law, University of Huddersfield
Roger Welch, Senior Lecturer in Employment Law, Anglia Polytechnic University and Secretary, Chelmsford TUC
Frank Wilkinson, Department of Applied Economics, University of Cambridge
Charles Woolfson, Lecturer in Industrial Relations, University of Glasgow

Introduction

The Future of Labour Law developed from a conference of the same name held in London in September 1994. The conference, which was organized by the Haldane Society's employment law sub-committee, brought together trade union and other activists, academics from the industrial relations and labour law fields and lawyers practising in the area. After 15 years during which workers' protections had been dismantled, their representatives shackled and their security removed, the aim was to stimulate debate about the possibilities for change.

The very length of time during which supporters of the labour movement could only criticize, react to and protest about what was being done by the government created a threat to their ability to advocate, create and design a new scheme of labour law. The prospect of a Labour government was beginning to look like more than a pipe-dream and there was a feeling that such an opportunity should not be wasted. The hope was that the conference would be one instrument by which the boundaries of a new debate might be fashioned.

The chapters in this volume give some indication of the variety of subjects discussed over the two days of the conference. Plenary sessions covered areas such as labour economics (Frank Wilkinson and Jonathan Michie), the works councils debate (John Kelly and Professor Richard Hyman) and the role of legal regulation in industrial relations.

Numerous workshops were convened on subjects including 'rights' and the workplace (Professor Keith Ewing), recognition and worker participation (John Foster and Sonia McKay), the role of international labour clauses in securing workers' rights (John Hendy QC), industrial action (Professor Gwyneth Pitt and Roger Welch), the threat posed to health and safety standards by government-driven deregulation (Charles Woolfson), the role of Europe (Damian Brown), work-related rights for people with disabilities (Sue Maynard Campbell), the continuing wage gap between men and women (Aileen McColgan) and job security (Michael Ford and Steve Gibbons). Other workshops included 'social security and a guaranteed income', 'marginal/atypical workers and homeworkers', 'accountability of pension schemes', 'sex discrimination', 'maternity rights' and 'migrant workers, xenophobia and racism'. Unfortunately, the main speakers at these events were unable to contribute chapters to the book.

The chapters in this collection are wide-ranging and the views represented therein are diverse. In particular, chapters such as those by Richard Hyman, John Kelly, Roger Welch and Gwyneth Pitt adopt radically different approaches to the subjects (works councils and the future regulation of industrial action, respectively) with which they are concerned. But whatever the differences of style and approach, a number of themes predominate. First is the general consensus about the unsatisfactory state of the current law: whether the issue is that of trade unions' ability effectively to represent their members or of workers' safety, their freedom to take collective action, their protection from arbitrary dismissal or from discrimination on the basis of disability or sex, the resounding message is that things must change. The finger of blame is pointed primarily at the present government: in many cases the problems identified have arisen, for the most part, since 1979. Even where (as with sex and disability discrimination) the problems pre-dated the current political regime, the past 17 years have exacerbated or, at the very least, done nothing to improve matters.

This first theme is not surprising given that the point of the conference, and of this book, is to suggest an agenda for change. What is perhaps more important is the direction of change that is suggested. Despite the problems that have beset the labour movement over the years since 1979, despite unions' falling membership and the historically low level of collective bargaining coverage, most of the contributors to *The Future of Labour Law* fix their faith in the collective as the way forward.

Keith Ewing starts the collection with 'Rights at the workplace: an agenda for labour law', in which he surveys what he sees as the unsatisfactory current state of affairs and suggests a 'new agenda' based on the five pillars of equality of opportunity, social justice, workplace, democracy, protection of civil liberties and fairness at work. Ewing's chapter is followed by John Foster's 'Rights at work: the union's role'. Foster outlines what he sees as the 'desperate' situation currently prevailing: declining union membership and collective bargaining coverage; legislative and judicial assaults on trade unions and the dismantlement of the public sector; derecognition of unions and the drive towards 'personal' contracts.

Sonia McKay's contribution 'Representation or recognition', picks up this theme and questions how workplace recognition can best be achieved. She considers the statutory framework for recognition that was set up by the Conservative government in the wake of the Donovan Commission report, together with the various proposals which have come from the Trades Union Congress (TUC) and the concerns which have been expressed, in particular over the issue of non-union workplace representation. In response to the TUC's proposal that trade union recognition rights might be linked to union membership thresholds, McKay questions the idea that density of membership is the sole legitimate test of a union's claim 'to represent the aspirations of workers', and warns of the potential danger to the union movement of legislative change by the UK government in the wake of the 1994 *Commission of the European Communities* v *UK* decisions.

McKay's concerns about the threat posed to trade unionism by a statutory requirement for workplace consultation are picked up by John Kelly in Chapter 4, 'Works councils: union advance or marginalization?' Kelly points out the increasing 'drift towards company works councils in Britain' and presents the case against embracing these bodies as the future of employee representation at work. Taking as his starting position the question of 'whether some form of works council would help or hinder the recovery of union membership and influence', Kelly analyses the arguments for and against works councils, surveys the evidence from continental Europe and elsewhere and argues that works councils might prove 'a dangerous and damaging diversion from the process of union resurgence'.

Kelly's conclusions stand in contrast to those of Richard Hyman's 'Is there a case for statutory works councils in Britain?' Hyman argues for works councils as, in his own words, the 'least-worst' option currently on the agenda for British trade unions. The changes that have taken place since the 1970s have, in his view, rendered a return to the voluntaristic tradition impossible, and trade union 'recovery and renewal' requires a 'supportive legal framework', which, in his view, is most likely to be supplied by a works councils approach.

In Chapter 6, 'International trade and international trade union rights', John Hendy QC surveys what he characterizes as the 'assault' on trade union rights that has taken place over the past 17 years. His comments in this regard are not confined to the UK, but locate the increasingly hostile environment in the context of the growth of the 'world market', advanced technology and multinational employers. The solution Hendy puts forward draws on international labour standards such as those laid down by the International Labour Organisation (ILO). He argues that international trade agreements should contain labour clauses based on ILO standards and be enforced by an international labour inspectorate and international boycotting of defaulting countries.

The following two chapters deal with the right to strike, Gwyneth Pitt suggesting in 'The right to strike: a shift in focus' that the way forward lies in the recognition, and protection of the exercise of, the *individual's* right to strike. Pitt considers the current legal position in the UK and abroad and argues that the right would be best protected by the doctrine of suspension of contract which was considered, but rejected, by the Donovan Commission.

Roger Welch contributes Chapter 8, 'Re-establishing trade union rights: for positive rights to strike'. While he agrees with Pitt on the issue of suspension of contract, Welch takes a much more belt-and-braces approach to the issue of the right to strike as well as to the more general question of trade union rights. In contrast with Gwyneth Pitt, who accepts that the trade union's right to call strike action (although not the individual's right to take it) could be made dependent upon a ballot, Welch calls for the repeal of all trade union legislation passed since 1979 and its replacement with a framework of positive rights to include the right to take secondary and political strike action, and to do so without formal balloting of the membership. Welch acknowledges that his proposals are at odds with much of current thinking, and that they go beyond the bare minimum required by ILO rules, but he suggests that any balloting requirement allows employers to organize to render strike action ineffective and to use dissenting members in order to have industrial action injuncted. He also argues that, while British history records several cases of unions calling industrial action without the support of their membership, it does not record any such action lasting for more than a very short time.

Economists are frequently heard to claim that a deregulated labour market is an efficient labour market. But Jonathan Michie and Frank Wilkinson, who contribute Chapter 9, 'Trade unions, productivity and unemployment', argue that deregulation, as well as resulting in an increase in inequality in the UK, has done little to counter unemployment and nothing to encourage the labour market stability that is essential to effective training and increased productivity. Michie and Wilkinson survey the evidence from the UK and the USA and conclude that deregulation results in a downward spiral of short-term cost cutting, de-unionization and the resulting proliferation of low-paying, inefficient firms whose future relies on government subsidy in the form of welfare payments to their workers. Such a policy, they warn, and particularly its legitimation through the 'currently fashionable "basic income" schemes', threatens a return to the eighteenth- and nineteenth-century British 'Speenhamland system' – a dehumanizing, grotesque and inefficient system of subsidizing poverty wages, which the authors describe in chilling detail before going on to suggest a new approach to the regeneration of the British economy.

Charles Woolfson and Matthias Beck continue the focus on deregulation in Chapter 10, 'Deregulation: the contemporary politics of health and safety'. They discuss the current government drive to 'cut red tape', and the threat posed by it to the current framework of health and safety legislation. Woolfson and Beck chart the development of that framework, which, because of its emphasis on self-regulation and its neglect of economic deterrence, they regard as deeply flawed. The drive to reduce the 'burden on business', they argue, ignores the real costs of work-related injury and illness. But the prospects for improvement either on the home or on the European front are dim. 'Deregulation', the authors conclude, 'poses a challenge to the trade union movement which ... may provide new opportunities to portray trade unionism in a positive light.'

Just as Woolfson and Beck are underwhelmed at the prospect of Europe-driven change on the health and safety front, so Damian Brown takes a relatively sceptical view in Chapter 11, 'EU labour law and UK workers'. Brown outlines the extent to which European regulation currently protects the interests of British workers before considering what the needs of those workers are (for the main part, he argues, job security and effective representation). He takes the view that legislation on the European level has been 'disappointing at best', and presents a fairly bleak prognosis of future developments in the European Commission, the European Court of Justice (ECJ) and various of the member states. His conclusion, like that drawn by Woolfson and Beck in Chapter 10, is that the struggle for change must take place at the national level.

In Chapter 12, Sue Maynard Campbell addresses the topical issue of 'Disability rights'. Analysing the substance and history of the Disability Discrimination Act, she argues that it is fundamentally flawed, based on an outdated 'medical' model of disability rather than on the social model championed by the advocates of the defeated Civil Rights (Disabled Persons) Bill, which proved such an embarrassment to the then minister, Nicholas Scott. Maynard Campbell criticizes the shortcomings of the new legislation in terms of its failure to deal adequately with the environment within which disabled people function, their access to education, transport and polling stations, as well as its individual enforcement mechanism and restricted employment coverage. She concludes by calling for a comprehensive legislative attempt to level the playing field and place people with disabilities firmly in the mainstream.

In Chapter 13, 'Equal pay: a new approach', Aileen McColgan outlines the present unsatisfactory state of British women's pay and warns that the continuing drive towards deregulation threatens to widen the gender pay gap. She argues that much of the existing gap is the result of the more general (and widening) levels of wage inequality in the UK, and that the implementation of a national minimum wage would go a long way towards addressing this issue. But McColgan claims that such action is not enough and that the elimination of that part of the gender wage gap which is the result of 'discrimination' requires a new, collective approach to the 'equal pay' issue. She concludes by considering, in the light of experiences in Canada and Australia, what form such an approach might take.

The concluding chapter, 'Remedying dismissal law' is provided by Michael Ford and Steve Gibbons. They argue that the recent fashion for looking towards the contract as the source of job security is misguided and that efforts should be made, instead, to revitalize the system of statutory protection. They point, in particular, to the unsatisfactory nature of remedies currently available (worse still, to those actually utilized by the industrial tribunals), and consider practice at home and abroad before providing a blueprint for improvement.

1

Rights at the Workplace: An Agenda for Labour Law

K. D. Ewing

INTRODUCTION

Few people will need to be reminded of the great changes which have taken place in British labour law since 1979.[1] Successive governments have moved gradually to dismantle the structure of trade union and employees' rights built up carefully in the 1970s. Although the change has been gradual, it has been relentless, with no fewer than eight major pieces of legislation having been introduced since 1980, an average of one statute every two years. In the process we have seen the deconstruction of collective bargaining procedures and the deregulation of employment standards. The only respite has been provided by Europe, in terms of both Council Directives and decisions of the ECJ, though even here we are playing less than our full part, with the Maastricht opt-out potentially denying workers in the UK rights enjoyed by their counterparts elsewhere in Europe.

THE COSTS OF DEREGULATION

What has been the effect of the policies of government, to which labour law has contributed? On the one hand we can point to a decline in both trade union density and collective bargaining coverage, and on the other to an increase in income inequality and job insecurity. So far as trade union density and collective bargaining coverage are concerned, the decline in a short period of 17 years is remarkable and perhaps unprecedented. Whatever indicator is examined, whether it be the Labour Force Survey for trade union density or the Workplace Industrial Relations Survey for collective bargaining

coverage, the result is 'a depressing picture'[2] of decline. Thus, trade
union density has fallen from an estimated 62 per cent in 1980 to 33
per cent in 1994; and collective bargaining coverage has fallen from 71
per cent of employees in 1984 to 47 per cent in 1990.[3] But although
the survey evidence is controversial, and although it ought not to be
exaggerated, it appears to be the case that two out of every three British
workers are not unionized, and, perhaps more significantly, that more
than one out of every two British workers have their terms and
conditions imposed by their employer, subject only to the requirements demanded by the floor of statutory rights, significantly weakened
by the repeal of the Wages Councils Act 1979.

So far as income inequality and job insecurity are concerned, the
extent of the former was traced by the influential Rowntree Inquiry into
Income and Wealth[4] published early in 1995, and also in the TUC's
Arguments for a Minimum Wage. According to the key findings of
Rowntree, income inequality in the UK grew rapidly between 1977 and
1990, and the pace of increasing income inequality was faster here than
in any other industrialized country, with the exception of New Zealand.
Others have pointed out that between 1977 and 1992 the average real
wages of the lowest 10 per cent of male earners were static, while the
real wages of the top 10 per cent increased by 44 per cent.[5] The
growing inequality of earnings, together with cuts in social security, has
led in the view of some to an increase in family poverty. Turning from
income inequality to job insecurity, we find a decrease in the number
of workers in permanent, secure, well-paid jobs, with a corresponding
increase in the number of disadvantaged workers engaged in insecure
and poorly paid employment. Recent figures in a study by two
Cambridge economists suggest that as many as one-third of British
workers live in either insecurity or comparative poverty, caused either
by a lack of employment or by the nature of work which is part-time,
temporary and poorly paid.[6]

A NEW AGENDA FOR LABOUR LAW

It is against this background that in 1994 the Institute of Employment
Rights supported a project designed to examine developments in
labour law, with a view to stimulating discussion and debate about the
future. The project is an ambitious one, which it is hoped will lead to
the drafting of a balanced framework of proposals to 'strengthen legal
rights for people at work',[7] setting out a range of options in a non-

prescriptive way. It is not in any sense a campaigning project, but is designed to contribute to the debates that may be taking place elsewhere.[8] A possible model for this type of activity was provided by the Institute for Public Policy Research, which has produced important and thoughtful work on the question of constitutional reform and related issues.[9] The aim is to synthesize the experience and ideas of people from a range of backgrounds, including those in the academic and legal communities, as well as trade union officials and industrial relations practitioners.

The first step in the process, which would build on and reflect obligations arising under ILO conventions and EU social policy, is to seek to develop a number of organizing principles upon which labour law should be built, and which ought to inform any possible developments in the future. Drawing directly or indirectly from the ILO, and in particular from the Declaration of Philadelphia of 1944, supposed to inspire the policies of the members, five such principles have been identified: equality of opportunity, social justice, workplace democracy, the protection of civil liberties and fairness at work. These principles are fairly fluid, and may be said to merge into each other. Some may see equality of opportunity as an aspect of social justice; or the protection of civil liberties as an aspect of workplace democracy. But for ease of presentation, we shall refer to these as five discrete, if overlapping, principles.

Equality of Opportunity

So far as equality of opportunity is concerned, as a guiding principle this means very simply that people should not be excluded from or disadvantaged in labour market participation by discriminatory employment practices. This requires in the first place effective measures designed to remove discrimination from the workplace. Important measures to extend the current base of protection are to be found in the (admittedly inadequate) Disability Discrimination Act, while the Labour Party has announced intriguing proposals to make it unlawful to discriminate against people over 50, and, it is hoped, will pursue in government the recent initiatives of Baroness Turner, whose Sexual Orientation Discrimination Bill would extend the provisions of the Sex Discrimination Act 1975 to make it unlawful for employers to discriminate on the grounds of sexual orientation. The implementation of these measures would go a long way to completing our recognition of the principle of equality and bringing us into line with some of the pace-setting jurisdictions in Canada and Australia, where the protection is characteristically much wider than a narrow protection against discrimination on the grounds of race or sex.

But as a guiding principle the principle of equality of opportunity also means confronting and overcoming the structural barriers that operate to deny labour market participation in the first place. Two areas in particular illustrate in different ways the need for the recognition of a more wide-ranging principle, one being the position of workers with disabilities, and the other being the position of workers with family responsibilities, whether these relate to young children or elderly dependants. The need for legislation in respect of the former has at last been recognized, though as already suggested there are many who question the adequacy of the Disability Discrimination Act 1995, despite important amendments made in Parliament. The Act makes it unlawful for an employer to discriminate against a disabled person, with discrimination being defined to mean either less favourable treatment or a failure to comply with the duty to make adjustments to workplaces. In both cases, however, the discrimination is subject to a defence of justification, and in the latter case the duty arises only where the disabled person is placed 'at a substantial disadvantage in comparison with persons who are not disabled'; even then, the employer's duty is to take only 'reasonable' steps to eliminate any disadvantage. There is no general duty to make workplaces accessible to people with disabilities, an important omission from any statute introduced with a genuine desire to promote equality of opportunity.

The other major area where barriers operate to restrict equal opportunity relates to workers with family responsibilities, condemned, according to the Labour Party's Social Justice Commission, by the belief that 'the only real job is a full-time job, and that a successful career demands a full-time, life-time commitment and the sacrifice of everything else'.[10] It is true that it may be possible to use the Sex Discrimination Act 1975 to remove barriers to more flexible employment patterns, with cases compelling employers to permit flexi-time working by women with young children,[11] and to allow women to return to work on a part-time basis after maternity leave.[12] But the modest gains under the Act are no substitute for a comprehensive and coordinated strategy to remove the obstacles to full and effective labour market participation if the goal of equality of opportunity is to be fully realized. This is what is invited by ILO Convention 156 – the Workers with Family Responsibilities Convention, 1981 – which provides that 'all measures compatible with national conditions and possibilities shall be taken', to 'enable workers with family responsibilities to exercise their right to free choice of employment'. This in turn invites statutory rights to time off work for family responsibilities, more flexible working arrangements and, perhaps above all, much better childcare facilities.

Social Justice

So far as social justice as a second guiding principle is concerned, this was referred to by the Labour Party's Social Justice Commission as meaning, among other things, the idea that 'everyone is entitled as a right of citizenship, to be able to meet their basic needs of income, shelter, and other necessities'.[13] Developing this, we might say that the principle of social justice embraces the right of individuals to participate fully as citizens within their community from a base of adequate social support and protection. This base of support and protection would guarantee a minimum framework of benefits (in the widest sense of the term), and would seek to promote the widest possible range of opportunities. The aim is to ensure that all members of the community have a chance to participate fully in the life of the community with dignity and respect. Clearly, the responsibility for promoting social justice, as that term is used here, does not rest on the shoulders of labour law or labour lawyers alone. But on the other hand labour law has a role to play in the development of these minimum standards, along with other legal and political instruments.

There are in fact three policy goals to which labour law can contribute, albeit in different ways in each case. These are by:

- promoting employment opportunities;
- the provision of a minimum framework of rights at work;
- guaranteeing income security during interruptions and retirement from work.

The concerns of labour law are thus many and varied if all citizens are to be given an opportunity to realize their potential by, and to be rewarded for, their labour. This is an area however, which has been dominated recently by the arguments about the statutory minimum wage and in particular the level at which the wage should be set. But although these debates about the level at which the national minimum wage is to be set are of the greatest importance, perhaps of even greater importance to the labour lawyer is the method by which the principle is to be implemented, whether by legislation or otherwise.

ILO Convention 26 (the Minimum Wage-fixing Machinery Convention, 1928) provides that each member of the ILO which ratifies the Convention thereby undertakes to 'create or maintain machinery whereby minimum rates of wages can be fixed for workers employed in certain of the trades or parts of trades in which no arrangements exist for the effective regulation of wages by collective agreement or otherwise and wages are exceptionally low'.[14] The Convention leaves members free to decide the nature and form of the minimum wage-fixing machinery, but it also provides for the consultation of employers' and workers' representatives as well as other qualified persons, before the machinery is applied in a trade or a part of a trade. Consistently with these measures, the Labour Party's Economic Policy Commission has proposed the creation of a new tripartite Commission, an aptly named Low Pay Commission, presumably statutory, 'involving the social partners and independent nominees', which will examine the economic and employment as well as social justice considerations before setting the wage rate.[15] But although there will thus be a new institutional framework for the regulation of pay, it is unclear whether there will be a flat-rate minimum or whether there will be sectoral, occupational or regional variations.

Workplace Democracy

The third guiding principle, workplace democracy, refers principally to the effective recognition of the right of collective bargaining. Yet it has been claimed recently that 'citizens who enter the workplace' are often 'required to leave their democratic rights at the door',[16] while others have written of the growing 'democratic deficit' in British workplaces, with the decline in the levels of trade union density and collective bargaining coverage being accompanied by a decline in the extent of trade union recognition. The Labour Force Survey of 1994 suggests that only 48 per cent of employees worked in workplaces where trade unions were recognized for collective bargaining over pay and conditions of employment. This means, of course, that in a majority of workplaces there are no procedures for the collective regulation of working conditions while other evidence reinforces the conclusion that only a minority of British workers have an opportunity to participate in workplace decision-making procedures. But what is to be done? Workers cannot be compelled to join trade unions, nor can they be compelled to demand representation by trade unions. They can, however, be encouraged and protected by law if they wish to do so, and government can help to create a climate in which collective bargaining can flourish, partly by the careful use of legislation to underpin the bargaining process.

Legislation can underpin the process of workplace democracy in three ways. The first is by protecting those who join, take part in the activities and enjoy the benefits and services of trade unions, the so-called *membership rights*. The *Wilson* and *Palmer* cases (in which it was held that an employer could pay more to those engaged on personal contracts than those whose working conditions were governed by a collective agreement,[17] together with s. 13 of the Trade Union Reform and Employment Rights Act 1993, suggest that there is work to be done if trade union membership rights are to be effectively protected. Second, the law has a role to play in promoting the *organizational rights* and security of trade unions. Building on ILO Convention 135 (the Workers' Representatives Convention, 1971) and ILO Recommendation 143 (the Workers' Representatives Recommendation, 1971), this might include the right of access to an undertaking by full-time and branch officials not employed there; the right to hold meetings and post notices at the workplace (at sites to which workers have easy access); and the right to such facilities as may be necessary for workers' representatives in the discharge of their functions. It is a matter for consideration whether these rights should be available to a union represented in a plant, rather than only to one which is recognized by an employer. In other words, trade union organization rights would be triggered by membership rather than recognition, unlike the current statutory arrangements for time off work for trade union officials and members.

The third role of legislation relates to the provision of trade union *representation and recognition rights*. A helpful contribution in this respect are the TUC proposals in the document *Your Voice at Work*, which builds on an earlier document of 1991,[18] but also responds to the demands of the decision of the ECJ in *EC* v *United Kingdom*.[19] As far as representation is concerned, the paper proposes that individuals should have the right to be represented by an independent advisor, and specifically for a trade union member to be represented by a trade union official in any matter relating to his or her employment relationship, effectively giving statutory force to the EAT decision in *Discount Tobacco and Confectionery Ltd* v *Armitage*.[20] But the paper implicitly rejects the proposal, expressly rejected by the TUC Annual Congress in 1995,[21] for collective representation whereby a union could insist on the right to represent its members on a collective basis on matters of common interest between them, regardless of the number of workers the union has in membership. This was proposed by the media unions in particular, as being desirable in principle and necessary in practice, in view of the fact that employers could insist on separate meetings to discuss a general grievance or wage claim made by, say, 100 members in an office of 300 employees, stretching the resources of small unions to breaking point.[22]

On the question of consultation and negotiation, the TUC paper proposes a staged approach, with the rights of the union depending on the level of its support in the workplace. A union with 50 per cent membership in the defined bargaining unit will be entitled automatically to negotiating rights. Below that, a union which can demonstrate majority support in a bargaining unit by those participating in a survey or ballot, to be conducted by a proposed new Representation Agency, will also be entitled to negotiating rights. A union with lower levels of support, but with at least 10 per cent membership, will be entitled to general consultation rights which would apply to matters other than the mandatory issues prescribed by EU law (notably collective redundancies and transfers of undertakings);[23] and in workplaces where there is no union support of this level, the employer would be required to establish what is in effect a standing works council (unlike the *ad hoc* measures now permitted by the government), referred to as 'elections as a fall-back' (EFB), in which unions would have an opportunity to nominate candidates, and with which consultations would take place on the European issues.[24]

These are interesting and important proposals, though there are a number of problems which have to be addressed, some more important than others. The first is the fact that the extensive discretion vested in this Representation Agency may mean that we are in danger of returning to the battlegrounds of the 1970s, when the Advisory Conciliation and Arbitration Service (ACAS) was severely undermined by judicial review proceedings, at a time when judicial review as we know it today was in its infancy. There is the possibility of problems arising in terms of how surveys are conducted;[25] of determining the scope and extent of the bargaining unit; and of deciding who is entitled to vote at the election. Second, it is not clear what is to happen to these elections as a fall-back body if the union should subsequently acquire consultation rights by securing 10 per cent support from the workforce. If the union candidates win a majority of the places in the election, it is proposed that the union should be granted general consultation rights and that the elected body would not then be established. But if the elected body is established and the union then acquires general consultation rights, is the elected body to be wound up, with the non-union members of the workforce (perhaps as many as 90 per cent of the workforce) disenfranchised, or is the employer to consult with both about the same issues?

There is also the problem of the enforcement of any recommendations of the proposed new Representation Agency. In the case of general consultation rights, it is proposed that the 'legislation should give a trade union with members in the workforce the competence to apply to the tribunals for compensation on their behalf, and then also to the court as a last resort for an order compelling the employer to comply with the duty to consult'.[26] Breach of the order would be remedied by an additional award of compensation, and, in 'extreme cases', 'according to the normal principles of contempt of court'. It is also proposed that court orders supporting the status quo would be available, 'so that reinstatement would be the normal remedy and any dismissals which took place without adequate consultation would be void'.[27] These thoughtful and interesting proposals contrast with the rather less detailed measures suggested for compliance with the duty to bargain in cases where the union can establish majority membership or support. Here, surprisingly, it is suggested simply that the Representation Agency would determine whether the employer had failed to bargain in good faith and if so refer the matter to the Central Arbitration Committee (CAC) 'to determine the sanction'. But what sanction is there, apart from a power to propose an award of compensation to both the union and workers involved?

The Protection of Civil Liberties

With the fourth principle, the protection of civil liberties, the concern is that civil liberties are capable of violation not only by the State and those who wield public power, but also by employers and others who wield private power. There is a need for protection from the latter just as there is a need for protection from the former. Although the possibility of liberty being violated by employers will be reduced where there is strong workplace representation by trade unions, this is not to deny that a framework of statutory principle respecting the civil liberties of the individual will be necessary. A useful starting point here is the European Convention on Human Rights, for although its provisions apply, as a matter of international law, mainly to regulate the activities of government, its principles are equally relevant to constrain those who wield private power, including the power of the employer over the worker. On what rational basis can it be argued that while the government must respect an individual's right to private and family life, an employer may be free to undermine it with relative impunity? The difficult question then, is not whether employers should respect the civil liberties of workers, but to identify what these liberties are.

As a starting point, there are four articles of the ECHR which seem particularly appropriate: Article 8, which protects the right to privacy; Article 9, which protects the right to freedom of religion and conscience; Article 10, which protects the right to freedom of expression; and Article 11, which protects the right to freedom of assembly and association. It is not suggested that these measures should be formally incorporated into domestic law; that is a separate argument.

Nor is it suggested that these measures are or should be unqualified, any more than they are in the convention itself. But it is suggested that these different articles of the convention embrace standards which could be made to apply in the workplace. Recognition of the right to privacy would, for example, regulate the storage of information about employees, the requirement to provide personal information about employees, and the right of access to information stored about the employee. The second of these concerns would clearly have been important in the *NATFHE* case, where the union was required to provide the employer with the names of its members, despite the claim of counsel that it was deeply offensive to union members who were entitled to keep their membership private.[28]

A number of benefits would also flow from the recognition of the right to freedom of expression and assembly, which would provide a framework for liberalizing the law relating to employer accountability, on the one hand, and peaceful picketing, on the other. Freedom of expression issues arise not just in the context of whistle-blowing, important though it is that this matter be addressed,[29] particularly in the light of a *Labour Research* survey, which revealed that as many as one in five disciplinary procedures 'specifically barred employees from disclosing confidential information regardless of the circumstances and threatened instant dismissal to employees who disregarded the rule'. Also important is the right to legitimate criticism of the way in which the business is run and the accountability of those who make business decisions, to protect people like David Wilson, first victimized for refusing to accept a personal contract, and then dismissed (three months after the House of Lords ruling) for being 'openly critical of the company, its profits, its dividend policies and the remuneration of various individuals'.[30]

Fairness at Work

The fifth and final principle referred to above is the principle of fairness at work, by which it is meant that all people at work have the right not to be treated unfairly by their employer in any matter relating to the employment relationship. This is a principle already recognized by the common law (to the extent that there is an implied term of the contract of employment that the employer will not treat employees 'arbitrarily, capriciously or inequitably' in matters of pay,[31] or will not 'without reasonable and proper cause' act in a way 'calculated to destroy the relationship of confidence and trust between employer and employee'[32]), and by legislation (to the extent that there is a right not to be unfairly dismissed[33]). In both cases, however, the scope and extent of the principle is limited, in the case of the common law by the fact that the implied terms are often unenforceable without the employee first leaving the job and the economic security which it provides, and in the case of the legislation by the fact that it applies only to decisions relating to dismissal.

If we are serious about the right of employees not to be treated unfairly at work, there is a need to consider whether the principle of fairness should be extended, and if so how this might be done. There are really two questions for consideration: the first is the application of the principle during the subsistence of the employment relationship; and the second is the application of the principle on termination of the relationship. So far as the former is concerned, is it right that the protection against unfair treatment should depend upon the implied terms of the contract of employment, particularly when these terms are for all practical purposes often unenforceable by the employee? In those cases where the term is enforceable, as in *Johnstone* v *Bloomsbury Health Authority*,[34] is it right that it should be necessary for the employee to seek relief in the High Court to prevent the employer from compelling him or her to work in a manner which is harmful to his or her health? And is there a case for statutory protection against unfair treatment at work generally, just as there is statutory protection against discriminatory treatment on the basis of race and sex, covering a wide range of employer decisions? If so, what would be the scope and content of this right?

Whatever the case for the better application of the principle of fairness while the employment relationship subsists, there is perhaps more strongly a case for the review of its application on termination of the relationship. Five problems in particular require attention. The first is the excluded categories, though this appears in the process of resolution, but is not yet completely resolved, as a result of EC law.[35] The second problem relates to the permitted grounds for dismissal, which are more permissive than ILO Convention 158 (the Termination of Employment Convention, 1982). The third relates to the fact that the tribunals are denied jurisdiction to deal with industrial action dismissals, again an omission which is incompatible not only with ILO Convention 158, which the UK has not ratified, but also with ILO Convention 87 (The Right to Organize and Freedom of Association, 1948) which it has. The fourth concern relates to the remedies available in the case of a successful unfair dismissal claim, with reinstatement being awarded in only 1.2 per cent of cases in 1993–94, and with the median award of compensation in 1993–94 being a modest £2773. The fifth and final problem relates to the effectiveness of the industrial tribunal system, with Roy Lewis and Jon Clark claiming in an influential publication that 'Cheapness, speed and informality have been undermined by a long term trend towards legalism within the industrial tribunals.'[36]

THE ROLE OF TRADE UNIONS AND COLLECTIVE BARGAINING

These then are the principles that ought to inform future strategy in this area. The question which now arises for consideration is simply this: how can they best be implemented? In a recent consultation document, *A New Economic Future for Britain*, Labour's Economic Policy Commission proposed that 'The government has the responsibility for defining minimum standards, including through legislation.' But this is also a responsibility which has traditionally been discharged by collective bargaining, in the UK and in other European countries, and is a responsibility which, it is contemplated, will continue to be conducted by collective bargaining by the architects of European Social Policy, as the Working Time Directive[37] makes abundantly clear. This provides not only for the setting of standards by collective agreements,[38] but also allows derogation from the prescribed standards by collective agreements.[39] There are, however, a number of matters which will need urgently to be addressed if collective bargaining rather than regulatory legislation is to continue to be the dominant method of standard-setting in British workplaces.

Collective Bargaining: Decline and Decentralization

The first of these relates to the declining coverage and decentralization of collective bargaining. As already pointed out, a minority of British workers are now covered by agreements. The decline in collective bargaining coverage has in fact been one of the most significant developments in the past 17 years, and appears to be without parallel in any of the other OECD countries, with a recent survey concluding that 'the decline in collective bargaining has been most pronounced in Great Britain'.[40] As already pointed out, collective bargaining coverage in Britain has fallen from 70 per cent in 1980 to 47 per cent in 1990. The position is in fact worse when we take into account that at least another 11 or 12 per cent were covered by wages council orders, pushing joint regulation up in excess of 80 per cent, perhaps as high as 85 per cent. On this basis, coverage has in fact fallen to 47 per cent from 80 to 85 per cent since 1980.[41] But not only is the UK's decline the sharpest, it is as a result among the OECD countries with the lowest levels of collective bargaining coverage. To put the matter in perspective, coverage in Australia stood at 80, Finland 95, France 92 and Germany 90 per cent.

Related to this is the decentralization of collective bargaining, now extending from the private sector into the public sector as well. This has seen the break up of national or sectoral bargaining arrangements (with only one in ten workers in the private sector now thought to be covered by multi-employer bargaining arrangements) and a greater emphasis on enterprise-based bargaining. One reason why this is important is that collective bargaining decentralization is sometimes associated with low levels of coverage, with the recent OECD study pointing out that 'Countries characterized by single-employer bargaining tend to have lower coverage rates compared with countries where bargaining is conducted at higher levels and where employer organizations and union federations are strong.' Although decentralization is also a feature of bargaining developments in other countries, 'there has been great variation between countries in the nature and extent of decentralization of industrial relations and of employers' flexibility initiatives'.[42] But few countries, it seems, have gone as far as the UK, and even as late as 1994 the OECD survey could record that 'in a majority of OECD countries the sectoral level has remained the principal arena for wage determination'.[43]

Rebuilding Sectoral Bargaining Machinery

If collective bargaining is thus to reassert a dominant role, it may need, as a matter of urgency, some form of state support. In view of the extent of the decline, the scale of that support may have to be substantial. But this raises a second problem, which relates to the form of state support. If the goal is to expand the coverage of collective bargaining, the obvious solution would be to seek to turn the tide and reassert the importance of sectoral bargaining arrangements,[44] while also retaining the arrangements which already exist.[45] Such a strategy appears to have a number of possible benefits, in the sense that it would contribute in no small way to the principles of equality of opportunity (to the extent that there is some evidence that the gender pay gap may be smaller in countries with more centralized bargaining arrangements[46]), social justice (to the extent that workers covered by collective bargaining are on average more favoured than those who are not covered and to the extent that there is thus likely to be a higher level of coverage of a wide range of benefits) and workplace democracy (to the extent that it is suggested by some commentators that centralized pay determination is likely to reduce employer resistance to a trade union presence in the company, perhaps more likely still if devolved flexibility bargaining were to be permitted).

Yet despite the social benefits, despite the fact that it happens elsewhere and despite the importance of collective bargaining as a method of workplace regulation, it would be very ambitious to seek to reassert the primary role of sectoral bargaining. In the first place, it would require a commitment to reconstruction as great as that demonstrated in 1917, but without the spectre of communism haunting Europe to drive the engine of reform. Second, it would mean setting up sectoral wages councils or statutory joint industrial councils in every industry, at a time when organization on the employers' side appears to have disintegrated. Third, it would mean having to have a procedure for exempting well-organized industries, while ensuring at the same time the extension of agreements to all working in the sector in question. Fourth, it would mean revising current policy commitments such as the proposed Low Pay Commission, which could be redundant in a regulated system of sectoral bargaining. Finally, it would mean confronting rather than appeasing the resistance of employers at a time when there is no ideological stomach for such a fight and no obvious political capital to be gained in picking one.

This last problem indicates that a determined effort to reassert the primacy of sectoral bargaining in Britain would be a heavy load for our voluntary system to bear and a great deal to contemplate. In the absence of a strong political commitment, it is open to question whether it could be done without the support and cooperation of employers,[47] and there is no evidence of any enthusiasm on their part for such structures. Indeed, the opposite appears to be the case, with Brown pointing out, for example, that 'Employers' determination to remain with single-employer bargaining if they are to have any sort of bargaining is strongly implied by their rejection of existing forms of employer collaboration.' Further evidence of employer resistance to the idea was indicated some time ago in the Confederation of British Industry (CBI) report of 1991 on UK inflation performance, which was clearly of the view that it would be unrealistic to turn back the tide given the trend towards decentralization in the 1980s. Despite the admitted advantages of a highly centralized system of pay bargaining, they thought it more sensible and in keeping with current practices and institutions to enhance wage flexibility by moving more rapidly towards decentralization in pay determination, taking advantage in the process of the weakened market power of trade unions.

Expanding the Frontiers of Enterprise–Based Bargaining

If we are seeking to expand the frontiers of collective bargaining, the alternative is to adopt the strategy of the TUC, which effectively proposes to expand the coverage of collective bargaining from the bottom up rather than the top down. As already pointed out, the TUC favours a step-by-step approach to trade union recognition, with unions entitled to a greater degree of recognition depending upon the scale of support which they have within a defined bargaining unit. So a union with 10 per cent membership (10 per cent drawn from the trigger mechanism in the European Works Councils Directive of 1994) will be entitled to consultative status with the employer, while a union with majority support (demonstrated in a survey or a ballot) will be entitled to negotiating rights with the employer, as will a union which can demonstrate majority membership. Where a union does not have 10 per cent support the employer will be required to establish what is in effect an elected works council of employees, for which the union would have the right to nominate candidates and campaign for election.

It remains to be seen how far this strategy will push back the frontiers of collective bargaining and help the unions to march into new territory, though we should not underestimate the flexibility and subtlety of the TUC proposals as a strategy for the extension of collective bargaining. As a package it ought to be able to meet the problems presented by the majority rule requirement of the US legislation and overcome the problems in the USA, where a union has to demonstrate 50 per cent support for certification in a 'death or glory' election. It is of the greatest importance that under the TUC proposals a union with 10 per cent will be entitled to general consultation rights, not just on what we might refer to as the European issues of redundancy and business transfers, but more generally to include 'management proposals involving significant changes in employment numbers or working conditions'. Admittedly, it is not clear how far this will go, but it is nevertheless a crucial measure, which will reward unions for support and give them encouragement to build up membership to secure full recognition rights, thereby giving workers the right to have their terms and conditions covered by a collective agreement.

Although these arrangements will undoubtedly help unions, we should also be realistic about what the proposals can be expected to deliver. If we return to the OECD survey, we are reminded of the fact that countries characterized by single-employer bargaining tend to have lower rates of coverage of collective agreements. More specifically, the survey points out that collective bargaining coverage in the USA is 18, in Japan 23 and in Canada 38 per cent. These countries are dominated by establishment-based bargaining, and also have legal frameworks for trade union recognition which are geared towards single-employer bargaining. It is true that the TUC proposals are predictably more union-friendly than the legal regimes operating in the USA or Canada. But it remains the case that under these proposals a union will need majority support in the bargaining unit to negotiate on pay, unless the employer agrees to collective bargaining on a voluntary basis. It may well be that in the brave new world of New Labour we will simply have to become accustomed to lower levels of bargaining coverage and a diluted form of trade union representation.

CONCLUSION

By way of conclusion, there are urgent problems waiting to be addressed. But before the process of reconstruction begins we must ask what it is that we expect labour law to be able to do. Drawing from the great human rights instruments of the ILO, there are five principles which should inform our thinking in the future, five goals which we should be seeking to promote. These principles can be promoted by legislation or collective bargaining or by a combination of the two. As far as collective bargaining is concerned, there is a need first to seek to extend the breadth of collective bargaining coverage. This might be done in one of two ways, either by the top-down approach attempted by Whitley in 1917, or by a bottom-up approach as is currently proposed by the TUC or, better still, by a combination of both.

As far as a top-down approach is concerned, there are good reasons why in principle we would want to move in the direction of more centralized arrangements, which would contribute to the effective implementation of the principles of workplace democracy, social justice and equality of opportunity. But none of these advantages could be secured if employers refuse to participate, and it is for consideration whether it is now too late for such an initiative, though it would be remarkably cautious to refuse to contemplate such a possibility by refusing to swim against the tide of recent developments. Although we might endorse the recommendations of the Whitley Committee in

1917 that the government should propose without delay to employers' associations and trade unions the formation of standing joint industrial councils, there is no reason to believe that anyone would pay any attention, even if the employers' associations still had a postal address. Nor has there been any suggestion that legislation could possibly be used to create sectoral bargaining machinery, tempting though it may be to contemplate statutory machinery of this kind in the case of the privatized utilities, particularly after the *South West Water* case and the derecognition of Unison.[48]

So far as a bottom-up aproach is concerned, if this is to be the primary device for the carriage of a collective bargaining strategy, we may be asking it to bear a heavy load. As proposed by the TUC this strategy ought almost certainly to help unions with low levels of membership to establish a role at the workplace and a voice for employees. But under the TUC proposals the unions will not be entitled to full negotiating rights on basic issues such as pay and working time unless they can establish high levels of support. It is true that the strategy might be reinforced by a range of other initiatives, such as contract compliance (to the extent that it is permitted by EU law) and derogation by collective bargaining from implemented EU directives (as in the case of guarantee payments and the unfair dismissal provisions of the Employment Protection (Consolidation) Act 1978 (EPCA)). Also helpful, as proposed by the TUC, would be the reintroduction, in line with the observations of the ILO committee of experts, of some power on the part of trade unions to take solidarity action in support of other workers engaged in a lawful dispute (which could include a recognition dispute),[49] though the effect of such action may be limited if it is to be preceded by a ballot.

We should, however, be alert to the limitations and implications of this particular strategy, even if it does offer a way forward. As a solution to the problem of declining collective bargaining coverage, an enterprise-based approach may be second best, even if it is most sensitive to industrial relations and political realities. Just as we would have to accept the possibility of lower levels of collective bargaining coverage, and a more consultative rather than standard-setting role for trade unions, so we would also have to accept the fact that a higher proportion of workers than would have been considered acceptable in the past would have to depend on the direct regulation of their working conditions by the State. It is thus difficult to disagree with Labour's Economic Policy Commission when it asserts that 'The government has a responsibility for defining minimum standards, including through legislation.' For unless a way can be found to extend the application of minimum standards agreements throughout industry,[50] it is difficult to see what alternative there is to a comprehensive framework of statutory rights if we are serious about promoting rights at the workplace, for all workers.[51]

NOTES

1. For a critique of these developments, see J. Hendy, *A Law unto Themselves. Conservative Employment Laws: a National and International Assessment* (Institute of Employment Rights, 3rd edn, 1993).

2. S. Milner, The coverage of collective pay-setting institutions in Britain, 1895–1990 (1995) 33 BJIR 69, at p. 88.

3. Admittedly the 1990 figure is thought to underestimate the position by a few percentage points. See W. Brown, The contraction of collective bargaining (1993) 31 BJIR 189.

4. Vol. 1 (1995).

5. See Institute of Employment Rights, *Just the Job?* (1995) p. 4.

6. K. Coutts and R. Rowthorn, *Employment in the United Kingdom: Trends and Prospects* Cambridge: ESRC Centre for Business Research, 1995.

7. J. Moher, *Trade Unions and the Law – The Politics of Change* (Institute of Employment Rights, 1995).

8. The first stage in the project was completed by the publication of Institute of Employment Rights, *Just the Job? A Consultation Paper on the Future of Employment Law* (1995).

9. See Institute for Public Policy Research, *The Constitution of the United Kingdom* (1991).

10. *Social Justice: Strategies for National Renewal.* The Report of the Social Justice Commission (1994), p. 188.

11. See *Public Service*, December 1994 (case of Susan Dawson).

12. *Home Office* v *Holmes* [1984] IRLR 299.

13. Report of the Social Justice Commission, *op. cit.*, p. 188.

14. This is very like the formula of the Trade Boards Act 1918, which extended the scope of the trade boards beyond the four set up initially in 1909 by the Trade Boards Act 1909. By s. 1(2), it provided that the Minister of Labour 'may make a special order applying the principal Act to any specified trade to which it does not at the time apply if he is of the opinion that no adequate machinery exists for the effective regulation of wages throughout the trade, and that accordingly, having regard to the rate of wages prevailing in the trade, or any part of the trade, it is expedient that the principal Act should apply to the trade'.

15. *A New Economic Future for Britain.* A consultation document from Labour's Economic Policy Commission (June 1995), p. 60.

16. TUC, *Representation at Work* (1995), p. 5. Also TUC, *Your Voice at Work* (1995), p. 5.

17. *Associated Newspapers Ltd* v *Wilson* [1995] 2 All ER 100.

18. TUC, *Trade Union Recognition* (1991). See also K. D. Ewing, Trade union recognition – a framework for discussion (1990) 19 ILJ 209.

19. [1994] IRLR 392, 412. The ECJ found the UK in breach of the Collective Redundancies and Acquired Rights' Directives on account, *inter alia*, of its inadequate provisions for the consultation of workers' representatives. On the government's response, see The Collective Redundancies and Transfer of Undertakings (Protection of Employment) Regulations 1995, SI 1995/1587.

20. [1990] IRLR 15, doubted by Lords Keith, Bridge and Lloyd in *Associated Newspapers Ltd* v *Wilson, op. cit.*

21. *Guardian*, 15 September 1995.

22. For full details of the proposal, see Press for Union Rights, *Workers' Rights: The Next Step* (1995). The proposal was said to be unworkable and a threat to union stability. See *Guardian*, 15 September 1995.

23. According to the report, 'The areas of consultation should cover management proposals

involving significant changes in employment numbers or working conditions.' But this would not include pay. See TUC, *Your Voice at Work* (1995), pp. 21–2.

24. TUC, *Your Voice at Work* (1995).

25. See *Powley* v *ACAS* [1978] ICR 123, and *Grunwick Processing Laboratories Ltd* v *ACAS* [1978] ICR 231.

26. TUC, *Your Voice at Work* (1995), p. 25.

27. *Ibid.*, pp. 25–6.

28. *Blackpool and The Fylde College* v *NATFHE* [1994] IRLR 227.

29. See L. Vickers, *Protecting Whistleblowers at Work* (Institute of Employment Rights, 1995).

30. *UK Press Gazette*, 3 July 1995. The same article reports Lord Rothermere, speaking to the Media Society on press freedom shortly after the dismissal, as saying that, 'Without free speech, which means free criticism as well as free thought and expression of new ideas, our institutions would stagnate like those of ancient China and Marxist Russia, which also had no true or efficient mechanism of change. If disclosure is the stuff of news, then suppression is the mask of power.'

31. *Gardner (FC) Ltd* v *Beresford* [1978] IRLR 63.

32. *Woods* v *WM Car Services (Peterborough) Ltd* [1982] ICR 692.

33. Employment Protection (Consolidation) Act 1978, Part V.

34. [1991] ICR 269.

35. See most recently *R* v *Secretary of State for Employment, ex parte Seymour-Smith* [1995] IRLR 464.

36. R. Lewis and J. Clark, *Employment Rights, Industrial Tribunals and Arbitration: the Case for Alternative Dispute Resolution* (Institute of Employment Rights, 1993).

37. Council Directive 93/104. For a full analysis, see B. Bercusson, *Working Time in Britain: towards a European Model* (Parts I and II) (Institute of Employment Rights, 1994).

38. See Articles 4 (rest breaks) and 6 (maximum weekly working time).

39. See Article 17(2) (derogations by legislation or collective bargaining permitted in the case of specified activities) and 17(3) (generally).

40. Collective bargaining: levels and coverage. In *OECD Employment Outlook 1994*, Chapter 5.

41. Milner, *op. cit.*

42. A. Ferner and R. Hyman, *Industrial Relations in the New Europe* (1992), p. xxi.

43. So, for example, in Germany decentralization has taken place in the form of devolved bargaining, which has been accommodated 'within existing procedures at enterprise level, and has been embedded within a solid structure of national and industry-level arrangements'. This is in marked contrast to Britain, where decentralization, in contrast to most European countries, has been paralleled by what Crouch refers to as a 'collapse of associational control', and hence 'multi-employer bargaining'. See Ferner and Hyman, *op. cit.*

44. For an account of such arrangements, which operated in the UK in the post-war period, see Ministry of Labour, *Industrial Relations Handbook* (1961).

45. On which see Nursing and Midwifery Staffs Negotiating Council Staff Side, *Evidence to the Review Body for Nursing Staff, Midwives and Health Visitors 1996* (September 1995).

46. See, for example, M. Thornton, Equal pay in Australia. In F. Eyraud (ed.), *Equal Pay Protection in Industrialised Market Economies: In Search of Greater Effectiveness* (Geneva: ILO, 1993), p. 23.

47. It is to be noted that when the mines and railways were decommissioned at the end of the First World War, the statutory bargaining regimes were made expressly conditional on the initial agreement of the employers in the case of the mines, and their continuing agreement in the case of the railways. See Mining Industry Act 1920 and Railways Act 1920.

48. *Griffin* v *South West Water Services Ltd* [1995] IRLR 15.

49. But note that the TUC resolution applied to solidarity action, 'particularly where an employer seeks to circumvent a lawful dispute', a kind of retaliatory action.

50. On which see *The Record*, August 1995, p. 1, where the General Secretary of the Transport and General Workers' Union refers to a campaign 'to guarantee Minimum Standards Agreements across industry' in order to 'guarantee decent pay, secure training as a universal right for all, extend the European social agenda with employers and win the right for all workers to be represented at work by an independent trade union'.

51. Admittedly, if this is the way ahead, then it would be decidedly unfortunate with workers subsisting on a thin gruel of diluted union influence, balanced by minimum statutory standards.

2

Rights at Work: The Union's Role

John Foster

A reduction in union power was an important aim of Conservative policy, even though it was couched in the language of checking abuses, democratising procedures and so on.[1]

On the doorsteps in the 1979 campaign, Tory canvassers were asked, 'What if the trades union leaders won't talk to Mrs Thatcher if she was the Prime Minister?' The right answer to that question was and is 'So what – who cares?'[2]

The real aim of 15 years' persecution of trade unionists has become increasingly clear to a British workforce left with few rights to protect jobs, pay or conditions.

In the past years, the government's position on workplace law has become more desperate at home and abroad. In Britain, it drew criticism from all sides for rushing through an amendment to the third reading of the Trades Union Reform and Employment Rights Bill, with the aim of reducing the effects of the Court of Appeal's decision in *Wilson* v *Associated Newspapers*,[3] a case taken up by the National Union of Journalists (NUJ). The Press for Union Rights Campaign was set up in 1989 with the aim of establishing a statutory right to recognition and an obligation to collective bargaining within the United Kingdom. The campaign has played a leading role in alerting the rest of the union movement and in formulating legal policy for the future. The 1994 TUC conference backed the campaign, and the TUC has now formed a working group to discuss how recognition can be protected in law.

In Europe, a legal challenge prompted partly by the campaign has led to an ECJ ruling that Britain is breaching EU directives which require employers to consult staff representatives on transfers of undertakings and collective redundancies.[4]

BACKGROUND

The government has removed legal restraints on employers, abolished legal rights and protection for working people and increased restraints on unions. The reduction of collective bargaining has been part of the systematic restructuring of industrial relations in our society. The overall decline of trade unions in Britain has been identified in two major surveys, the third Workplace Industrial Relations Survey (WIRS3) and the second Company Level Survey of Industrial Relations (CLIRS2).

The WIRS3 has revealed that in the period from 1984 to 1990 total union density fell from 58 to 48 per cent and collective bargaining coverage from 71 to 54 per cent. If workplaces employing under 25 workers are included, collective agreement coverage fell to 47 per cent and union membership to 38.8 per cent.

This attack on union rights has been a fundamental part of the government's economic strategy and has left four million people unemployed. The desperation of the unemployed has been used to introduce more 'flexible working', including casualization, part-time working, lower wages and poorer conditions. The Trade Union Reform and Employment Rights Act 1993 (TURERA) abolished wage councils and introduced yet more measures to restrict industrial action. It also interfered with the check-off system for union subscriptions.

The government's established Commissioner for Rights of Trade Union Members has the sole task of advising and funding members to sue their unions. Significantly, the government has not established a commissioner to support workers' legal rights against their employers. Legal aid is not available to support the 54,000 people who submitted applications to industrial tribunals in 1994.

The NUJ, together with the RMT, won a significant victory in the Court of Appeal in the *Wilson* v *Associated Newspapers* and *Palmer* v *Associated British Ports*[5] cases. The Court of Appeal ruled that it was unlawful to withhold a pay increase to people who refused to sign personal contracts which contained clauses requiring them to give up their right to be represented in a collective agreement negotiated by an independent and recognized trade union. As a result of this decision, Viscount Ullswater, on behalf of the government, introduced a late amendment on the third reading of TURERA, to neutralize the Court of Appeal's decision. Despite this change to the law Associated Newspapers and Associated British Ports appealed to the House of Lords against the Court of Appeal ruling and were successful.[6] The appeal was upheld on the basis of an interpretation of the wording of the relevant Act, and the judges found that the omission of withholding a pay rise was not an 'action' and therefore not covered. This view was taken despite earlier cases having been decided on the basis that an omission was as discriminatory as an action. This judgment is of fundamental importance because the decision appears to give employers the right to victimize trade union members. It has undermined two other major decisions in British law: *Ridgeway* v *National Coal Board* (1987)[7] and *Discount Tobacco* v *Armitage* (1990).[8] The latter gave people the right to be represented on all matters relating to their employment. The House of Lords' decision has denied this principle except where a trade union is recognized.

In the public sector, the 'next steps' programme of the civil service means there are now 76 separate agencies employing 216,370 workers – over half the total of civil servants. The formation of 29 agencies is part of the government's announced programme to introduce compulsory competitive tendering and 'market testing' within the civil service. This means derecognition and poorer wages and conditions.

Recognition has been withdrawn from teachers' unions for pay bargaining in primary and secondary education in England and Wales. In higher education, the National Association of Teachers in Further and Higher Education (NATFHE) is facing the effect of trusts, the imposition of personal contracts and the end of collective bargaining. The mining industry has been devastated by the privatization of the electricity supply industry; London Underground permanent staff have been replaced by contract labour for the provision of ancillary services and drivers have had new contracts introduced on a personal basis. London buses have been privatized, with the introduction of inferior pay and conditions.

In the private sector, anti-union legislation has been used to introduce personal contracts, derecognize unions and end collective bargaining. This has been accompanied by a fall in wages and conditions. There is another significant development, as reported in the WIRS3, which found that 'workplaces that were less than ten years old recognised unions in twenty three per cent of cases compared with fifty two per cent of those that were more than twenty years old'. In addition to this, of the 69 per cent of companies that recognized unions within their existing establishments, 60 per cent reduced the role of trade unions in collective bargaining. The report goes on to reveal the extent to which collective bargaining has undergone a significant shift. Even the presence of union representatives at the workplace suffered a substantial decline from 1984 to 1990: in the private manufacturing sector from 98 to 90 per cent and in private service from 67 to 57 per cent.

The impact of the recession fuelled by the government's economic strategies has been a further fall in union membership. Cadbury-Schweppes has withdrawn recognition for two-thirds of shop stewards at its factories at Somerdale (Bristol) and Bourneville (Birmingham). Within the engineering sector, the collapse of the national agreement in 1989 led, in establishments employing fewer than 200 workers, to a pay system unilaterally determined by management. The main employers in the oil sector – British Petroleum, Esso, Shell – have derecognized their workforces. Unipart ended the collective bargaining for all its workers and claimed a significant increase in profits, to £15.4 million, as a result.

Unemployment, privatization, personal contracts and performance-related pay all form part of the government's economic strategy. The climate of fear and intimidation among many workers, particularly union representatives, is part of this pattern. A Green Paper from the European Union suggests that: 'Having a job also, is about more than just having money. Employment gives people a place in society. It gives dignity, social contacts, self esteem. It is essential to our well being.' The European Convention of Human Rights, Article 11, protects freedom of association, in particular the worker's right to join a trade union for 'the protection of his interest'.

The government has introduced its programme of anti-union laws to prevent people combining together with the aim of maintaining or improving the conditions of their working lives. As the Director General of the Institute of Personnel Management put it, we are on the verge of creating a 'permanently casualised industrial peasantry'. And the government has acted unlawfully. It stands condemned by the United Nations International Labour Organisation over its employment laws.

Britain is a signatory to the ILO's international conventions. Two of the most important of the Conventions are Nos 87 and 98, which protect union autonomy and activity from state interference. The ILO committee of experts has, since 1989, condemned many aspects of the government's anti-union legislation. In 1992 the British government tried to persuade the ILO general assembly to reject the committee of experts' report for that year. The general assembly rejected the British government's argument. The government has not exercised its right to appeal to the International Court of Justice in the Hague.

The relationship between the employer and employee really matters to the economy and to the community. Workers are not simply a disposable resource. A decent industrial relations framework establishes a decent working environment. Security at work and the right to representation are part of a crucial relationship which benefits social conditions, the family and the wider community.

The faults are becoming more apparent every day. Unions have a role in fighting for the change. The rights which we must establish are:

1 Everyone should have the opportunity to earn his or her living in an occupation freely entered into.
2 All workers have the right to just conditions of work.
3 All workers have the right to safe and healthy working conditions.
4 All workers have the right to a fair remuneration sufficient for a decent standard of living for themselves and their families.
5 All workers and employers have the right to freedom of association in national or international organizations for the protection of their economic and social interests.
6 All workers and employers have the right to bargain collectively.

WHAT IS TO BE DONE

The Press for Union Rights Campaign is aiming to establish the following principles and the European Charter states quite clearly that there is a commitment for the British government to the following:

1 To promote joint consultation between workers and employers.
2 To promote, where necessary and appropriate, machinery for voluntary negotiations between employers or employers' organizations and workers' organizations, with a view to the regulation of terms and conditions of employment by means of collective agreements.
3 To promote the establishment and use of appropriate machinery for conciliation and voluntary arbitration for the settlement of labour disputes.
4 To recognize the rights of workers and employers to collective action in cases of conflicts, including the right to strike, subject to obligations that might rise out of collective agreements previously entered into.[9]

NOTES

1. N. Lawson, *The View from No. 11* (1992).
2. N. Tebbit, *Upwardly Mobile* (1989).
3. [1993] IRLR 326.
4. *European Commission* v *United Kingdom* (Cases 382 & 383/92) [1994] IRLR 392 & 412.
5. *Op. cit.*
6. [1995] ICR 406.
7. [1987] IRLR 80.
8. [1990] IRLR 15.
9. Turin, 18 October 1961.

3

Representation or Recognition

Sonia McKay

According to at least two recent surveys,[1] most people believe in a right to representation by trade unions. After more than 15 years of anti-union legislation, and a significant weakening of union powers to defend their members, these findings are perhaps surprising. But access to proper representation requires a system which both encourages collective bargaining and guarantees union recognition.

Those who support the need for workers' organization would have little difficulty in accepting the results of these surveys. Questions only arise when one attempts to determine how a transition from representation to recognition can be achieved. Is it best achieved through a formal system of statutory recognition, on the lines of that in existence through most of the 1970s? Or is union recognition best arrived at by first giving every worker a general right to be represented through a consultative body, even at the risk of creating non-union organizations?

These are the issues this chapter is seeking to address. It does this by examining the history of statutory recognition from the Donovan Commission[2] onwards, and by counterpoising this with the European model of worker representation bodies, with their well-established rights to information and consultation.

REPRESENTATION AND DONOVAN

The world of work appears to have changed fundamentally since the time, some 30 years ago, when Donovan began taking evidence. First, there has been a decline in union recognition.[3] This has been matched by a fall in union density (the proportion of the workforce in unions) to 35 per cent in 1993. This fall is partly explained by a decline in the traditionally male workforce and a growth in female work. But the main reasons for the change are: the differences between full-time and part-time work; the growth of smaller workplaces at the expense of larger ones; and the decline of sectors where union membership has traditionally been stronger, most notably in manufacturing.[4] As the proportion of part-time jobs has increased, so too has non-unionism: unions overall continue to experience recruitment difficulties among this group of workers. Even within the public sector there is a difference of at least ten percentage points in the density levels of full- and part-time staff.[5] Union membership is also much lower for the under twenties, a problem that clearly is of concern for the long-term future of trade unionism.

It is in this context that the TUC published its 1995 consultative document on trade union representation.[6] This, as will be noted later, was one of a line of documents going back to the mid-1980s, in which unions, together with academics and occasionally the Labour Party, have attempted to grapple with the issue of union representation in the workplace. While the consultative document, and the TUC proposals which followed it[7] reflect the TUC's growing interest in systems of worker representation in other European Union countries, they nevertheless echo themes that have been around for at least 30 years, in particular fears over multi-unionism and concern about the potential for third-party involvement in internal union matters.

As has already been noted, union density in 1993 was just 35 per cent. Thirty years ago, when Donovan began taking evidence, density stood at 42.6 per cent. There was, however, already some concern (expressed forcefully in the Commission's report) about what it noted as a dramatic fall in union membership, from its peak in the early post-war years. It was this fall in membership, and its impact on collective bargaining, that had been a compelling reason for the inquiry.

According to Bain, there had been 'a gradual, but certain decline in union density' from the late 1940s onwards.[8] By 1964 the density rate had reached a low of 42.6 per cent. Bain traced this decline to changes in the labour force itself, changes which still appear all too familiar. There had been a shrinkage of employment in a number of basic industries that had a long tradition of union activity (railways, coal mining and national government) and an expansion of employment in areas with a traditionally low level of union organization. A corresponding growth in white-collar employment, in particular, was seen as a reason for the decline in union density. While one in four trade unionists was a white-collar worker, fewer than two-thirds (65 per cent) were in TUC-affiliated unions.

Bain reviewed a number of proposals as to how best to deal with the issue of recognition.[9] He favoured the proposal, put by Flanders, for the establishment of an independent tribunal to which recognition and other procedural disputes might be referred by the government, on its own initiative, or at the request of unions or employers. Its advantages were seen as applying to all workers and all procedural disputes, avoiding 'administrative inflexibility and legalistic procedures'.

The issue for Bain, and for others at that time, was how to strengthen recognition rights without encouraging the formation of company unions and breakaways. Thirty years on these remain equally strong pressures in any demands for recognition rights.

Today, it is difficult to conceive that governments once viewed the collapse of collective bargaining with alarm. Yet that was the starting point for the commission's enquiry. In dealing with the extension of collective bargaining, Donovan began with the words: 'properly conducted, collective bargaining is the most effective means of giving workers the right to representation in decisions affecting their working lives, a right which is or should be the prerogative of every worker in a democratic society'. For those who gave evidence to the Commission there could be no separation between collective bargaining and representation: the latter flowed from the former. Collective bargaining rights inevitably meant recognition rights.

Since Donovan the world has moved on: there have been major challenges to the ethos of nationalization and the welfare state, a removal of funds from the public sector, increasing privatization and changes in industrial structures. Some may argue that those earlier aspirations are no longer achievable, or perhaps even desirable, goals. What this chapter will do is focus on a number of issues, including:

- how to determine what is meant by the concept of a representative body;

- whether concerns over competition for members should determine how recognition rights are formulated;

- whether unions can survive where worker representation is encouraged, but where union recognition remains no more than a distant goal.

Although the Donovan Commission was set up during the period of a Labour government, that government did not remain in office long enough to do much more than set up a Commission on Industrial Relations (CIR) with voluntary powers to hear recognition disputes. It was left to the Conservative government of 1970–74 to formalize this arrangement by giving new powers to the CIR. The 1971 *Industrial Relations Code of Practice* stated:

82. A trade union may claim recognition for negotiating purposes either when management already has agreed bargaining arrangements with other unions or where no arrangements exist. In either case management should take into account:

(i) the extent of support for the claim among the employees concerned, whether members of the union or not;
(ii) the effect of granting recognition on any existing bargaining arrangements;
(iii) whether or not recognition should be granted to the same union in respect of supervisors and of members of their work groups.

83. Management is entitled to know the number, but not the identities of the employees covered by the proposed bargaining unit who are members of the union making the claim; where the extent of support cannot be agreed it should be determined by arrangements agreed between the parties, for example, a ballot.

99. Employees need representatives to put forward their collective views to management and to safeguard their interests in consultation and negotiation. It is also an advantage for management to deal with representatives who can speak for their fellow employees.

The code's overall tone shaped the conduct of negotiations between employers and employees throughout the period of the Conservative government and beyond.

In 1975 the new Labour government introduced the Employment Protection Act, the first time such legislation had been introduced with union support. Under s. 11, unions could refer recognition disputes to ACAS. There was provision for dealing with non-compliance under s. 15 and under s. 16 for a CAC award. There has since been much criticism of the 1975 Act's provisions. This has included a questioning as to whether the procedures contributed at all to the growth in recognition that did take place.[10] ACAS is on record as stating that s. 11 had no more than a marginal effect.

Later analysis has suggested that a complete picture cannot be obtained merely by counting the number of references to ACAS. While the majority (1115) of the 1610 references were withdrawn, ACAS reported that 46 per cent of the withdrawals were fully successful in gaining recognition and that in a further 36 per cent some form of recognition was achieved. Dickens and Bain[11] say that the indirect impact of these procedures was a 'tendency to engender a climate of opinion which encourages the voluntary recognition of unions', and that this has to be taken into account. In the view of Ewing,[12] the recognition procedures were not total failures, since nearly 100 new employers a year recognized unions.

Dickens and Bain[13] argue that the absence of a recognition procedure in the 1980s has impeded the development of unions. In their detailed analysis of recognition procedures from 1970 onwards, they found that the main problems with the 1975 law arose because of a lack of agreed recognition criteria and the absence of effective sanctions. There was no agreed formula for how bargaining agents would be chosen. And the threat of arbitration over terms and conditions meant that there was little incentive for employers who already provided reasonable terms to recognize.

Traditionally the trade unions had been wary of statutory recognition procedures, and in their evidence to Donovan had not put the proposal forward as a solution to the decline in union density. There were two main concerns. The first was that statutory recognition might assist in the development of non-affiliated or sweetheart company unions. There is some evidence that this did occur during the operation of the s. 11 arrangements. According to Dickens and Bain, although company unions did not, in general, gain recognition from either the CIR or ACAS, some 86 non-TUC unions were formed.

The unions' second major concern was over union rivalry. Simpson[14] notes that a 'recurring concern in these responses was how they would affect inter-union competition'. The TUC, in a document published more than ten years after Simpson, reaffirmed that viewpoint by suggesting that rights to represent individuals should be limited to appropriate unions. [15] Even in its latest proposals (see below), concern over inter-union competition remains powerful.

Experiences of the statutory procedures, and in particular the difficulties involved in what was probably the highest profile recognition dispute of the period (that at the film processing plant at Grunwick), helped to swing trade union opinion away from a statutory framework.

HOW UNION POLICY DEVELOPED

Despite the reservations mentioned above, TUC policy, right until the late 1980s, backed the idea of some form of statutory support for recognition. At its 1985 congress, there was a call for 'statutory support for unions to achieve recognition'. In 1988, congress called for 'effective triggers' to union recognition. In 1989, it demanded 'a legally enforceable threshold of membership', declaring union recognition a priority area.

In its 1990 report to congress, the TUC noted that 'unions continued to find it difficult to achieve new recognition agreements with employers, particularly in the newer sectors and in the southern half of Britain', and that industrial action aimed at securing recognition was almost unknown. The latest government statistics for industrial stoppages[16] reveal that this continues to be the case. Between 1991 and 1994, only 36 (3.5 per cent) of 1024 stoppages concerned trade union matters (a general category including recognition). ACAS, too, now deals with many fewer recognition cases. In 1982 it conciliated on 232 cases, and in 1983 on 216. By 1990 this figure had fallen to 159, and by 1993 it had reached an all-time low of just 94 cases.[17]

At the beginning of 1991, the TUC held a seminar on recognition for union officers. Five expert academics and two international trade union representatives from the USA and the Netherlands were invited. Under project TUC 2000,[18] recognition was to be a priority. The stated task was to 'develop TUC policy on employment law with special reference to union recognition, taking account of the European and wider international dimensions'.

By September of the same year a new consultation document, *Trade Union Recognition*, had been published. This began by making the case for collective representation and bargaining: 'only the collective organization of an independent union can provide any effective counterweight to the power of an employer'. It demonstrated that workers fared worse in non-union workplaces, quoting a Citizens Advice Bureaux (CAB) report, *Hard Labour*. The new document proposed a staged recognition procedure:

1 Any worker had the right to individual representation.
2 Once 10 per cent of the workforce had been recruited there would be a right to facilities.
3 At about 20 per cent membership there should be the right to consultation on certain issues.
4 Negotiation would be achieved at about 40 or 50 per cent.

This phasing-in would be accompanied by rights to time off for trade union duties and possibly for check-off facilities. The call for a phased approach with different degrees of recognition depending on the level of membership had already been suggested by McCarthy and Ewing.[19]

The TUC proposal accepted that unions with significant member-ship should be accorded the status of representatives of the workers for the purposes of EU legislation. But a dominant theme throughout the document is their concern that representative bodies on the lines of works councils might create rival organizations and that if they were given wide powers there might be a corresponding restriction on union agreements with employers.

There was also concern that, if a statutory procedure was adopted, it would need to avoid the difficulties which had manifested themselves in the course of the Grunwick dispute; in particular, the unions wanted to be sure that there would be no need to rely on the cooperation of the employer. One proposal envisaged a system of joint representation in circumstances where a single union had difficulty in reaching a particular level of membership.

The document suggested that what the bargaining unit should be was to be left to the union itself to decide. And to avoid inter-union conflict (on the lines of that arising from the 1975 legislation), there should be provision that independent unions not be barred by non-independent staff associations. There was even a proposal that once a single union sought recognition other unions would be excluded from seeking recognition.

By 1991, one of the issues that was becoming more important to unions was derecognition. A survey published in the magazine *Labour Research*[20] revealed that derecognition had become much more widespread, with four times as many cases recorded in the period 1988–92 as in 1984–88. One of the dangers in the staged system was that it could encourage derecognition if membership fell.

The 1991 seminar on recognition, with its emphasis on a comparative approach, inevitably took account of the experiences of a number of other jurisdictions. The outcome of this research was to separate the jurisdictions analysed into two distinct models. In Northern Ireland, for example, there was a 'reasonably strong public policy commitment to collective bargaining'. In contrast, in the USA this was not the case. It was an inescapable conclusion that public policy was an essential component of any successful statutory procedure.

At this stage the TUC was still taking a cautious approach to European legislation, wishing to ensure that new laws 'should benefit trade unions where they are recognised and promote recruitment into unions', so that employers did not use the opportunity to create alternative channels of communication with workers, 'which might weaken trade unions'. The 1991 paper concluded by posing a series of questions:

- What would be the appropriate percentage to trigger each stage?
- How would membership be verified?
- Who would determine the appropriateness of the union?
- How could inter-union disputes be minimized?
- How could the risk of derecognition be reduced?
- What were the appropriate enforcement measures?

In 1992, congress adopted the statement *Employment Law – a New Approach*. This called for the right of representation 'where no union is recognized'. Where there were recognized unions individuals should be confined to representation by those unions. Where there was none, representation would depend on the union being appropriate.

At the 1994 congress, Bill Morris, from the Transport and General Workers' Union (TGWU) and the General Council, introduced the latest TUC proposals[21] by stating that the 'central goal of a trade union is the right to bargain on behalf of its members'. He was aware that the TUC's latest proposals could open the door to non-union representatives. Congress debated the interim report and agreed that a further document should be drawn up. It is this document that was published in 1995.[22]

The new proposals signalled a clear departure from the position previously taken by the TUC. Instead of the staged approach there was to be a new model, encompassing the following:

- an individual right to representation on all matters regarding the employment contract and in cases of dismissal;
- a right to a general consultative body, with the unions having the right to nominate candidates and seek wider support;
- a new public agency responsible for determining what the bargaining unit should be, which are the appropriate unions, what the threshold of support should be and the extent of the employer's duty to bargain;
- new rights to join and to be active in a union.

Although the first of these proposals also formed part of the staged approach, the remaining proposals are quite new. Nevertheless, they still reflect the central union concerns already referred to, particularly when the role of the public agency is examined. This is primarily to determine the appropriateness of contending unions, the coverage of the bargaining unit and the threshold of membership. The intent once again is to prevent multi-unionism.

The thrust of the proposals is that employers would see advantages in granting recognition, since either way they would end up with some form of representative body. The danger is that unions might conclude that securing recognition depends on their convincing employers that union organization presents fewer industrial relations problems. This moves perilously close to the concept of unions as a disciplinary force in the workforce.

Although it might be argued that it was outside the remit of the TUC document, there is little within it which looked at how unions could win members to guarantee recognition. There is some suggestion that individuals seeing the union at work in the consultative committee would want to join. However, it is equally arguable that the reverse is possible: individual experiences of a weak consultative body, without negotiating powers, may present unions themselves as weak organizations incapable of securing real improvements at work. There is no evidence to suggest that the involvement of workers in the consultative machinery, in the absence of a statutory framework supportive of collective bargaining, pushes workers in the direction of demanding negotiations. Dickens and Bain,[23] in their study of the s. 11 recognition procedures, found that many groups failed to get recognition under ACAS because they could only demonstrate a low level of support.

The proposed consultative bodies would only be appointed where unions had sought, but not been granted, recognition. Unions could stand candidates for the new bodies, whose model comes directly from the European Works Council Directive and the directive's procedure for the establishment of a special negotiating body to determine the composition of the works council. The new bodies would, in effect, be fall-back committees, leading the TUC to have coined the term 'elections as a fall-back' (EFB). These bodies would not have competence to bargain. 'Collective bargaining would remain the exclusive preserve of recognised trade unions.'

The decision of the ECJ in June 1994 (see below) was a major influence on the direction taken by the TUC. Important too was Wedderburn's opinion to the TUC on the ECJ decision. Wedderburn argued that to comply with the ruling it would not be enough for employers to create *ad hoc* employee representatives on any occasion when requirements for consultation over redundancies or transfers was contemplated. Basing itself on this, *Representation at Work* stated that, for the requirements to be met:

- there must be provision for designating workers' representatives in all cases;

- the representatives must be independent of the employers and not subject to any control by the employer as to selection or composition;

- the representatives must have continuity (it would not be an acceptable response to the ECJ to provide for the designation of representatives only at the point when redundancies or a transfer are to be effected);

- the representatives must have adequate resources and access to sufficient information and contact at the workplace to enable them to represent the workers involved.

One notable difference between the latest proposals and the earlier documents, including those presented to the 1994 congress, is the absence of any reference to ILO conventions, in particular Conventions 87 and 98,[24] and to the reports of the ILO's committee of experts.[25]

ESTABLISHING REPRESENTIVITY

This analysis of the theories that have helped to form TUC policy on recognition and representation leads inevitably to an attempt to understand how representivity itself is established.

The traditional view on how to determine what is representative is to look simply at the proportion in membership. Thus, a union with 70 per cent of the workforce in membership is deemed to be more representative than one with 20 per cent membership. It was this mathematical relationship that was the basis of the staged approach to recognition.

The 1991 TUC document on trade union recognition advanced a simple mathematical formula. This accepted without question that there was a link between legitimacy and the proportion of the workforce recruited into membership. But membership levels are not the sole way of establishing legitimacy. Trade unions may legitimately represent the aspirations of workers even where they do not represent anything approaching a majority. In France, for example, employers are under a legal obligation to negotiate with unions, despite exceptionally low levels of membership in the three main union federations. Even where status is linked to union size (as, for example, in Italy), the UIL federation, with a membership of just over one million (representing just 4 per cent of the Italian labour force[26]) is nevertheless accorded representative status and is a body with whom employers must bargain.

Even in the UK, the procedures for registration for independence do not demand that unions show their representivity by reference to density. The agricultural workers' union (now a section of the TGWU) is representative of agricultural workers despite a density rate of just 11 per cent.[27] When the opinions of insurance workers are sought, no one presumes it odd that the media should consult the relevant unions, even though union density is just 35 per cent. The reality is that it is unions which represent and express worker aspirations and it is this which makes them the representatives of workers.

Representation and its relationship with union strength is a complex issue. This has been recognized by the courts. Three cases are particularly relevant.

In the first, *Discount Tobacco and Confectionary* v *Armitage*,[28] the Employment Appeal Tribunal (EAT) had to rule on a claim of dismissal for trade union reasons. Armitage sought from her employers a statement of her written particulars, but received no response. She then contacted her trade union official, asking him to intervene. In response to a letter from the union, Armitage was sent a copy of her contract, but soon after she was dismissed. She could not claim under unfair dismissal legislation since she did not meet the service qualification. Instead she claimed under s. 58 EPCA (now s. 152 TULR(C)A 1992), which provides that a dismissal is unfair if the reason is that the employee 'was or proposed to become a member of an independent trade union'.

Armitage was not dismissed because she was a member of a union, but because she had contacted her union. The EAT had no hesitation in ruling that the essence of the right not to be dismissed for trade union membership included dismissal for seeking representation, since a right to be a member, without representation, is an empty right.

The TUC 1995 document makes reference to *Armitage*, stating that it establishes the right to individual representation. However, *Armitage* could equally be viewed as offering wider rights. If it can be said that individuals have a right to involve their union over individual issues, then surely two or more individuals could also have the right to involve their union over their collective complaint. According to Mr Justice Knox, representation was the consequence of membership. It ought to follow that collective representation is the consequence of collective membership.

The 1995 decision of the House of Lords in *Associated Newspapers* v *Wilson*[29] might seem to cast doubt on *Armitage*. Here the issue was the denial of certain employment benefits to those who refused to transfer to personal contracts. Wilson argued that the employer's actions were aimed at preventing or deterring trade union membership or penalizing individuals for membership. The Law Lords disagreed, ruling that the employer's actions were aimed at encouraging employees to move on to the new contracts and had no relationship to their rights to trade union membership. There was no question of dismissal, and *Armitage* was not argued.

The issue of representation was also relevant in the *South West Water* case.[30] Following privatization, South West Water Services (SWW) derecognized Unison and established a staff consultative committee consisting of 14 elected representatives. Unison members won eight of the 14 seats. With all employees entitled to participate, the new committee appeared on the face to be representative, particularly since Unison membership was low, estimated at no more than 15 per cent by the time that the case began in the High Court.

Following an internal review, the company decided that redundancies would be necessary and agreed that these should be discussed with the consultative committee. Unison commenced an action in the high court. It submitted that the EU directive on collective redundancies[31] was directly enforceable against SWW. In addition, the union argued that the company was in breach of the requirement to consult with workers' representatives and that as far as its members were concerned Unison remained their representative, despite derecognition. Although the union failed in its substantive claim on direct effect, Mr Justice Blackburne did go on to rule on the status of the union. UK law was not sufficiently clear as to who union representatives might be. But Article 1(1)(b) of the Directive had a clear definition of worker representatives. They were 'the workers' representatives provided for by the laws, or practices, of the members states'. Since UK law was unclear it was necessary to look at UK practices. Two industrial relations experts were called: Lord McCarthy and Neil Millward (author of the WIRS studies). Having considered their evidence, Blackburne J was in no doubt that:

> the consultative machinery established by SWW in the shape of the staff council and the area consultative committees was very much the exception in the field of modern-day industrial relations and that despite an increasing trend towards derecognition of trade unions for collective bargaining purposes, many employers

Sonia McKay

still continue to recognise trade unions for other purposes, including dealing with collective redundancies.

His conclusions were that 'Unison and not the staff-side representatives' should be regarded as the representatives for the purpose of consultation.

The case established that unions remained the dominant practice of representation in the UK context. The danger is that this position could alter as a result of the Collective Redundancies and Transfer of Undertakings (Protection of Employment) (Amendment) Regulations 1995, which lay down a new statutory framework of non-union consultative committees. The successful establishment of such bodies would in effect reverse Blackburne's findings on the issue.

The final UK case is the Northern Ireland Court of Appeal decision in *Northern Ireland Hotel and Catering College and North East Education and Library Board* v *NATHFE*.[32] This, too, arose from a claim over a failure to consult. The union concerned (NATHFE) was one of two recognized unions. However, it had no members in the college where the redundancies were to occur, and the employer consulted only with the other recognized union. The Lord Chief Justice of Northern Ireland, Brian Hutton, upheld the NATHFE claim.

Since it was a recognized union it had the right to be consulted, regardless of its own membership's involvement in the redundancies.

The SWW and NATFHE cases taken together point to an extension of union rights. They provide that a non-recognized union may be consulted because it has members, while a recognized union may be consulted even where it has no members. At a point in time when the courts appear to be open to the assertion of union rights over consultation, the establishment of non-union bodies is extremely damaging for unions.

REPRESENTATION MODELS IN OTHER EU STATES

Trade union strength varies greatly across European Union member states and it is for this reason that, when each state came to adopt formal legal mechanisms for consultation, the models approved of could include or exclude trade unions, depending on that state's own history.

In Belgium, France, Germany, Greece, Luxembourg, the Netherlands and Portugal only registered trade unions are competent bodies, and therefore only they can conclude collective agreements. In Belgium, France, Luxembourg and Spain there are further requirements that unions establish that they are sufficiently representative. In Spain, for example, to conclude agreements the unions must hold at least 10 per cent of the works council seats and employers must equally meet a 10 per cent standard. In Greece and Portugal, only employers' organizations can conclude agreements. In France, the requirement that the employers' organization be widely representative applies where extension of a collective agreement is under consideration. In Ireland, to register a collective agreement the employer needs to be 'substantially representative'.

There does not appear to be any direct relationship between the existence of a formal recognition machinery and high levels of membership. In the USA, for example, although a formal procedure exists, union membership is low and has been falling for some time. One explanation must be that it is not the procedure itself which makes the difference but the industrial relations climate within which the procedure operates. States with a strong public policy commitment (like the Netherlands and Sweden) have higher levels of membership than those where this does not apply.

European unions at sectoral level, where most bargaining takes place, do not necessarily have 50 per cent or higher membership, yet they are the negotiating parties recognized under the Maastricht protocol as capable of concluding agreements. The union responsible for European-level negotiations in the building and construction industry, for example, is the European Federation of Building Workers (EFBWW). The French unions affiliated to the EFBWW represent just 3 to 5 per cent of French building workers. The UK unions represent just 30 per cent of the UK workforce, while the Italian unions cover just 38 per cent of the construction labour force in Italy. Despite these low density figures, the EFBWW is considered competent to conclude agreements on behalf of European building workers.

The formal position adopted by the European trade unions is that there should be a 'right of every worker to be covered by a collective agreement'.[33] By contrast, the EU directives, of which the directive on works councils is merely the latest example, recognize a fundamental right to information and consultation that is not linked to union organization and does not lead to union bargaining rights.

The concept of a directive giving workers general rights to information and consultation was first proposed in 1980 as the ill-fated Vredling Directive. Vredling, perhaps not surprisingly, was opposed by the UK government. Selwyn Gummer, then Under Secretary of State for Employment, said of the proposed directive that it 'fails the key test of whether it will help or hinder recovery from the recession'. There was no need for any new mechanisms, since there had already, in the UK, been a growth in joint consultation committees.[34]

The UK government put forward, as its own alternative to Vredling, requirements in the Employment Act 1982 placing a duty on employers with over 250 employees to give details in their annual reports on their activities that provided employees with information, consulted them or rewarded them for the company's performance. However, in 1985 a survey of 311 companies found that fewer than 13 per cent were in full compliance with the Act.[35]

Throughout the 1980s there were attempts to resurrect Vredling, but in the end the member states adopted a much more limited directive on works councils. Despite its more limited coverage, the UK government lost no time in opposing it because it was 'inflexible, bureaucratic, costly and unnecessary'. The UK government supported 'voluntary' employee involvement: it had no objection to setting up works councils, provided that companies wanted them.

The stated purpose of the directive is 'to improve the right to information and consultation of employees'. The directive presumes that consultation will take place with employee representatives defined, as in the earlier directive on collective redundancies, as 'employees' representatives provided for by national law and/or practice'. Article 2 defines consultation as 'the exchange of views and establishment of dialogue between employees' representatives and central management or any more appropriate level of management'.

Thus, for the directive, the central issue is the exchange of information. Works councils would have no bargaining role. In most other EU states, this separation between information and bargaining is already well established in practice, and worker consultation bodies do not, and cannot, cut across the role of unions as collective bargainers.

The directive relies heavily on the German model of works councils, but whether this in itself is enough to conclude that its adoption would lead to the growth and development of independent trade unions is questionable. Ewing suggested that the introduction of a German model might undermine the influence of trade unions and collective bargaining, and that 'employers would be happy to create such institutions which would simply be another way to undermine trade union organization'.[36]

The TUC accepts that the range of consultation issues under EU law is narrow and supports their extension. But it is convinced that unions with a reasonable membership base will be strengthened. At the same time it accepts that in countries like France, where there is a low union membership, universal consultation rights may have undermined unionization still further. Wedderburn is more cautious, pointing out that while EU practices may in fact secure a significant role for trade unions, any mechanism for compelling or encouraging employers to bargain would have to be devised and implemented at national level.[37]

GERMANY, FRANCE AND ITALY

It is well known that in Germany employment and collective bargaining are closely regulated. Article 9, para. 3, of the basic law states:

> The right to form associations to safeguard and improve working and economic conditions is guaranteed to everyone and to all trades, occupations and professions. Agreements which restrict or seek to impair this right shall be null and void; measures directed to this end shall be illegal.

Although some bargaining takes place at plant level between employers and worker representatives, the most important agreements are concluded between employers' federations and unions. These agreements are so important that they are implemented even by employers not party to them. Overall, the German Labour and Social Affairs minister estimates that 90 per cent of employees have their terms and conditions determined by collective agreements.[38]

The influence of collective bargaining is therefore extensive, and is separate from the role of the works councils. But the ability to conclude collective agreements which bind most employers has not in itself been enough to stop a decline in union membership. In 1991 it was estimated that around 41.7 per cent of employees were in trade unions. The DGB (the main German trade union federation) had been growing from a low of 7.6 million in 1984, reaching 7.9 million just before unification which itself brought in an additional four million members from the former East Germany. But the 1980s growth has proved not to be sustainable. From a combined 11.8 million in 1991, membership has fallen to an estimated 9.8 million.[39] A recent union survey of members revealed that 40 per cent of West German members and 54 per cent of East German members were considering leaving the union. They blamed not the failure to reach collective agreements, but the lack of action by unions and growing unemployment.

The second largest EU state is Italy. There, too, legislation guarantees 'the free right of trade unionism' (Article 39 of the 1948 Constitution). Unions which are recognized nationally – that is, which meet four requirements covering democracy, substantial membership, significance throughout the country and representation of all categories of worker – are the only legitimate negotiating bodies. Union membership has declined in Italy as elsewhere. In 1980 it was just over nine million, giving a union density rate of 49.8 per cent. Although in numerical terms it is larger today, an estimated 40 per cent or more of the current membership is made up of retired members no longer in work.

In France, too, there are rights to join and organize in unions (Article L 412-1 of the Code du Travail) and employers must negotiate with union representatives (Article L 132-27). Collective agreements have widespread impact, with some 85 to 95 per cent of French employees having their pay determined at least in part by them. Yet union membership is low and still on a downward path, with one European Trade Union Institute (ETUI) estimate putting it at somewhere between 12 and 16 per cent of employees.

It can be seen, therefore, that the works council directive comes at a point of declining union membership. Ewing argued that any means to introduce worker consultation should come after, rather than before, trade union organization and that a failure to do so could lead to the introduction of devices which 'may serve only to chill support'.[40]

It is in this context that one of the most significant developments on recognition and representation, the decision of the ECJ in June 1994, should be analysed. In *Commission of the European Communities* v *UK*,[41] the issue was whether the UK was in breach of the directives on collective dismissals and on acquired rights owing to its failure to designate who was to be consulted in the absence of trade union recognition. Both directives interpreted representatives of employees as 'the representatives of the employees provided for by the laws or practice of the member states', the same definition as appears in the works council directive. Under UK law, as the SWW case noted, there is no provision for the designation of employee representatives where this does not occur voluntarily in practice. The European Commission therefore brought the case on the basis that the directive required member states to ensure that there was employee representation in an undertaking. The Commission argued that it could not be inferred from the directive that this should only apply where there was employer consent, and said that 'the state guarantee must accordingly cover all cases in which effective protection is not ensured by other means'. The UK approach had rendered the directive largely ineffective. The Commission stressed that its interpretation 'does not impose trade union recognition in UK undertakings', and suggested that it might be adequate for a member to designate representatives 'only in order to comply with the obligations of the Directive'. The Advocate General supported the position taken by the Commission, but also said that there was nothing in the directives to suggest an intention to require even partial harmonization.

The ECJ delivered its ruling on 8 June 1994. Community legislature was 'intended both to ensure comparable protection for employees' rights in the different member states and to harmonise the costs which those protective rules entail for Community undertakings'. The only thing that the directive left to member states was to determine the arrangements for designating the employee representatives who must be informed and consulted: 'National legislation which makes it possible to impede protection unconditionally guaranteed to employees by a Directive is contrary to community law.' The court ruled that although Article 6(5) does envisage the possibility of there not being any employee representatives in an undertaking, it cannot be read in isolation from other provisions. The intention of community legislature was not to allow a situation where no representatives are designated. The directive required member states 'to take all measures necessary to ensure that employees are informed and consulted through their representatives'. This was not designed to bring about harmonization of practice but harmonization of costs.

The ECJ ruling required the UK government to bring forward the necessary legislation to comply. The 1995 regulations, effective from 1 March 1996, are its response. Those are already subject to a legal challenge by a number of trade unions which began in the High Court on 29 February 1996. The unions argue that the regulations fail to set down standards for fair and free elections and that they do not provide for consultation where the workforce does not have the resources to organize an election. A victory for the unions in the courts would be a significant blow to government attempts to weaken union organization. As yet it is unclear what form this will take. But given the government's history of anti-union legislation, it is unlikely that any amendment to the law will be framed in such a way as to assist union organization.

CONCLUSION

From 1 March 1996 new laws have regulated the appointment of worker representatives in the UK. Whether the structure adopted hinders or aids the growth of trade unions is at issue at the time of writing. Trade union membership is continuing to decline (by 6 per cent in 1994 alone[42]). Cases of derecognition appear to be escalating,[43] and they are now involving major companies like BP, Shell and Mobil, with companies like Zeneca and Cadbury proposing a new limited role for unions.

Other factors that may play a part include the decline in the closed shop. The existence of 100 per cent membership agreements not only helped unions to maintain high levels of membership, but also kept at bay the problem which dominates union thinking – the threat of multi-unionism. In this context, if non-union representative bodies are formed, then consideration also needs to be given to how such organizations could maintain themselves as autonomous bodies without union finance and expertise. But it is equally the case that unions, attempting to advance their cause through such bodies, would need to devote resources and energies within workplaces where they have few or no members, possibly at the expense of organizing in areas where there is a significant membership.

Union organization might be classed as being at a crossroad. The absence of a public policy to defend trade unionism makes the future of unions significantly less clear than it was those 30 years ago when Donovan sought ways of extending the role of unions.

NOTES

1. At the beginning of 1995 the TUC published the results of an NOP survey conducted in January, which found that 95 per cent wanted the right to be represented by a union for conditions of employment, with 93 per cent wanting this extended in regard to pay. In a 1994 survey, the manufacturing union MSF found that 88 per cent of the public believed that there should be a legal right to representation by a union.

2. *The Royal Commission on Trade Unions and Employers' Associations 1965–68* (Cmnd 3623). Chaired by Lord Donovan, the Commission had the task of attempting to find solutions to changing workers' organization in the 1950s and 1960s, in particular the growth of a shop stewards movement, which advanced workers' interests through plant-level bargaining. The Commission took evidence over three years before presenting its report in 1968.

3. The Workplace Industrial Relations Survey, *Workplace Industrial Relations in Transition*, showed a fall in recognition from 66 per cent of all establishments in 1984 to 53 per cent in 1990. The 1993 Labour Force Survey revealed a further drop to 49 per cent.

4. The exception is in banking and finance, where higher membership levels have been achieved in smaller, rather than larger, workplaces. Trade Union Recognition, *Employment Gazette*, December 1994 (data from the 1993 Labour Force Survey).

5. *Ibid.*

6. TUC, *Representation at Work – a TUC Consultative Report* (London: Trades Union Congress, 1995).

7. TUC, *Your Voice at Work: TUC Proposals for Rights to Representation at Work* (London: Trades Union Congress, 1995), discussed in Chapter 5 by R. Hyman.

8. G. Bain, *Trade Union Growth and Recognition*. Royal Commission on Trade Unions and Employers' Associations, Research Paper 6.

9. These included: a strengthening of the Fair Wages Resolution, proposed by Hughes and Alexander; extension of recognized terms and conditions (Wedderburn and the Amalgamated Engineering Union, AEU); amendment to the Companies Act to require companies of a certain size to engage in collective bargaining (Wedderburn); arbitration (TUC); and a recognition tribunal (Flanders).

10. By 1980, according to the survey by Daniel and Millward, *Workplace Industrial Relations in Britain, 1983*, 67 per cent of workplaces had recognized unions.

11. L. Dickens and G. Bain, A duty to bargain. In R. Lewis (ed.), *Labour Law in Britain* (1986).

12. K. Ewing, Trade union recognition – a framework for discussion (1990) 19 *Industrial Law Journal* 209.

13. *Op. cit.*

14. B. Simpson, Judicial control of ACAS (1979) 8 *Industrial Law Journal* 209.

15. TUC, *Trade Union Recognition* (London: Trades Union Congress, 1991), consultative document.

16. Department of Employment, *Employment Gazette*, December 1991, 1992, 1993 and 1994.

17. ACAS, *Annual Report* 1982, 1983, 1990, 1991, 1992, and 1993.

18. The TUC's document on unions by the year 2000.

19. J. McCarthy, *Freedom at Work* (London: Fabian Society, 1985); Ewing, *op. cit.*

20. The union derecognition bandwagon, *Labour Research*, November 1992.

21. TUC, *Representation at Work* (London: Trades Union Congress, 1994), interim report to the 1994 congress.

22. TUC (1995), *op. cit.*

23. Dickens and Bain, *op. cit.*

24. Convention 87 on Freedom of Association and Protection of the Right to Organise, and Convention 98 on the Right to Organise and Collective Bargaining.

25. In 1990 the seafarers' union, the National Union of Seamen, made a formal complaint against the UK government over violation of trade union rights. The complaint was upheld by the committee (case 1540). In 1989 the National Union of Teachers had its complaint against the UK government upheld (case 1518).

26. 1990 figures.

27. Lies, damned lies and union density, *Labour Research*, June 1994.

28. [1990] IRLR 15.

29. [1995] ICR 406.

30. *Griffin and others* v *South West Water Services* [1995] IRLR 15.

31. Council Directive 75/129, Directive on the approximation of the laws of the member states in relation to collective redundancies.

32. [1995] IRLR 83.

33. ETUI 1988.

34. The Workplace Industrial Relations Survey showed that as many as 70 per cent of establishments of over 1000 employees had such committees.

35. Why get involved?, *Labour Research*, November 1985.

36. Ewing, *op. cit.*

37. B. Wedderburn, The Italian Workers Statute – some British reflections (1990) 19 *Industrial Law Journal* 154.

38. This figure only applies for workers in the former West Germany. The situation in the former East Germany is more complex. Labour Research Department, *Across the Table – Collective Bargaining in Europe, a Trade Union Negotiators' Handbook* (1993).

39. *Guardian*, 14 January 1995.

40. Ewing, *op. cit.*

41. [1994] ICR 664.

42. *Financial Times*, 19 January 1995, reported that the latest TUC estimates of affiliated members showed a decline from 7.2 million in 1993 to 6.8 million in 1994. In 1979, membership was at its peak of 12 million.

43. G. Gall and S. McKay, Trade union derecognition in Britain 1988–1994, (1994) 32(3) *British Journal of Industrial Relations* 433.

4

Works Councils: Union Advance or Marginalization?

John Kelly

INTRODUCTION

The parameters of British trade union decline since 1979 are by now sufficiently well known that there is no need to repeat them. Membership, density, strike activity, national influence and, in many sectors of the economy, workplace influence have all declined, albeit to varying degrees and unevenly across the economy as a whole. Equally familiar is the list of policies attempted by unions over the years to restore membership and density and recover their influence with employers and government. According to Towers[1] five major types of policy have been pursued by most unions at one time or another, with varying degrees of failure, i.e. merger with other unions, new recruitment strategies, improving individual and collective services to members, political campaigning (particularly in general elections) and the redefinition of union purpose.

While the incidence of mergers has accelerated dramatically since the early 1980s, there is no evidence to suggest that union merger in and of itself has slowed down, let alone arrested, membership decline. Evidence of 'new' recruitment strategies, such as the campaigns to attract part-time workers or the concerted TUC-inspired recruitment drives in London and Manchester, suggests the results have been disappointing, with few additional members signed up.[2] Individual membership services, such as free legal and financial advice, are now almost ubiquitous, yet research on the reasons given by new members for joining trade unions shows they are important only for a very small minority. [3] Political campaigning has significantly increased the number of unions with political funds but has failed to prevent the Conservatives winning general elections in 1979, 1983, 1987 and 1992. That leaves redefinition of union purpose, whose most extreme form was the former Electrical, Electronic, Telecommunications, and

Plumbing Union's (EETPU, now AEEU) vigorous advocacy of so-called no-strike agreements with employers. The expulsion of the EETPU from the TUC in 1988 was sometimes interpreted as the death-knell of such agreements, but in fact it is more likely that the continuing decline in strike activity devalued such agreements in the eyes of employers.

Increasingly, therefore, the redefinition of union purpose has taken the more subtle form of an emphasis on the prospects of union cooperation with employers. Under the leadership of John Monks, the TUC has given a renewed priority to union–management partnership. The arguments for and against 'social partnership' have been examined elsewhere,[4] but one issue that has attracted increasing attention is the institutional form (or forms) through which such partnership should be pursued. Would it, for instance, be feasible to pursue such relations with individual employers exclusively through enterprise or establishment collective bargaining? Or is the collective bargaining forum, with its clearly demarcated sides, opposing interests and high degree of formality, too irredeemably adversarial to facilitate such relations? Many American writers on enterprise or establishment level labour–management cooperation have long favoured an approach in which separate cooperation committees are created alongside bargaining committees in order to create a different, more cooperative, climate of industrial relations.[5] More recently, a growing number of writers have begun to promote works councils as a viable and desirable form of employee representation, and their lead has now been followed by the US Commission on the Future of Worker–Management Relations.[6] British union interest in new types of institution has increasingly centred on the European-style company works council as a possible vehicle of social partnership.[7] Britain is in fact one of the few countries in the European Union which makes no statutory provision for employee or union-based workplace bodies to consult and/or negotiate with the employer at company and/or establishment level.[8] In this chapter, I first set out the various definitions of works councils, and then examine the cases for and against their adoption in Britain from the perspectives of the unions. My principal concern is whether some form of works council would help or hinder the recovery of union membership and influence, since I take these outcomes to be the prerequisites for sustained improvements in the quality of people's working lives. I am not therefore concerned with the much debated issue of whether works councils (in whatever form) help or hinder productivity or profitability (or other employer interests), except insofar as these variables impinge on unions and their members.[9]

John Kelly

DEFINITIONS

The works council is defined by Freeman and Rogers as a 'mandated form of plant-based worker representation alternative to unions'.[10] The key component of this definition is contained in the final phrase, since works councils throughout Europe are elected by all employees in a plant (or company), whether or not they are union members, and works councillors themselves are not obliged to be union members. Moreover, works councils are typically consultative and information-receiving bodies, with few if any formal bargaining rights, and ordinarily they cannot exercise the right to strike. It is in terms of *constituency, composition, role* and *powers* that the European-style works councils can be designated as an alternative to unionism. In practice matters are more complicated. First, where unions are well organized at workplace level, many works councillors will in fact be active trade unionists, e.g. in Germany, Austria and Spain.[11] Second, works councils vary significantly in the scale of their rights: while councils in most countries have some limited co-determination rights, where changes cannot be made without the agreement of the workforce, there is wide variation in the range of issues subject to the rights of information and consultation. Third, while most works councils are exclusively employee bodies, some countries, e.g. Belgium, Denmark and France, have joint management employee councils, usually chaired by the employer.[12] Fourth, the German works councils are forbidden by law from organizing strike action, and the Belgian works councils 'exist to promote collaboration between employer and employee'.[13] Spanish works councils, on the other hand, undertake collective bargaining and do have the right to strike, so there is significant variation in the rights of these bodies, notwithstanding their identical titles.[14] Finally, while most works councils in Europe have their rights and powers laid down by statute, a few do not, e.g. Denmark.

THE DRIFT TOWARDS COMPANY WORKS COUNCILS IN BRITAIN

In its evidence to the 1977 Report of the Committee of Inquiry on Industrial Democracy, the TUC argued that any system of worker representation above and beyond collective bargaining should be based exclusively on the trade unions. Workers' interests should be formulated and pursued through a 'single channel of representation'. Proponents of company works councils have abandoned the idea of the single channel as no longer realistic or workable, and argue instead for a dual system on the following grounds.

European Trends

First, works councils are coming into existence in Britain in any event, because of the 1994 Directive on European Works Councils (EWCs). Despite the British opt-out from the Maastricht Treaty, British companies with at least 1000 employees and branches in at least one other EU state will be obliged to create an EWC for their non-British employee representatives. It is unlikely that such firms will exclude British trade unionists, as the recently established United Biscuits EWC suggests, and there is evidence that other British firms are likely to follow suit.[15]

It has also been argued that a recent ECJ decision has driven a coach and horses through Britain's *de facto* single-union channel. In 1994 the court ruled that consultation with employee representatives over redundancies and transfers of undertakings could *not* be based exclusively on trade unions, as the British government had maintained, because this position would leave the non-union workforce with no collective rights on these two issues.[16] The court ruled that, in the absence of trade unions, some other form of stable and enduring system of worker representation, such as works councils, would have to be created to satisfy European legal requirements.[17]

The 'Representation Gap'

The decline of union density and influence, in both the UK and the USA, has led to the emergence of what some American commentators refer to as the representation gap – the difference between the rights that employees *want* and the rights they actually *have*. (A second, and subsidiary, component of the same gap is the difference between the type of collective voice that employees *need* in order to function effectively and the type they *have* or, more commonly, do not have.[18]) Many of the American commentators believe it is unlikely that this gap can be filled quickly by the recovery of collective bargaining and trade unionism, not least because of employer hostility, and so they have increasingly turned their attention to alternative forms of worker representation that will prove more acceptable to employers. These have included works councils,[19] 'employee involvement',[20] 'joint governance',[21] 'co-management'[22] and a 'mutual gains labor policy'.[23] In Britain, it has been argued that even the best conceivable union recognition laws are unlikely to generate a radical and rapid recovery of union membership and density and that, consequently, a twin-track approach, emphasizing union rights and employee rights, should now be favoured over the previous commitment to a single channel of representation.[24] In any case, a union-based system of worker representation such as worker directors would leave large areas of the current workforce untouched.[25]

The Employers' Need for Labour Cooperation

A third reason for advancing the case of works councils is often only implicit in some of the criticisms of collective bargaining, but is important none the less. This is the idea that in an increasingly competitive, global, capitalist economy, the adversarial character of collective bargaining is unacceptably costly and is therefore less appropriate than in the past.[26] According to Terry, production issues such as the restructuring of work require 'a retreat from purely autonomous, antagonistic workplace union organization'[27] (although he acknowledged that the less adversarial works council model could undermine employee support for unionism[28]). Works councils could constitute a mechanism for satisfying some of the interests of both parties, without imposing heavy costs on either. Workers obtain a form of collective voice that provides them with influence and employers experience an improvement in the quality of their decision-making.[29]

Works Councils and Union Stability

It has been argued that levels of union membership and influence have held up significantly better in countries such as Germany and Austria, where employee rights have been institutionalized in workplace collaborative bodies such as statutorily based works councils.[30] The figures are shown in Table 4.1.

Table 4.1 *Union density in selected OECD countries, 1980 and 1990 (as percentage of employees)*

	1980	1990
Germany	37	34
Austria	54	46
Netherlands	35	26
UK	51	39
Ireland	57	52*
France	19	10
Italy	49	40*

* 1989
Sources: Visser; OECD.[31]

Works Councils as a Step to Union Recognition

In establishments where unions were not yet able to demonstrate sufficient membership support to justify a claim for full recognition, a statutory all-employee body with consultation and information rights

> should be viewed as a springboard for new forms of membership growth and influence, enabling unions to approach a point where bargaining rights are much more easily obtained ... They could provide lay activists with unparalleled opportunities to demonstrate the value and role of union membership and participation.[32]

This theme echoes the idea, set out in an earlier TUC report, that unions could obtain different types of rights (individual representation, information, consultation, full collective bargaining) at different levels of membership support.[33] The reasoning was that demonstrations of effectiveness through individual representation or consultation would encourage more employees to unionize, so that union support could gradually be built up to levels sufficient to obtain recognition for full collective bargaining.

Finally, because of the problems faced by trade unions in recruiting workers and obtaining full recognition for collective bargaining, it has been argued that unions today face a Hobson's choice between some form of all-employee works council body with information and consultation rights or nothing at all.[34] This argument, stark though it may seem, is perhaps the most fundamental of all, because, I believe, it

underpins all the detailed claims about the desirability of works
councils. Insofar as it captures a mood of pessimism, nurtured by
nearly two decades of defeat and decline, it is at one and the same time
the least frequently articulated defence of works councils and yet, for its
advocates, far and away the most compelling.[35]

THE CASE AGAINST COMPANY WORKS
COUNCILS IN BRITAIN

One point on which both critics and proponents of works councils
would agree is that there is a growing 'representation gap' between the
collective rights that employees would like and the ones they 'enjoy'.
The principal case against works councils is that, at best, they would do
little or nothing to fill this gap and, at worst, they would promote the
ideology and practice of non-union labour–management collaboration.

The Variable Impact of Works Councils

If we start with the impact of works councils on union density, it is clear
that the frequently cited German case is rather unusual. There are
quite a number of countries with works councils whose union
movements have shown dramatic declines in density, if not in
influence, and Table 4.1 confirms that Austria, the Netherlands,
France and Italy all fall into this category. (So too in all probability does
Spain, although its union membership data are fairly unreliable and
subject to a considerable margin of error.[36]) Since there is significant
variation in the composition and rights of works councils, it is perhaps
not surprising that there is corresponding variation in the fortunes of
the associated union movements. At the very least, these findings
caution against the naive view that works councils in Britain would
reproduce the stability of German unionism, rather than the collapse of
French unionism.[37] According to Terry, one significant determinant of
the varied fortunes of trade unionism is the degree of union security
provided by the law.[38] The union bargaining role is far better protected
in Germany than in France or Italy, for example.

It is important in the German case to appreciate the role of factors
other than works councils in the genesis of union stability. These would
include: the legal protections for union security and for the union role

in collective bargaining (mentioned above); the formal separation of the rights and powers of works councils (operating within firms) and trade unions (operating above the level of the firm); the high degree of collective organization on the part of German employers (sufficient to inhibit significant free-riding in the form of anti-unionism); the long-standing employer commitment to 'social partnership', an ideology reinforced by the major political parties (CDU, SPD and FDP); and the strength of the economy in the post-war period and its capacity to defuse distributional conflicts between labour and capital.[39] It remains unclear whether union density and influence has been stabilized through the 1980s and 1990s by works councils, or whether a secure and strongly institutionalized union movement have helped to ensure that works councils actually do exercise some influence. It is also possible that neither of these hypotheses is correct and that union stability and works councils are not causally connected in any way at all. Certainly, in the absence of any agreement on the direction of causation (if any) between the presence of works councils and the stability of unionism, it would be a leap of faith to imagine that the introduction of works councils would have a significant and positive impact on British trade unionism.

Militancy and Union Stability

If we examine union movements across the capitalist world in order to discover successful 'models', it becomes clear that 'works councils' provide only one possible route to stability, contrary to the pessimistic advocates of Hobson's choice. If we take union density figures for 1980 and 1990 (Table 4.2), then there are six advanced capitalist countries with density declines as small as, or smaller than, the figure for Germany. Only one of these (Luxembourg) has a system of works councils.[40]

Denmark, Sweden and Norway have systems of workplace representation firmly based on unions, not on works councils, with extensive legal rights for unions and their members, as well as strong political support from social democratic governments.[41] Industrial militancy in the period 1980–89 compared with 1960–67 rose more significantly in these countries than in any other OECD country apart from New Zealand (measured by workers involved per 1000 employees).[42] Likewise, the Canadian union movement has responded to the economic pressures of the 1980s and 1990s by 'aggressively follow[ing] the path of social unionism emphasising the adversarial culture in collective bargaining with management and political action over broader working class issues'.[43]

Table 4.2 *Trade union density in 1980 and 1990 in selected countries (percentage employees in employment)*

	1980	1990
Sweden	80	83
Finland	70	72
Norway	57	56
Canada	35	36
Luxembourg	52	50*
Denmark	77	73
West Germany	37	32*

* 1989
Sources: Visser; OECD.[44]

It remains unclear whether union militancy has helped to maintain union density (which is certainly plausible), or whether stable density has facilitated a policy of militancy (which is equally plausible), or some combination of the two. On the assumption that *successful* militancy demonstrates union effectiveness and therefore encourages workers to unionize, eventually raising (or stabilizing) union density, then in principle a strategy of militancy through collective bargaining and political action could prove to be at least as effective as cooperation through works councils.

The Growing Hostility of Employers to Restrictions on Their Power

The works council proposals rest on a critical assumption about employer attitudes, namely that they would be willing to engage in meaningful consultation with all-employee bodies, either in union or in non-union workplaces. According to Rogers and Streeck,[45] employers would act this way because it is in their best interests to cooperate with organized labour even if they themselves do not yet realize this. Since employer responses to works councils may differ in the union and non-union sectors, I shall consider each in turn.

In the unionized sector the proponents of works councils assume that, while they would be all-employee bodies, they would not be anti- or even non-union bodies to any significant extent. In Germany, after all, approximately 80 per cent of all works councillors are trade unionists (and many are trade union activists), and the councils are not only consultative bodies but also have rights of co-determination (change cannot be made without agreement) on issues such as overtime and dismissal.[46] But the question to be asked in the British context is this: why should employers with a record of growing hostility to trade unionism be even remotely interested in cooperating with legally based consultative bodies dominated by trade unions?

The growth of employer hostility to trade unionism has been extensively documented and will only be briefly summarized here.[47] Employers have become increasingly hostile to granting union recognition, even where unions have recruited a clear majority of workers in an establishment and demonstrated their support for recognition through a secret ballot. This is shown by Table 4.3.

Table 4.3 *Union success rate in recognition cases handled by ACAS, 1976–1993*

	1976–82	1983–86	1987–93
Success rate (%)	45	32	27
Average no. of total cases per annum	426	207	145

Source: Kelly.[48]

Unionized employers have also become increasingly willing to derecognize unions either partially (for collective bargaining purposes) or totally (unions cease to have any function at the workplace). Practically unknown before the mid-1980s, the incidence of derecognition rose to about 25 cases per annum in 1987 and 1988 and, by 1994, had reached at least 70 cases per annum. Moreover, the practice is starting to spread from its origins in printing, publishing and shipping into other sectors of the economy, such as the highly organized oil industry.[49] Employers also ensured that the scope of collective bargaining contracted through the 1980s and that issues once subject to joint regulation with unions came more and more to be determined unilaterally by the employer. According to the Workplace Industrial Relations Surveys, the contraction in bargaining scope was particularly severe in the early 1980s, but in the late 1980s appeared to be confined to manufacturing and industry (both public and private).[50] Since these data only cover unionized establishments, they leave out of the picture the growing number of firms in the late 1980s that contracted the scope of collective bargaining to zero by an act of partial or total derecognition. Finally, we have evidence from a number of studies of attempts by employers to circumvent shop stewards as a channel of

communication and deal directly with their own workforces.[51] All of
this evidence points to a significant rise in the level of employer
hostility to unionism, making it difficult to understand why these same
employers would be willing to entertain the idea of works councils,
particularly if they came to be dominated by trade unionists and
enjoyed certain rights of co-determination. On the other hand, if
employers thought that works councils might prove to be a viable
alternative to unionism then their interest might be aroused, but this
process would in turn arouse the suspicions of many trade unionists
about the employers' motives. Employer interest in such bodies has
already been reported in a number of hospital trusts, which have
recently created works councils alongside trade union negotiating
committees.[52]

What about the non-union sector and the argument that works
councils could provide a springboard for trade union growth?[53] The
reasoning behind this claim appears to be that works councils would be
sufficiently effective to persuade workers of the virtues of collective
representation but not so effective as to satisfy their desire for such
representation. Unions would thus be able to present themselves to
collectivized employees as the inevitable next step required for
effective representation. This scenario is undoubtedly possible and
its supporters could draw on the evidence of white-collar workers'
dissatisfaction with staff associations in the 1970s, and their turn to
independent trade unionism, as consistent with it. But it is equally
possible to stress the long historical period (of about 50 years) during
which the staff associations set up by sophisticated anti-union employers, in the building societies and banks, for instance, succeeded in
keeping independent trade unionism at bay. More recent British
evidence shows that employer-initiated company councils (similar in
many respects to works councils) have helped to maintain a long-
standing non-union status or consolidate a more recent shift to non-
unionism.[54] It was the fear of such anti-union bodies that led American
unions in the 1930s to press successfully for legislation preventing
employers from creating non-union representation in the face of an
imminent or actual union organizing drive. Spanish experience with
works councils suggests that where unions are weak, the institutional-
ization of worker cooperation with employers can limit the scope of
union activity.[55] All we can say at this stage is that the notion of works
councils as a springboard to full unionism is neither more nor less
convincing than the proposition that they will constitute a roadblock to
union growth.

The Ideology of Works Councils

Works councils in many European countries, and certainly in Germany, are premised on the formal (often legal) duty of employees to collaborate or cooperate with employers on matters of mutual interest. In Germany, for instance, there is a legal obligation to cooperate with management 'in a spirit of mutual trust for the goal of the employees and of the establishment'.[56]

The other side of this coin is a so-called 'peace obligation', the legal prohibition on German (and Dutch) works councils from organizing industrial action (the right to call strikes resides exclusively in unions). The class collaborationist character of the first post-war Works Councils Act (1952) explains why the Social Democratic Party and the DGB (the principal union confederation) opposed the legislation and attempted (unsuccessfully) to create British-style shop steward systems alongside works councils.[57] There is evidence that works councils have enjoyed some success in achieving the goal of a form of workplace unionism that is functional for the employer. According to the manager of a US car plant in Germany:

> There are three major advantages of councils. First, you're forced to consider in your decision-making process the effect on the employees in advance. ... This avoids costly mistakes. Second, works councils will in the final run support the company. They will take into account the pressing needs of the company more than a trade union can on the outside. And third, works councils explain and defend certain decisions of the company toward the employees. Once decisions are made, they are easier to implement.[58]

Moreover, such enterprise or establishment level cooperation may lead workers to identify their interests evermore closely with those of their employers.[59] The above quote, and the associated arguments about the benefits for *employers* of works councils, underline the legitimate fear that works councils may provide employees with 'voice', but on the employer's terms.

Yet the antagonistic interests of employers and employees, sharpened by the years of recession and restructuring, and manifest in growing employee concerns over job insecurity, work intensification and earnings inequalities, require more than employee voice – they require *effective* voice based on the right of workers to exercise collective power through independent organizations that they regard as legitimate:[60]

Without power and legitimacy the concept of voice is rendered virtually meaningless ... as scholars begin to employ a definition of voice encompassing the concepts of power and legitimacy, it will be clear that unions are the natural and primary vehicle for the expression of voice.[61]

For all the reasons set out above, works councils are unlikely to be of very much value to British trade unionism, and will do little to fill the 'representation gap'. Any positive impact of works councils on union stability appears to depend on contextual features, such as employer support and legalized union security, that are largely absent from Britain. Worse still, the 'social partnership' ideology inscribed in works councils could undermine the serious and credible alternative of militant trade unionism that has been so important in the Scandinavian countries and in Canada in recent years.

COUNTER-ARGUMENT: THE CONTINGENT CHARACTER OF EMPLOYER POLICIES

It might be objected that employer hostility is directed towards unionized collective *bargaining*, but not the *consultation* which lies at the heart of works councils. It might also be objected that once employers were faced with *statutory* works councils, hostility would give way to a pragmatic desire to make them work. Employer hostility, in other words, is best seen as contingent on particular circumstances and therefore likely to change as circumstances change.

One way of testing the first argument is to see whether the decline in collective bargaining coverage since 1984 has been matched by a rise in the incidence and/or significance of joint consultation (Table 4.4).

The evidence suggests that, outside the public sector, the incidence of joint consultative committees has fallen very much in line with the decline in collective bargaining coverage. Even more striking is that the incidence of consultative committees declined far more rapidly in the unionized sector than in the non-union sector, refuting the suggestion that unionized employers are substituting consultation for collective bargaining.[62] Equally revealing is the decline in union influence over the selection of consultative committee representatives. In 1984, such representatives were chosen by unions in 62 per cent of establishments which recognized unions, but by 1990 this figure had fallen to 48 per

Table 4.4 *Trends in collective bargaining coverage and joint consultation, 1984–1990*

	Private manufacturing		Private services		Public sector	
	1984	1990	1984	1990	1984	1990
Establishments with union recognition (%)	56	44	44	36	99	87
Establishments with consultative committee (%)	30	23	24	19	48	49

Source: Millward *et al.*[63]

cent. This trend is, again, consistent with employer hostility to unions, and rather alarming for those who believe that union-influenced works councils will be acceptable to employers.[64] The growing preference of employers is for one-way communications between junior managers and their subordinates, and it is notable that the largest increase in the incidence of such communications was in the unionized sector of the economy, suggesting that employers are seeking to bypass unions, not engage with them in consultative bodies.[65] Given the desirable and feasible options of weakened unions or no unions at all, why should employers see any attraction in works councils, particularly on German lines, with strong union influence and rights (however circumscribed) of co-determination?

This question brings us to the second rejoinder to the objections raised against works councils, namely the contingent character of employer opposition. Historical evidence suggests one set of conditions under which many employers might well come to appreciate the value of works councils and in which they could therefore be implemented on a wide scale. The resurgence of union militancy towards the end of long waves in the economy has almost invariably encouraged employers to seek out less adversarial and less powerful channels of worker voice. Towards the end of the First World War it was Whitley committees (or joint industrial councils), interlocking structures of union–management negotiation that would institutionalize conflict and serve to defuse the growing political and industrial militancy of sections of the industrial working class. During the Second World War it was joint consultative committees that seemed to hold out the prospect of union–management cooperation on management-defined issues, and in ways that posed the least threat to the employers' prerogatives. The strike wave of 1968–74, and the associated union interest in 'workers' control' and industrial democracy via extended collective bargaining, provoked considerable employer interest in rival schemes of 'employee participation'.[66]

It is quite conceivable that any recovery of union militancy consequent on the ending of the current long downswing could well generate an upsurge of employer interest in alternatives to trade unionism, such as works councils. In *that* context works councils could well be implemented without significant employer opposition, and might even provide some degree of influence for employees over particular issues, albeit with employers having the final say. But in that context, works councils would come to play exactly the type of anti-union role that critics so fear. If, indeed, there were a recovery of union membership and militancy, it would be utter folly to derail such a movement by colluding with employers in the promotion of weaker forms of worker representation.

CONCLUSIONS

In a period of union weakness and employer power, works councils are likely to prove ineffective at best, and ideologically disarming at worst. There are, in any case, no convincing grounds for believing that in present circumstances British employers will have any interest in adopting works councils unless they are forced to do so by law. If a form of worker representation is to be legislated and imposed on employers then it should be independent trade unionism. Equally devoid of merit is the Hobson's choice defence of works councils, that it is them or nothing at all, because comparative evidence suggests that industrial and political militancy has contributed to union stability in Scandinavia and Canada. Of course, militancy is not a panacea for success, as the French and Italian union experience shows, but then works councils are no panacea either, as is clear from the Dutch case. In a period of recovery of union membership and militancy, works councils could turn out to be a dangerous and damaging diversion from the process of union resurgence, their attraction to the employer corresponding to their potential for derailing the rising fortunes of the union movement. In either case, continuing union weakness or union recovery, there are no really persuasive grounds for embracing the institution of works councils.

ACKNOWLEDGEMENTS

I would like to thank Richard Hyman, Aileen McColgan, David Metcalf and Robert Taylor for comments on an earlier draft of this chapter.

NOTES

1. B. Towers, Running the gauntlet: British trade unions under Thatcher 1979–1988 (1989) 42(2) *Industrial and Labour Relations Review* 163.

2. J. Kelly and E. Heery, Full-time officers and trade union recruitment (1989) 27(2) *British Journal of Industrial Relations* 196; J. Kelly and E. Heery, *Working for the Union: British Trade Union Officers* (1994); J. McIlroy, *Trade Unions in Britain Today* (2nd edn, 1995), pp. 402–8.

3. A. Kerr, Why public sector workers join trade unions: an attitude survey of workers in the health service and local government (1992) 14(2) *Employee Relations* 39; A. Sapper, Do members' services packages influence trade union recruitment? (1991) 22(4) *Industrial Relations Journal* 309; J. Waddington and C. Whitston, Collectivism in a changing context: union joining and bargaining preferences among white-collar staff. In P. Leisink, J. van Leemput and J. Vilrokx (eds), *Innovation and Adaptation: Trade Unions and Industrial Relations in a Changed Europe* (1995).

4. J. Kelly, union militancy and social partnership. In P. Ackers *et al.* (eds), *The New Workplace and Trade Unionism* (1996).

5. T.A. Kochan, and L. Dyer, A model of organizational change in the context of union-management relations (1976) 12 *Journal of Applied Behavioural Science* 59; T.A. Kochan, H.C. Katz and R.B. McKersie, *The Transformation of American Industrial Relations* (New York: Basic Books, 1986); M. Schuster, Models of co-operation and change in union settings (1985) 24 *Industrial Relations* 382.

6. Commission on The Future of Worker-Management Relations, *Report And Recommendations* (Washington, DC: Departments of Labor and Commerce, 1994); R.B. Freeman and J. Rogers, Who speaks for us? Employee representation in a non union labour market. In B.E. Kaufman and M.M. Kleiner (eds), *Employee Representation: Alternatives and Future Directions* (Madison, WI: Industrial Relations Research Association, 1993); T.A. Kochan and M. Weinstein, Recent developments in US industrial relations (1994) 32(4) *British Journal of Industrial Relations* 483; T.A. Kochan and P. Osterman, *The Mutual Gains Enterprise. Forging a Winning Partnership among Labor*, Management and Government (Boston: Harvard Business School Press, 1994); P. Weiler, Governing the workplace: employee representation in the eyes of the law. In Kaufman and Kleiner, *op. cit.*

7. The company works council should be distinguished from the European works councils that must be established in all companies operating in more than two EU member states and employing more than 1000 people. These EWCs only cover multinational companies, and do not apply to purely national companies falling below the EWC directive's 1000 employee threshold.

8. Freeman and Rogers, *op. cit.*, p. 47; W. Lecher and R. Naumann, The current state of trade unions in the EU Member States. In W. Lecher (ed.), *Trade Unions in the European Union: a Handbook* (1994), pp. 102–5.

9. J.T. Addison, K. Kraft and J. Wagner, German works councils and firm performance. In Kaufman and Kleiner, *op. cit.*

10. *Op. cit.*, p. 68.

11. R. Bean, *Comparative Industrial Relations* (2nd edn, 1994), p. 34; O. Jacobi, B. Keller and W. Muller-Jentsch, Germany: codetermining the future. In A. Ferner and R. Hyman (eds), *Industrial Relations in the New Europe* (1992), p. 243; S. Mielke, P. Rutters and K.P. Tudyka,

Trade union organization and employee representation. In Lecher, *op. cit.*, p. 166; F. Traxler, Austria: still the country of corporatism. In Ferner and Hyman, *op. cit.*, p. 281.

12. Lecher and Naumann, *op. cit.*, pp. 102–5.

13. Freeman and Rogers, *op. cit.*, p. 46.

14. D. Metcalf, *Works Councils: Power, Organization and Impact* (London: London School of Economics, Centre for Economic Performance, 1994), Working Paper 668.

15. Labour Research Department, Works councils: a will and a way (1995) 84(5) *Labour Research* 17.

16. *European Commission* v *United Kingdom (Case 382/92)* [1994] IRLR 392, *European Commission* v *United Kingdom (Case 383/92)* [1994] IRLR 412.

17. M. Hall, The right to employee representation: works councils, union recognition and collective bargaining (Lecture to the London School of Economics Trade Union Seminar, March 1995); TUC, *Representation at Work: Interim Report to the 1994 Congress* (London: Trades Union Congress, 1994), pp. 14–17; TUC, *Representation at Work: a TUC Consultative Report* (London: Trades Union Congress, 1995) pp. 12–13, 23–7. In fact it seems unlikely the government will legislate to create 'stable and enduring' bodies: see Labour Research Department, The right to a collective voice (1995) 84(6) *Labour Research* 9.

18. Freeman and Rogers, *op. cit.*; Weiler, *op. cit.*

19. Freeman and Rogers, *op. cit.*; Kochan and Weinstein, *op. cit.*; Weiler, *op. cit.*

20. Commission on the Future of Worker–Management Relations, *op. cit.*, p. 8; T.A. Mahoney and M.R. Watson, Evolving modes of workforce governance: an evaluation. In Kaufman and Kleiner, *op. cit.*

21. A. Verma and J. Cutcher-Gershenfeld, Joint governance in the workplace: beyond union-management co-operation and worker participation. In Kaufman and Kleiner, *op. cit.*

22. S. Rubinstein, M. Bennet and T. Kochan, The Saturn partnership: co-management and the re-invention of the local union. In Kaufman and Kleiner, *op. cit.*

23. Kochan and Osterman, *op. cit.*

24. TUC (1994), *op. cit.*, pp. 18–19.

25. W. McCarthy, *The Future of Industrial Democracy* (London: Fabian Society, 1988), Fabian Tract 526, p. 13.

26. Freeman and Rogers, *op. cit.*, pp. 33–4; Kochan and Osterman, *op. cit.*, p. 94; McCarthy, *op. cit.*, pp. 5–6; Mahoney and Watson, *op. cit.*, pp. 156–9.

27. M. Terry, Workplace unionism: redefining structures and objectives. In R. Hyman and A. Ferner (eds), *New Frontiers in European Industrial Relations* (1994), p. 237.

28. *Ibid.*, p. 248.

29. Freeman and Rogers, *op. cit.*; Kochan and Osterman, *op. cit.*, pp. 127–30; Metcalf, *op. cit.*; J. Rogers and W. Streeck, Workplace representation overseas: the works councils story. In R.B. Freeman (ed.), *Working under Different Rules* (New York: Russell Sage Foundation, National Bureau of Economic Research, 1994); TUC (1995), *op. cit.*

30. M. Hall, *Works Councils for the UK? Lessons from the German System* (Coventry: University of Warwick, Industrial Relations Research Unit, 1993), Paper in Industrial Relations 46, p. 2; Terry (1994), *op. cit.*, p. 227.

31. J. Visser, The strength of union movements in advanced capitalist democracies: social and organizational variations. In M. Regini (ed.), *The Future of Labour Movements* (1992), p. 19; OECD, *1994 Economic Outlook* (Paris: Organization for Economic Cooperation and Development, 1994).

32. TUC (1995), *op. cit.*, p. 31.

33. TUC, *Trade Union Recognition* (London: Trades Union Congress, 1991); and see J. Kelly, Trade union recognition: a critical analysis of the TUC's proposals (paper to BUIRA Conference, Manchester, July 1991) for criticism.

34. Weiler, *op. cit.*, p. 101.

35. I readily concede that this argument is pure speculation for which I can offer no tangible evidence. On the other hand, I am convinced that it is right!

36. M.M. Lucio, Spain: constructing institutions and actors in a context of change. In Ferner and Hyman, *op. cit.*

37. Rogers and Streeck, *op. cit.*, noted the variation in union fortunes under works council regimes, but argued that other positive effects, such as worker voice, outweigh such considerations.

John Edmonds also remarked on the variation but was prepared to take a chance: see R. Taylor, *The Future of The Trade Unions* (1994), pp. 214-15.

38. *Op. cit.*

39. Jacobi *et al., op. cit.*; C. Lane, *Management and Labour in Europe: The Industrial Enterprise in Germany, Britain and France* (Aldershot: Edward Elgar, 1989); Lecher and Naumann, *op. cit.*; Mielke *et al., op. cit.*; L. Turner, *Democracy at Work: Changing World Markets and the Future of Labor Unions* (Ithaca, NY: Cornell University Press, 1991).

40. G. Tunsch, Luxembourg: an island of stability. In Ferner and Hyman, *op. cit.*

41. J.E. Dolvik and D. Stokland, Norway: the 'Norwegian model' in transition. In Ferner and Hyman, *op. cit.*; A. Kjellberg, Sweden: can the model survive? In Ferner and Hyman, *op. cit.*; K. Lilja, Finland: no longer the Nordic exception. In Ferner and Hyman, *op. cit.*

42. M. Shalev, The resurgence of labour quiescence. In M. Regini (ed.), *The Future of Labour Movements* (1992), p. 105; and see also P.K. Edwards and R. Hyman, Strikes and industrial conflict: peace in Europe? (in Hyman and Ferner, *op. cit.*, pp. 260-2) for similar findings on strike frequency trends in Sweden and Norway.

43. P. Kumar, Canadian labour's response to work reorganization (1995) 16(1) *Economic and Industrial Democracy* 39, p. 46.

44. *Op. cit.*, p. 19; *op. cit.*

45. J. Rogers and W. Streeck, Productive solidarities: economic strategy and left politics. In D. Miliband, (ed.), *Reinventing the Left* (1994).

46. Hall, *op. cit.*, p. 5.

47. Kelly (1996), *op. cit.*; P. Smith and G. Morton, Union exclusion and the decollectivization of industrial relations in contemporary Britain (1993) 31(1) *British Journal of Industrial Relations* 97; P. Smith and G. Morton, Union exclusion in Britain - next steps (1994) 25(1) *Industrial Relations Journal* 3.

48. Kelly (1996), *op. cit.*

49. G. Gall and S. McKay, Trade union derecognition in Britain, 1988-1994 (1994) 32(3) *British Journal of Industrial Relations* 433.

50. N. Millward, M. Stevens, D. Smart and W. Hawes, *Workplace Industrial Relations in Transition* (1992), pp. 251-2.

51. M. Marchington and P. Parker, *Changing Patterns of Employee Relations* (1990); J. Storey, *Developments in the Management of Human Resources* (1992).

52. Labour Research Department, Human resource management (1995) 148 *Bargaining Report* 7.

53. TUC (1995), *op. cit.*, p. 31.

54. IDS, *Company Councils* (London: Incomes Data Services, 1989), Study 437; IDS, *Company Councils* (London: Incomes Data Services, 1994) Study 561; Labour Research Department, *op. cit.* (notes 15 and 52).

55. Lecher and Naumann, *op. cit.*, p. 86.

56. Jacobi *et al., op. cit.*, p. 242.

57. V.R. Berghahn and D. Karsten, *Industrial Relations in West Germany* (1987), pp. 167-87; Mielke *et al., op. cit.*, pp. 164-7.

58. Freeman and Rogers, *op. cit.*, p. 51.

59. R. Hyman, Changing trade union identities and strategies. In Hyman and Ferner, *op. cit.*, pp. 134-5.

60. Terry (1994), *op. cit.*, pp. 247-8.

61. P.A. Greenfield and R.J. Pleasure, Representatives of their own choosing: finding workers' voice in the legitimacy and power of their unions. In Kaufman and Kleiner, *op. cit.*, pp. 193-4.

62. Millward *et al., op. cit.*, pp. 71, 152.

63. N. Millward, *The New Industrial Relations?* (1994), pp. 78-9.

64. *Ibid.*, p. 81.

65. *Ibid.*, p. 87.

66. M. Poole, *Towards a New Industrial Democracy* (1986); H. Ramsay, Cycles of control: worker participation in historical perspective (1977) 11(3) *Sociology* 481.

5

Is There a Case for Statutory Works Councils in Britain?

Richard Hyman

John Kelly (Chapter 4) has written a forceful and systematic rebuttal of the familiar arguments for statutory works councils in Britain.[1] I accept most of his evidence and agree with a number of his inferences, but do not reach such confidently negative conclusions. Twenty years ago I would have endorsed these too; but times have changed, and today I incline to the view that a statutory system of employee representation is – to put it no more strongly – the least-worst option for British unions.

In this chapter I offer some comments on the operation of German works councils, questioning whether these can be regarded simply as vehicles for collaboration with management; consider the implications of the EU directive establishing European works councils; and discuss whether, and how, the council route might form part of a strategy for trade union recovery and renewal. First, though, it is important to place the debate within a broader context: the 'tradition of voluntarism'[2] in British industrial relations, the impact of developments in the past two decades and the case for a system of positive employment rights. My underlying theoretical assumption should be emphasized: that according to differences of time and place, similar institutions can have different effects and different institutions can have similar effects.

THE END OF VOLUNTARISM?

The institutions of British industrial relations – including the traditional characteristics of labour law – contrast significantly with patterns in most other European countries, and reflect distinctive features of both socio-economic and juridical context. In the words of Kahn-Freund, 'British industrial relations have, in the main, developed by way of industrial autonomy'.[3] For most workers, collective bargaining became a far more important method than legal enactment for the regulation of employment conditions; and most participants, for much of the past century, shared Kahn-Freund's estimation of the virtues of such a 'voluntarist' system.

In comparative terms, the British state apparatus has traditionally been relatively underdeveloped, and the institutions of civil society correspondingly prominent. The rise of industrial capitalism brought the political ascendancy of the doctrine of *laissez-faire*: that the government and the law should interfere as little as possible in economic activity. Such 'non-interventionism' applied, of course, against the background of the common law, which embraced the principles of property rights and the sanctity of individual contracts. The full weight of common-law doctrine was evidently to render collective organization and action illegal; the force of socio-political tradition ensured that when the legislature agreed a remedy, it followed the route of negative immunities rather than positive rights.

The most influential employers came to find 'collective *laissez-faire*' acceptable. When the familiar system of British industrial relations was shaped in the mid-nineteenth century, British capitalism was dominant in expanding world markets; in large measure, successful employers felt confident of their ability to handle their employees – and, where collectively organized, their unions – without the need for state assistance.

Trade unions in the main supported the evolving system for rather different reasons. Their experience of hostile rulings by anti-union judges – who displayed remarkable creativity in construing both statute and common law to the unions' disadvantage – made them anxious to maintain their distance from the courts. Even seemingly supportive legislation might fall foul of judicial ingenuity; hence a system of immunities which excluded the courts from intervention in everyday industrial relations seemed far preferable to one founded on positive rights.

As well as setting their sights against positive collective rights, most union representatives viewed with at best ambiguity the principle of statutory rights for individual employees, particularly in respect of issues that were central to the collective bargaining agenda. It was commonly argued that if workers had employment rights guaranteed by law – for example, minimum wages, maximum hours or protection against dismissal – their incentive to unionize would be undermined: far better to rely on *de facto* rights underpinned by 'free collective bargaining'. Hence comes the tradition that most continental observers have always found difficult to comprehend: trade union support for a system where 'in strict juridical terms, there does not exist ... any "right" to organise or any "right" to strike'.[4] The law, as defined by the pivotal Acts of 1871, 1875 and 1906, left workers free to organize collectively and employers equally free to victimize those who did so; permitted unions to bargain collectively while leaving employers at liberty to refuse to negotiate; enabled unions to call a lawful strike 'in contemplation or furtherance of a trade dispute' without restricting employers from dismissing strikers for breach of contract (or even suing them individually for damages). This contrasts radically with other national labour law regimes, which oblige employers to respect workers' rights to unionize, to bargain 'in good faith' with representative unions and to impose no penalty (beyond withholding wages) on those who strike legally; and which also provide an extensive range of individual employment rights.

The powerful commitment to 'free collective bargaining' contained evident contradictions. 'No state, however benevolent, can perform the function of trade unions in enabling workpeople themselves to decide how their interests can best be safeguarded', declared the TUC in its submission to the Donovan Commission in 1966. This suspicion of state regulation presents clear affinities with the ideology of 'business unionism' which underpinned American labour organization for most of this century. Yet British trade union traditions also involve a strong class identity, commonly articulated in terms of socialist principles. The formation in 1900, on the initiative of the TUC, of what was soon to become the Labour Party is one of the movement's proudest points of historical reference.

The paradox is real, but has usually been managed pragmatically. From pre-capitalist popular struggles against feudal aristocracy, the British labour movement inherited notions of plebeian assertiveness which helped to create an adversarial tradition in industrial relations;[5] but unions have (almost) always been content to seek the best available deal within the socio-economic order as it is. It is not too cynical to suggest that even radical trade unionists normally concentrate on bread-and-butter issues through the week and reserve socialist rhetoric for their weekend speeches. 'Politics' and 'industrial relations' have traditionally been conceived as separate spheres; the unwritten rule was that the Labour Party did not encroach uninvited in the field of collective bargaining, while the unions did not attempt to dictate party policy on non-industrial issues. The complex interaction of class, politics and collective bargaining has often attracted the title 'Labourism':[6] an admixture of beliefs, institutions and practices which could enable remarkable displays of militancy and determination yet in effect proved typically defensive and hence accommodative.

British trade unions had longer than those of any other country to learn the lessons of survival: that militancy could bring results, but refusal to compromise invited frontal counter-attack by the unrestrained force of employers or the state (or both in alliance). For most of their history, the objectives of even militant trade unions have been surprisingly modest; and negotiations have been approached in the spirit of give-and-take. In a system of 'free collective bargaining', sustaining the long-term bargaining relationship with employers was paramount. In Wright Mills's famous expression, union negotiators learned to act as 'managers of discontent';[7] and this was true not only of full-time officials but also of shop stewards. Long before American academics had theorized the value to companies of an institutionalized system of collective employee 'voice', sophisticated British employers had recognized in practice that independent workplace organization – even (or perhaps particularly) if led by militants – could ease the task of managing the shopfloor. The detailed study some three decades ago by Turner and his colleagues[8] showed stewards in the motor industry as a buffer between company and workforce, a kind of cut-price personnel department:

> the leading stewards are performing a managerial function, of grievance settlement, welfare arrangement and human adjustment, and the steward system's acceptance by management (and thus in turn, the facility with which the stewards themselves can satisfy their members' demands and needs) has developed partly because of the increasing effectiveness – and certainly economy – with which this role is fulfilled.[9]

It is important to emphasize this dialectic of militancy and compromise, for it casts doubt on the adequacy of any simple dichotomy between adversarial and collaborative industrial relations institutions and practices. Uncompromising militancy is a recipe for defeat and exclusion; unqualified collaboration invites grass-roots alienation and perhaps revolt. Any effective system of representation is a contradictory combination of conflict and accommodation. Paradoxically, then, those who probed beneath the surface of Britain's adversarial system of trade unionism could identify an underlying bias towards orderly industrial relations: 'the desire of both sides of industry to provide for, and to operate, an effective system of collective bargaining is a stronger guarantee of industrial peace and of a smooth functioning of labour–management relations than any action legislators or courts or enforcement officers can ever hope to undertake'.[10]

As a further caution against over-romanticizing the potential of trade union militancy within the framework of 'free collective bargaining', it should be added that the archetypal beneficiary of the traditional British system was the male manual worker with 'industrial muscle'. Bargaining strength could derive from a variety of factors: scarce skills (perhaps buttressed by union control of occupational entry); a strategic position in the production process, which made strike action a potent threat; a cohesive occupational community, which reinforced the bonds of collective solidarity; and so on. In many cases, and despite contrary rhetoric, trade union policy seemed primarily oriented to defending the relative advantages of the stronger sections of the working class against possible encroachment by the weaker (whether unionized or not), rather than challenging the system on behalf of the class as a whole. 'Solidarity' was normally construed in particularistic terms.

This discussion has used the past tense. The system of industrial relations which prevailed, mainly with only gradual alteration, between roughly 1870 and 1970 has since then undergone rapid and radical transformation. Does the tradition of voluntarism, and within it the ideology of 'free collective bargaining', still have significant purchase? There are many reasons for scepticism.

First, the coverage of collective agreements, as indicated by the 1990 Workplace Industrial Relations Survey,[11] has fallen below the symbolic threshold of half the workforce. In part this reflects the decline in union membership – already discussed by Kelly[12] – but it is also a consequence of the decentralized autonomy inherent in the British system. As Visser has shown,[13] the norm in Europe – partly because of more centralized bargaining structures, partly because of provisions for legal extension of agreements – is that these cover far more workers than are trade union members. In any event, if only a minority of the workforce is covered by collective agreements, it is not easy to argue that 'free collective bargaining' should remain the central method of employment regulation. Add to this fact the impact of some two decades in which feminists and other critics have challenged the primacy of collective bargaining for its anti-egalitarian implications, and the political logic points to the need for new approaches by the unions.

The second key determinant of change has involved management initiative. Employer acquiescence was an important basis for the emergence and persistence of voluntarism. As argued earlier, the self-confidence of successful mid-Victorian capitalists faced with moderate trade unions encouraged the flowering of collective bargaining as a mode of employment regulation. By deliberate action or by default, their role remained of crucial importance. For example, the fiasco of the 1971 Industrial Relations Act was explained in trade union mythology as the result of coordinated defiance by the labour movement; but in fact it owed much to the reluctance of *employers* to utilize the penal sanctions that the legislation made available.

The situation has now changed radically. British capitalism has faced unprecedented competitive challenges, making survival dependent on urgent cost-cutting rationalization. The militant defensiveness of British trade unionism, which could be accommodated in better times, was no longer tolerable, and the result was a series of traumatic struggles in such industries as motor vehicles and newspaper printing. Production and employment collapsed in many of the traditional trade union strongholds; to maintain the viability of the enterprise, and a continued negotiating relationship with management, workplace union representatives were forced to undertake a distinctive British form of 'concession bargaining' in which an extensive range of traditional job controls had to be abandoned. As Kelly documents, many employers – because they were faced by more intransigent unions or encouraged to exploit the change in the balance of power – abandoned union recognition altogether. More significantly in numerical terms, the expanding sectors of service and sweatshop employment – typically characterized by small units (even if as part of giant multinationals), low pay, insecure status and a female or ethnic minority workforce – are largely outside the coverage of collective bargaining. Despite some strenuous recruitment efforts, unions remain excluded across much of this sector, partly because insecurity makes workers keep their heads down, while the succession of legal restrictions on 'secondary' industrial action make it virtually impossible for unions to apply external pressure on anti-union employers.

The third key factor is the shift in the political environment. The most obvious aspect was the election of the Thatcher government in 1979 and the succession of anti-union laws that followed. But the abandonment of voluntarism was presaged by earlier legislation: not simply the 1971 Act, but also the Trade Union and Labour Relations and Employment Protection Acts that replaced it. From the 1960s, it might be argued, there was a process of incremental juridification, which reached its apogee in the 1980s.

Can there be a return to voluntarism? For at least two reasons, this seems impossible. One is that the 'new' Labour Party leadership clearly judges many of the Conservative initiatives to be electorally popular, and is running scared of contemplating any legislative changes that might be denounced as a 'militants' charter'. The second is the European perspective: within the framework of the Maastricht social protocol (which the UK will almost certainly endorse after the next election), the agenda for employment regulation is increasingly shaped by continental norms and principles. These imply more, not fewer, legislative prescriptions. The political realities are that any successful mobilization for a union-friendly legal environment must perforce connect with the discourse of positive employment rights, which is the taken-for-granted background of industrial relations in the rest of Europe.

WORKS COUNCILS IN GERMANY

The post-war German system of 'co-determination' (*Mitbestimmung*) comprises two elements: the works councils, whose structure and functions are defined by the Works Constitution Acts (*Betriebsverfassungsgesetze*) of 1952, 1972 and 1988;[14] and the representation of employees on supervisory boards, established in larger companies in 1951 and 1952 and extended by the *Mitbestimmunggesetz* (Co-determination Act) of 1976, with varying provisions for different categories of enterprise. Most observers would consider that the two institutions are interdependent and complementary, and that neither can adequately be analysed in isolation. However, for reasons of space I will focus exclusively on works councils, as does Kelly in his chapter. It should be noted, however, that at the time of the previous 'industrial democracy' debate in Britain two decades ago, associated with the appointment and report of the Bullock Committee, the subject of discussion was board-level rather than workplace representation.

German law prescribes the election of works councils in all private companies with five or more employees.[15] If an employer fails to initiate an election, a trade union with members in the establishment (or any three eligible employees) may do so. In practice, many smaller establishments do not possess works councils; but the great majority of employees in the private sector are so represented. The size of works councils varies according to the size of the establishment. Manual and white-collar workers must be represented in proportion to their numbers in the workforce. Councillors hold office for four years, are legally protected against dismissal and must be allowed facilities (including necessary paid time off work) to perform their functions. In workplaces with over 300 employees, the council may elect a prescribed number of its members with full release from work.

Works councils possess three types of rights in relation to management decision-making: information, consultation and co-determination. The scope of each is legally prescribed in fine detail: in brief, there exist extensive information rights, somewhat narrower consultation rights, while co-determination – which gives the council at least a provisional veto over management action – is much more closely circumscribed. Council and employer are enjoined to operate 'collaboration in good faith' (*vertrauensvolle Zusammenarbeit*) and to maintain industrial peace. Issues in dispute, if irresoluble domestically, can be adjudicated in the labour courts.

The final key feature of German law is the demarcation between the sphere of collective bargaining and that of the works councils. Only trade unions can negotiate over those issues defined as appropriate for collective bargaining, and only unions may legally call a strike; works councils are supposed not to negotiate with the employer, and not to encroach into the territory of collective agreements.

So much for the legal formulae; what happens in practice? There are three key issues: how significant are the rights possessed by works councils as a protection for workers' interests; is the 'dual system' of worker representation a source of weakness and division; and does the formal prescription of collaborative council–management relations prevent effective mobilization of resistance to objectionable employer initiatives?

The formal rights of German works councils – while more extensive than in any other European country – should certainly not be exaggerated. As Briefs has commented, 'the more important the matter for the company as a whole, the weaker the rights of the works councils'.[16] Even the right to information is limited in respect of business strategy and other aspects of economic planning; yet decisions on such policy issues confine the room for manoeuvre over those personnel and other 'social' matters on which councils possess stronger rights.[17]

Three points should be made here, however. First, this does not mean that collective bargaining provides any better basis for defending workers' interests; here, too, negotiations occur within the context of managerial strategies that are not part of the bargaining agenda. Swedish experience underlines this point. In the 1970s, unions came to recognize that – because 'voluntarist' industrial relations could not influence the production, investment and location decisions of major companies – they were losing their ability to shape employment conditions. In consequence, they pressed for a more legally regulated structure, drawing on the German system in the Co-determination Act 1976 (*Mitbestimmunggesetz*).

Second, the powers assigned to works councils are by no means negligible. In particular, they wield considerable ability to restrain management's autonomous ability to hire and fire – a capacity which some powerful workplace union organizations in Britain once enjoyed, but which in hard times has virtually disappeared in this country. As Streeck has frequently argued,[18] this has made a low-cost deskilling response to intensified competition far more difficult for German employers to contemplate than is the case in Britain: a conclusion reaffirmed in the cross-national comparison of rationalization by Turner.[19]

Third, there is much evidence that effective works councils can use their formal powers – notwithstanding the letter of the law – as a platform for negotiation. In practice, 'collaborative' industrial relations can imply significant constraints on employers. The scope for a self-confident works council to question, complain and delay can make life well-nigh intolerable for a management that insists too arrogantly on its own formal rights.[20]

The 'dual system' of German industrial relations was once widely viewed as a source of trade union weakness, institutionalizing a mutually damaging bifurcation between trade unions entitled to mobilize industrial struggle, but formally excluded from the workplace, and councils confined to the workplace and prohibited from militant action.[21] On the left within German trade unions, the British shop steward system was regarded in the 1960s and 1970s as a superior model to be emulated by strengthening the status and influence of trade union shopfloor representatives (*Vertrauensleute*).[22] The challenge failed – partly because, as Streeck has argued, union officials themselves wished to sustain their monopoly of the strike weapon and had no intention of allowing the development of a counter-force to their own authority. Rather than the *Vertrauensleute* capturing the works councils, as some activists had hoped, almost the reverse occurred, with councils often utilizing *Vertrauensleute* to undertake routine communications on their behalf.

Nevertheless, the development of German industrial relations – particularly after the amendments to the law on works councils in 1972 – has ensured that any notion of a segmented representation structure is inaccurate: 'the two levels in the dual system are mutually reinforcing'.[23] It is not simply that the great majority of successful candidates for election to works councils are official nominees of DGB unions;[24] each is dependent on cooperation with the other. Works councils cannot function effectively without access to the resources that unions offer;[25] unions 'use the works council system as the institutional framework and the major source of support for their activities at the workplace and in the enterprise'.[26]

Today it is notable that the former debates between left and right over the 'dual system' have been silenced;[27] erstwhile critics now regard the legalized rights of the works councils as a primary source of trade union stability and resilience in difficult economic and political circumstances. In Germany there are *no* 'legal protections for union security and for the union role in collective bargaining' – *pace* Kelly – apart from the rights of the councils themselves. There is no statutory requirement for an employer to recognize a trade union, and indeed some refuse to do so.[28] What in practice sustains the representative status of German unions, despite a level of membership density somewhat lower than in Britain, is first the high degree of employer solidarity (the great majority of firms are members of employers' associations and thus party to collective bargaining), and second the system of works councils. It scarcely makes sense for an employer to pursue a union exclusion strategy if the workforce is legally entitled to elect a works council that is in turn likely to be dominated by union activists (with special protection against victimization).[29]

This leads to the final issue: the practical effects of the peace obligation imposed on works councils. The law offers some interesting ambiguities that permit sophisticated workplace activists significant discretion. Works councils may not call a strike: that much is clear. Yet works councillors as individuals have the right to participate in strikes called by the unions to which they belong. However, they may not exploit their position as councillors in order to canvass support for such a strike. In practice – as in the case of the dispute in the German engineering industry at the beginning of 1995 – this allows works councils a free hand to campaign on behalf of their union's programme of demands, and to denounce the inadequacy of the employers' response; only when it comes to the point of 'warning strikes' and formal strike ballots is it necessary to allow the *Vertrauensleute* organization, or the outside trade union apparatus, to take over the running.[30] While complying with the letter of the law, it is possible to stretch considerably the spirit of 'collaboration in good faith'. And even in respect of workplace-specific issues that are not part of the collective bargaining agenda, and thus in principle not legally open to strike action, pressure tactics exist within the law. For although the works council may not call a strike, it has the right to convene a general works meeting (at the employer's expense!) to report on issues under discussion with management. As Hege and Dufour[31] describe, this can concentrate the mind of the employer very effectively.

The key conclusion of this discussion of the German system is thus that, as in Britain, shrewd workplace representatives can often bend the rules to their advantage. My strong impression is that in large, well-organized workplaces, the everyday activities of works councillors display more similarities to than differences from those of British shop stewards. In smaller and less well-organized firms, the German model probably allows trade unions significantly greater leverage than is available in Britain. And in hard times, it seems scarcely disputable that the institutionalized rights of workplace representation provide far greater scope for unions to defend existing points of strength and to advance where they are weak than is available in Britain.

EUROPEAN WORKS COUNCILS

The directive of September 1994, 'on the establishment of a European Works Council or a procedure in Community-scale undertakings and Community-scale groups for the purposes of informing and consulting employees', is the first concrete achievement of the Maastricht social protocol, which enabled the other EU member states to regulate employment issues without involving the UK. The directive applies not only to the 11 signatory states but also to the three new members of the EU and to those members of the European Economic Area (EEA) which remain outside: a total of 17 countries.

This initiative follows more than two decades of abortive efforts to legislate on employee representation in European multinational companies. The draft European Company Statute of 1970 sought to provide an optional corporate status for European transnationals, with employee representation on supervisory boards a required element; later drafts suggested a menu of alternative participatory mechanisms. The draft fifth directive of 1972 likewise proposed a 'German' two-tier structure in large companies; this was made more flexible in subsequent drafts. The Vredeling proposals of 1980 covered information and consultation arrangements in large companies with complex structures.

The EWC directive ultimately adopted may be seen as the end result of the Vredeling initiative. Each of the 17 countries is required to incorporate into national law a requirement that companies meeting the specified criteria (at least 1000 employees in all the countries, and at least 150 in each of two of these) shall – unless employee representatives determine otherwise – introduce information and consultation arrangements at European level. It is estimated that over 450 companies with headquarters in the 17 countries are covered by the directive.[32] While there is currently no obligation to apply these provisions to establishments in the UK (if a future government reverses the Maastricht opt-out this will of course change), British multinationals – like those with headquarters outside the EEA – are required to observe them within the participating countries if employment levels there meet the criteria. This may bring at least another 400 companies within the jurisdiction of the directive. In these circumstances, it would be surprising if a firm were to establish a procedure for continental employees only and exclude British worker representatives.

As Kelly notes, a more immediate issue for the UK government is raised by the ECJ judgment in June 1994 that the directives on employee consultation in cases of redundancies and transfers of undertakings had not been adequately implemented, since British law requires such consultation only where the employer recognizes trade unions. Legislation has now been introduced, providing for consultation with elected employee representatives where no trade union is recognized. In this respect, British law has imported elements of continental notions of dual representation,[33] even though the government's grudging and tokenistic response is seen by many experts as insufficient to meet the ECJ requirements.

The combined effect of the post-ECJ legislation and the EWC directive is to introduce the principle of directly elected employee representatives to fill the increasing vacuum in the coverage of collective bargaining. In neither case is there an obstacle to maintaining the 'single channel' of representation for those employees who are represented by a recognized trade union; in such circumstances, the principle of subsidiarity allows established British practice to continue. More generally, the framing of the EWC directive has been designed to encourage voluntary agreements at company level – as in the 40 or more multinationals where arrangements were in place before September 1994 – with the statutory imposition of a mechanism only as a last resort.[34]

The formal powers specified in the directive are modest: the right to at least one annual meeting for information and consultation relating 'in particular to transnational questions which significantly affect workers' interests'. While German notions of management–council collaboration are replicated in references to working 'in a spirit of cooperation', there is little in common with the array of rights and functions assigned to German works councils. In this sense, the very title 'European works council' is a misnomer. Nevertheless, the significance of the directive is more than symbolic. Under its provisions, worker representatives in multinationals are able to meet to discuss corporate issues, with the employer covering wages, travel and accommodation, translation facilities and expert assistance. Given current constraints on trade union finances, it is surely a major advantage for unions that transnational firms will be obliged, in effect, to bankroll a system of Europe-wide joint shop stewards' committees.

Intelligent trade unionists should have little difficulty in turning these facilities to advantage in their handling of collective bargaining. Some anti-union employers will doubtless attempt to evade or minimize their obligations. It is reported, for example, that Marks & Spencer is attempting to establish a 'European council' consisting primarily of British representatives appointed by non-union 'house committees'.[35] It remains to be seen whether such mechanisms will be judged to comply with the requirements of the directive; and, if they do, whether non-union representatives on such bodies will remain immune to the obvious attractions of formal union backing.

WHAT STRATEGY FOR TRADE UNION RECOVERY?

Given the scale of economic and political adversity, it is possible to argue that British trade unions have shown considerable resilience in the 1980s and 1990s, and that alarmist assessments of the condition of the movement are misplaced. In part, the debate involves questions of emphasis: is the glass half full or half empty? In addition, the issue is one of comparators; as Kelly notes, membership decline in Britain has been worse than in many countries but better than in some others. Density has not collapsed to the depths reached in France or the USA, for example. Nevertheless, it is sobering to reflect that it is now near the point from which the labour movements in those countries commenced their disastrous decline.

What is to be done? Here is the core of Kelly's answer: 'on the assumption that *successful* militancy demonstrates union effectiveness and therefore encourages workers to unionize, eventually raising (or stabilizing) union density, in principle a strategy of militancy through collective bargaining and political action could prove at least as effective as a strategy of cooperation through works councils' (emphasis in original). I am all in favour of successful militancy; but how far is this really on the agenda in Britain in the 1990s?

There are still some unionized groups that can wield traditional methods of industrial struggle with some success: the railway workers in 1994 provided one example. But the proportion of the labour force possessing old-style 'industrial muscle' is ever diminishing, and in the past 15 years even this segment has found that militancy more often results in traumatic defeat than in clear-cut victory. Some other categories of trade unionists have been able to mobilize widespread support in specific campaigns, to considerable effect; the school-teachers' resistance to testing was such a case. But victories of this kind are also exceptional.

A plausible strategy has to start from the realities of contemporary industrial relations. As Hall notes,

> many employees will have little or no experience of union membership or working in a unionised environment. The scale of the challenge facing unions is encapsulated in the 1990 Work-place Industrial Relations Survey finding that unions had members but no recognition in nine per cent of trading sector establishments, but no members at all in forty nine per cent of such establishments.[36]

For workers who do not perceive a serious conflict of interest with their employer, or conversely are so fearful of losing their job that they dare not step out of line, appeals to militancy are unlikely to prove an effective recruitment tactic. I have come, somewhat reluctantly, to accept the argument that union vitality and effectiveness require a favourable framework of law.

British unions today increasingly face a familiar vicious circle. Without recognition, they cannot offer the collective representation and bargaining achievements that are a major incentive to member-ship.[37] Yet without membership – perhaps a substantial majority of the workforce – they are unlikely to persuade hostile employers to concede recognition voluntarily. It is sobering to compare unions' current predicament with the situation in the 1970s: a decade of trade union advance when, for the first time in British history, density passed the 50 per cent threshold. Also for the first time, unions sought and obtained statutory support for recognition: the provisions in the 1975 Employ-ment Protection Act were drafted with the advice of the most eminent union-friendly legal experts. Yet the Grunwick case showed that a determined back-street employer could make a mockery of the procedures.

Kelly's survey of the current 'union avoidance' strategies of a growing number of employers shows that the problem of winning recognition – and of winning membership in advance of recognition – is far greater today. In such a climate, an effective union recognition law would be immensely difficult to devise and to enforce; it is not easy to envisage a statutory procedure that would transcend the problems of the 1970s in a far more uncongenial context.

It is against this background that we need to evaluate the idea of works councils in Britain, and more specifically the changing balance of opinion in the TUC. The proposals drafted by its Task Group on Representation at Work and approved by the 1995 congress, are presented as the basis for 'a new legal framework which combines the best traditions of British collective bargaining with new rights under European law'.[38] The report is a judiciously drafted political compromise, which moves cautiously away from the commitment to the single channel without ever embracing the terminology of works councils.

The report begins by noting the 'insecurity and injustice' faced by a growing proportion of employees in Britain today, and argues that only a new framework of legal rights can tackle the problem. Its proposals are developed in three sections. The first covers the right of the individual worker to representation, in particular in relation to discipline and grievances. This would include a right for members to be represented by their union, would prohibit victimization of members and representatives, and would provide rights for unions to recruit and distribute information at work. Trade union rights are also discussed in the third section, which proposes a statutory procedure for adjudicating claims for recognition and considers how a 'duty to bargain' might be enforced on recalcitrant employers.

In its central section the report discusses employee consultation rights against the background of European law. It distinguishes between the limited agenda (redundancies and transfers of undertakings) covered by the 1994 ECJ judgment, and 'general consultation rights' which would encompass 'management proposals involving significant changes in employment numbers or working conditions'.[39]

To meet both the ECJ requirements and the broader consultative proposals, the report suggests a twin-track approach. The preferred option is for consultation arrangements agreed between an employer and an independent trade union or unions. Realistically, however, this option will not be available where union membership and/or recognition is absent. Here, the report draws on the provisions of the EWC directive to propose a system of 'elections as a fall-back': workers would acquire a statutory right to elect representatives for the purposes of consultation, and trade unions would be entitled to nominate candidates for election.[40] If union nominees won a majority of seats, an award of general consultation rights could be made by a new representation agency, which would also adjudicate on recognition disputes.

The report argues that such a system could function 'as a springboard for new approaches of membership growth and influence',[41] since 'elections held as a fall-back would provide a way of establishing a legitimate trade union voice in the workplace [and] would in fact provide unions with a legally guaranteed basis for workplace organization'. These arguments seem to imply a rather more developed institution with a more extensive jurisdiction than the representative structure actually outlined: something rather like a works council, indeed.

Kelly is unimpressed. Ironically, however, he devotes rather more space to rehearsing arguments *in favour* of works councils than to developing the case *against*. He details five of the former, while presenting just three main counter-arguments. First, councils might as easily constitute obstacles to unionization as supports; second, they institutionalize an ideology of social partnership which inhibits militancy; third, if councils should assert their autonomy then anti-union employers would refuse to deal with them. Hence 'works councils are likely to prove ineffective at best, and ideologically disarming at worst'.

Clearly, any institutional experiment in British industrial relations will have results which are in large measure uncertain. The issue is one of the balance of probabilities, and these would be significantly conditioned by the precise content of any legal innovations: the devil is in the detail. Why take the risk? Because the current circumstances of British trade unionism are bad and in the absence of a more supportive legal framework are likely to deteriorate further; and because I am convinced that Kelly overstates the negative case. Let me address each of his three central arguments in turn.

Would statutory works councils assist or obstruct unionization? As Kelly points out, the relationship between councils and (changes in) union density is internationally variable.[42] What influences the patterns of variation? One factor would appear to be the degree of cohesion in the trade union movement: the three Western European countries with particularly sharp declines to dangerously low levels – France, Spain and the Netherlands – all have ideologically divided trade unionism, a factor which is likely to obstruct cooperation between unions and councils. Another obvious consideration is the extent to which councils possess significant rights of intervention in managerial decisions, and the degree to which links with trade unions are legally prescribed.

Where elected structures of employee representation possess significant functions, they typically find these impossible to perform effectively without the support of an external trade union. In this respect, the conclusions of the detailed case studies of Hege and Dufour[43] are persuasive. In Britain, I would take the experience of the staff associations in the finance sector as supporting instances. Kelly cites these as mechanisms which over a 'long historical period ...

succeeded in keeping independent trade unionism at bay'. But this was possible only while independent unionism faced an uphill struggle because a career in the sector seemed to guarantee security, status and material advantages. Once the material circumstances changed, staff associations could survive only by adopting a more autonomous and more militant stance; the end result was typically for them to assume the status of an independent union or to merge with a TUC-affiliated organization. In the absence of alternative suggestions for winning support among non-unionized workforces, the idea that councils could serve as a springboard for organization seems the best available strategic option.

Does the 'ideology of works councils' inevitably disarm trade unionism? I have already argued that notions of 'social partnership' need not act as too severe a straitjacket. German unions have in recent years mobilized some of the most effective displays of targeted militancy in any Western European country. At the same time, however, it is necessary to recognize – and to respond strategically to – the degree to which rank-and-file employees, regardless of institutional context, are susceptible to cooperative rhetoric. As product market competition has intensified, the notion that 'we are all in the same boat' has acquired considerable resonance, even if accompanied by other contradictory ideas. Within any establishment, employees – from shopfloor workers to plant managers – do possess a common interest in avoiding closure, whatever other areas of conflicting interests exist. This area of common interest can be as salient for a 'single-channel' shop stewards' committee committed to militant principles as for a 'cooperative' works council. Of course, institutions do make a difference; what is uncertain is how much, and how. And here it is important to emphasize a theme that Kelly disregards: the growing resort of employers to individualized forms of 'direct participation', such as in-house communications systems, quality circles and team briefings. Such channels of ideological dissemination are already in place. A specifically *collective* structure of employee representation, with rights of involvement by independent unions, offers the best potential for counteracting such channels by articulating the common interests of workers that conflict with those of the employer.

There is a related problem that Kelly does not explicitly address: as noted above, there are material as well as ideological pressures towards what Streeck has called 'wildcat cooperation'. [44] In hard times, any system of workplace employee representatives – whether comprising shop stewards, similar shopfloor union negotiators or a works council (unionized or otherwise) – may feel constrained to agree conditions which undercut official trade union policy. As suggested earlier, British industrial relations in the past 15 years may be read in terms of 'concession bargaining' by erstwhile workplace militants. Arguably, British trade unions, with their strong traditions of decentralized rank-and-file democracy, face particular difficulties in controlling a cumulative drift towards the undermining of general standards.[45] Works councils would alter the form of this problem; but not, I think, its underlying sources. Whatever happens, there is an urgent need for unions in Britain to achieve a more effective redefinition of the articulation between policy and practice at centralized and decentralized levels.

Would an anti-union employer refuse to cooperate with an assertive works council? This is Kelly's third argument, but here I feel that he conflates two issues. First, if British legislation imported continental institutions of management–employee consultation, would British employers embrace continental principles of social partnership? It would be naive to imagine so. But, second, could employers be constrained to deal 'in good faith' with such bodies? Here, the question is one of employer pragmatism rather than principle. The answer will depend partly on the nature of the legal obligations and the efficacy of the mechanisms of enforcement; and partly on the degree to which extra-legal resources can be mobilized (notably, by trade unions) to influence employer strategies. At a time when British unions have few power resources at their disposal, a system of statutory representation rights could help to fill the gap.

To conclude, I would emphasize that the concept of a works council is open to a diversity of procedural specifications and ideological evaluations. Some forms would undoubtedly be of little benefit to trade unions and could present serious dangers. If British unions adopt the demand for works councils they must do so without illusions and must be as concerned with the detail as with the principle.

Finally, I would stress that the question of works councils should not be seen as a free-standing issue, nor necessarily as the most important element in the debate over positive employee and trade union rights. The consolidation and renewal of British trade unionism must rest on an interlinked and complementary programme of institutional and legislative reforms, capable of reversing the regressive impact of 17 years of Tory vindictiveness and building bridges between the British labour movement and its continental comrades. Statutory rights of employee representation, to be advantageous, would need to be linked to the creation of a programme of individual rights of job security and employment conditions; the removal of unwarranted restrictions on trade union action; positive rights for union recruitment and organization; and, not least, a strengthening of workers' labour market position by a serious strategy of job creation.

The case for a 'continental' system of positive rights rests on a realistic assessment of existing trade union weakness. Voluntarism and 'free collective bargaining' offer only limited prospects of sustaining the remaining strongholds of union organization and effectiveness, and few if any hopes of making inroads into the growing majority of unorganized workplaces. A supportive legal and institutional framework could make a substantial difference. Within a different institutional order, it is even possible that 'successful militancy' may become a plausible option for a significant proportion of British workers. Alas, at present it is certainly not.

ACKNOWLEDGEMENTS

My thanks go to Mark Hall and Michael Terry for comments on a draft of this chapter. However, the usual disclaimers apply.

NOTES

1. Kelly is concerned in part to challenge the recent writings of American advocates of a works council system. It seems to me that the American debate differs significantly from that in Britain, in that supporters of works councils place far greater emphasis on the contribution of such institutions to workplace consensus than do their British counterparts. This may in part reflect the more devastated condition of trade union organization in the USA. In any event, I am here concerned only with the relevance of European (and particularly German) institutions to the British case.

2. A. Flanders, The tradition of voluntarism (1974) 12 *British Journal of Industrial Relations* 352.

3. O. Kahn-Freund, Legal framework. In A. Flanders and H.A. Clegg (eds), *The System of Industrial Relations in Great Britain* (1954), p. 44.

4. K.W. Wedderburn, *The Worker and the Law* (1980), p. 69.

5. A. Fox, *History and Heritage* (1980).

6. P. Anderson, Origins of the present crisis. In P. Anderson and R. Blackburn (eds), *Towards Socialism* (1965); J. Saville, The ideology of labourism. In R. Benewick, R.N. Berki and B. Parekh (eds), *Knowledge and Belief in Politics* (1973).

7. C. Wright Mills, *The New Men of Power: America's Labor Leaders* (New York: Harcourt, Brace, 1948), pp. 8-9.

8. H.A. Turner, G. Clack and G. Roberts, *Labour Relations in the Motor Industry* (1967), pp. 205-16.

9. This analysis helped to inspire the description of the shop steward in the Donovan Report as 'more of a lubricant than an irritant'; see also the case study by Batstone and his colleagues a decade later (E. Batstone, I. Boraston and S. Frenkel, *Shop Stewards in Action*, 1977). In passing, it is not a little surprising that Kelly does not mention shop stewards at all in the course of his chapter, given

that shop steward representation has traditionally been seen as the main alternative to works councils as a mechanism of workplace employee representation.

10. Kahn-Freund, *op. cit.*, p. 43.

11. N. Millward, M. Stevens, D. Smart and W.R. Hawes, *Workplace Industrial Relations in Transition* (1992).

12. Though he presents statistics only up to 1989. Sadly, what makes British trade unionism so exceptional is the *continuous* year-to-year decline in membership from 1980 to the present day.

13. J. Visser, European trade unions: the transition years. In R. Hyman and A. Ferner (eds), *New Frontiers in European Industrial Relations* (1984), p. 99.

14. Many of the features of the modern works council system are based on the legislation adopted by the Weimar Republic in 1920, which in turn reflected far longer historical traditions.

15. An analogous system of 'personnel councils', with somewhat weaker rights, exists in the public sector.

16. U. Briefs, Co-determination in the Federal Republic of Germany: an appraisal of a secular experience. In G. Széll, P. Blyton and C. Cornforth (eds), *The State, Trade Unions and Self-Management* (1988), p. 68.

17. A. Sorge and W. Streeck, Industrial relations and technical change: the case for an extended perspective. In R. Hyman and W. Streeck (eds), *New Technology and Industrial Relations* (1988).

18. See, for example, a number of the essays compiled in W. Streeck, *Social Institutions and Economic Performance* (1992).

19. L. Turner, *Democracy at Work: Changing World Markets and the Future of Labor Unions* (Ithaca, NY: Cornell University Press, 1992).

20. See W. Müller-Jentsch, Auf dem Prüfstand: das deutsche Modell der industriellen Beziehungen (1995) 2 *Industrielle Beziehungen* 11, p. 17.

21. See W. Müller-Jentsch, Neue Konfliktpotentiale und institutionelle Stabilität. In J. Matthes (ed.), *Sozialer Wandel in Westeuropa* (1979).

22. Literally 'trust-people', often misleadingly translated as shop stewards. Unlike British shop stewards, *Vertrauensleute* exercise no collective bargaining functions; their tasks involve recruitment, communications and (at times) mobilization of support for union policies.

23. K.A. Thelen, *Union of Parts: Labor Politics in Postwar Germany* (Ithaca, NY: Cornell University Press: 1991), p. 16.

24. In the most recent elections, in 1994, the DGB captured 'only' two-thirds of all seats; including minority unions, the total trade union share was 73 per cent. However, some of the remainder were 'unofficial' trade union candidates; and there is evidence that elected non-unionists often subsequently become union members.

25. A. Hege and C. Dufour, Decentralization and legitimacy in employee representation (1995) 1 *European Journal of Industrial Relations* 83.

26. Streeck, *op. cit.*, p. 153.

27. O. Jacobi, B. Keller and W. Müller-Jentsch, Germany: codetermining the future? In A. Ferner and R. Hyman (eds), *Industrial Relations in the New Europe* (1992), p. 220.

28. There does exist the possibility for a collective agreement to be extended to employers who are not party to it (*Allgemeinverbindlichkeit*), but in practice this procedure is inoperative.

29. Exceptions that prove the rule: in 1995 a works council dominated by the union HBV was established for the first time in the strongly anti-union Schlecker chain of chemist shops (U. Wohland, Kampf um soziale Mindeststandards: 6 Monate Auseinandersetzung um die Drogerie-kette Schlecker, *Express*, April 1995); while NGG achieved a similar success in the German offshoot of fast food chain McDonald's (U. Böhlefeld, Pionierarbeit bei McDonald's, *Die Mitbestimmung*, April–May 1995).

30. One example I can cite is the main Opel factory at Rüsselsheim: a workplace with almost 30,000 employees, the majority of whom are IG Metall members. There is a strong left-wing tradition dating back at least half a century. Two years ago I interviewed the works council president: surely, I asked, a set of full-time works councillors closeted in the same office block as the personnel department must risk becoming isolated from the workplace. Not in the least, he retorted. The committee of full-timers worked closely with the other works councillors, each of whom held frequent meetings with the *Vertrauensleute* in their own sections of the factory. Regular information leaflets were circulated to every worker, signed jointly by himself and the chair of the *Vertrauensleute*; in an emergency, virtually every worker could be contacted within an hour.

Certainly, the leaflets distributed in conjunction with the 1995 bargaining round express sentiments more militant than the much less frequent communications of most shop steward committees in Britain.

31. *Op. cit.*, pp. 95–6.

32. M. Hall, M. Carley, M. Gold, P. Marginson and K. Sisson, *European Works Councils: Planning for the Directive* (1995).

33. P. Davies, A challenge to the single channel (1994) 23 *Industrial Law Journal* 272; Hall, *op. cit.*

34. H. Krieger and P. Bonneton, Analysis of existing voluntary agreements on information and consultation in European multinationals (1995) 1 *Transfer* 188, p. 190, refer to this approach as 'enforced voluntarism'.

35. IRS, European Works Councils and the UK, *IRS Employment Trends*, April 1995, p. 581.

36. M. Hall, Beyond recognition? Employee representation and EU law (paper to Industrial Law Society Conference, May 1995). Note also that the WIRS data exclude establishments with fewer than 25 employees, where non-unionism is considerably more prevalent.

37. I share with Kelly considerable scepticism towards the notion that individual membership services can alone attract many workers to unionize.

38. TUC, *Your Voice at Work: TUC Proposals for Rights to Representation at Work* (London: Trades Union Congress, 1995), p. 7. An earlier version, *Representation at Work*, was published as a consultative document and discussed at a special conference in March 1995. Presentationally there are significant differences between the two versions; the main change of substance is that the latter makes far more detailed proposals on trade union recognition.

39. *Ibid.*, p. 2.

40. *Ibid.*, pp. 23–4.

41. *Ibid.*, pp. 26–7.

42. The evidence used and inferences drawn are, however, open to question. Membership density data cover only the two years 1980 and 1989. Kelly uses these figures to argue 'that Austria, the Netherlands, France and Italy' are 'countries with works councils whose union movements have shown dramatic declines in density'. It is misleading, to say the least, to describe Italy in the 1980s as a country with works councils; ever since the enactment of the *Statuto dei Lavoratori* (workers' statute) in 1970, workplace organization has been explicitly linked to trade unions. (In passing, one may note that the TUC proposals for workplace trade union rights seem to be strongly influenced by the Italian law.) As for Austria, its experience since 1980 is open to different interpretations; Visser (*op. cit.*, p. 83) includes it among the countries with 'more or less stable union membership levels'.

43. *Op. cit.*

44. W. Streeck, Neo-corporatist industrial relations and the economic crisis in West Germany. In J.H. Goldthorpe (ed.), *Order and Conflict in Contemporary Capitalism* (1984).

45. M. Terry, Workplace unionism: redefining structures and objectives. In Hyman and Ferner (eds), *op. cit.*

6

International Trade and International Trade Union Rights

John Hendy QC

INTRODUCTION

Trade union rights are under attack all over the world. The ICFTU *Annual Survey of Violations of Trade Union Rights* is horrifying testimony to that fact and to the fact that the attacks are increasing. A year's toll measures murders of trade unionists in hundreds; injuries and detentions in thousands and dismissals in tens of thousands. No one knows how many trade unionists or workers wishing to join trade unions were intimidated from defending their interests by the threats of the use of the law against them, or by threats of illegal action.

There are reasons for this increasing assault on trade unionism and there are also ways forward. Before considering them it is worth recapping on the UK situation.

THE ASSAULT ON UNION RIGHTS IN BRITAIN

In the UK we are now in the seventeenth year of continuous legislative attack on workers and their trade unions. This blitzkrieg has not been confined to the heavy bombardment of the seven major anti-union Acts of Parliament: the Employment Act 1980, the Employment Act 1982, the Trade Union Act 1984, the Employment Act 1988, the Employment Act 1989, the Employment Act 1990, the Trade Union Reform and Employment Rights Act 1993.

Other Acts of Parliament have also removed long-established rights and freedoms. New curbs were placed on picketing and demonstrations by the Public Order Act in 1986. The Criminal Justice and Public Order Act prohibits the organization of industrial action among prison officers despite the governmental recognition of the Prison Officers Association and its right to call industrial action since 1938.[1] Doubtless this presages further restriction on the right of public servants to take industrial action.[2] There are many other such examples.[3]

Many incursions are not found in Acts of Parliament at all. There are two Codes of Practice, one on picketing and one on industrial action ballots. These codes are taken into account by the courts,[4] where they are applied as if they were the law.[5] There is also a multitude of statutory instruments. One example of the latter is worth a moment's mention.

Even before the legislation referred to, back in 1979 within months of its election, Mrs Thatcher's government used a statutory instrument to withdraw the protection against unfair dismissal of the many millions of our workforce who have not worked for the same employer continuously for more than one year,[6] subsequently amended to two years.[7] This apparently minor change continues to be of profound significance to employee protection. Every employment lawyer in the country is aware of the well-established personnel managers' practice, in so many industries, of sacking staff in the week before their two years expires, so as to deny them protection. In some industries, such as construction, most employees never achieve protection against unfair dismissal at any point in their working lives, moving as they do from one site to the next, from one employer to the next, their periods of work interspersed with spells of self-employment and unemployment.

This extension of employers' immunity against unfair dismissal claims was meant to help to lift 'the burden of regulation' from employers, particularly small employers.[8] It was part of the shrill propaganda of 'deregulation'. The propaganda concealed the totality of the equation, namely that the burden lifted from the employer falls on the employee sacked unfairly, unreasonably and unlawfully, but deprived of all redress.

The policy of deregulation of legal restraints on employers has been accompanied by the imposition of legal restraints on trade unions. In both cases the effect is the same. Legal rights and protections of working people are abolished. Though the seven Acts do limit many important freedoms for working people (for example, the abolition of Wages Councils[9]), it is the withdrawal of trade union rights that characterizes this legislation.

To describe the effect of the seven Acts and the web of deceptive propaganda which still surrounds them would take a book,[10] not a short chapter. To set the scene, however, I will sketch out some of the major changes together with a couple of minor but telling points.

The first area of change is the invasion of trade union autonomy. This involves measures such as the requirement of fully postal elections for union leaderships.[11] Predictably, and contrary to the propaganda that this was a means of enforced democracy by 'handing unions back to their members',[12] the observed effect of the balloting requirements in union elections has been an 'immediate and universal fall in the rate of electoral participation'.[13] Another example is that a union informing its members of the details of a proposed merger is prohibited from expressing any recommendation or even opinion on the proposed merger in the notice setting out the proposal.[14]

There are many incursions into the use that unions may make of their funds. Wide-ranging powers of intervention have been given to the Certification Officer.[15] Apart from further restrictions (including more balloting requirements) on the use of their funds to pursue objectives politically,[16] unions were singled out for a unique prohibition on the use of their funds for paying off members' fines.[17] This applies regardless of the wishes of the membership expressed by ballot or otherwise, and does not apply to companies or other institutions. The 1993 Act has also come between member and union to set up a number of significant difficulties to discourage check-off of union subscriptions from wages and so impede union income and membership.[18] Regardless of a union's rulebook, restrictions have been placed on its power to admit, expel or discipline members.[19]

The infiltration of these statutory provisions into union autonomy is, of course, in addition to the long-established and easy penetration of the common law via the contract of membership. To facilitate the legal encroachment, first to enforce statutory, and later also common law obligations, the government established a Commissioner for the Rights of Trade Union Members (CROTUM). Her sole task is to advise and fund members suing their unions.[20] Like the telling evidence of the dog which did not bark in the night, the government has not established a commissioner to support workers' legal rights against their employers. Indeed, Legal Aid was not even available to support those who made the 69,612 applications to industrial tribunals which were disposed of in 1993–94.[21]

But the intrusion into union internal affairs goes much further than simple interpolation of new laws into union constitutions created by members. Now we have the jurisprudential anomaly by which a failure of an internal *intra vires* procedure can, in effect, provide to a non-member a cause of action against the union. A union can be sued by employers,[22] and even by members of the public,[23] on the grounds that it has failed properly to ballot for industrial action – even if the members themselves (for whom this democratic rule was introduced) have no complaint. No other body in British law is subject to comparable legal invasion of its autonomy.

The attack on trade union internal autonomy has been a serious blow to British unions but the damage done to their ability to engage with employers and represent their members has been yet more severe.

In 1980 the only legal machinery which enabled unions to compel employers to listen to representations on behalf of their members was abolished.[24] Now, at a time of diminishing union power, the 'British disease' in industrial relations is, without doubt, derecognition,[25] a phenomenon barely known across the Channel. The most recent and authoritative study shows that in only six years from 1984 to 1990 the number of workplaces with recognized unions declined from 52 to 40 per cent and the number of employees in such workplaces dropped from 58 to 43 per cent.[26] The change is doubtless more dramatic if the years from 1980 (when recognition machinery was abolished) to 1984 and from 1990 to 1994 (during which it is plain that the momentum to derecognize has continued) are taken into account.

In the absence of legislation for works councils, worker directors or any form of industrial democracy, with negligible, easily evaded and unenforceable duties to consult,[27] with the ability to exert pressure by industrial action virtually non-existent,[28] and with all forms of statutory machinery for fixing wages or other terms abolished,[29] workers are denied the right to have their unions represent them and unions are increasingly denied the opportunity to do so. Collective agreements are torn up by employers and the government proclaims that it 'will continue to encourage employers to move away from traditional, centralised collective bargaining'.[30]

The ability to take industrial action – never in law a right – has, of course, been shot to pieces by the Conservative governments' legislation. On the firm foundation of the unlawfulness of industrial action at common law, the scope of the legal 'immunity' has been reduced,[31] picketing curtailed[32] and all forms of sympathetic action outlawed,[33] along with action in support of a closed shop[34] or to seek recognition of a union.[35] There are hideously complicated (fully postal) balloting provisions, with obligations to notify the employer at every stage – including the duty to notify the identity of potential strikers to the employer.[36] Unions are made directly liable for damages and, unless they repudiate their members' actions, they are liable for unofficial industrial action.[37] If they do repudiate, unofficial strikers can be dismissed unfairly, selectively and otherwise unlawfully, without the right to claim unfair dismissal.[38] Official strikers are only a little better off.[39] Members of the public can sue for injunctions financed by the new Commissioner for Protection against Unlawful Industrial Action.[40]

Other changes to the law have increased accessibility to this new armoury of legal weapons against trade unions. In addition to the government-funded Commissioners, receivership is more easily obtainable, and propping the doors of the arsenal open there remains that deadly weapon, the interlocutory injunction.[41] Available on the flimsiest of untested evidence on the slender basis of an 'arguable' case and at the judge's discretion 'on the balance of convenience', the interlocutory injunction is a launcher for all these warheads.

Yet this legal onslaught has not come to an end with the coming into effect of the Trade Union Reform and Employment Rights Act 1993 on 1 September 1993. Section 36 of the Deregulation and Contracting Out Act repealed the provision that makes selection for redundancy in breach of a customary or agreed procedure automatically unfair. This mean little provision, encouraging employers to renege on agreements, was inserted in response to an amendment forced on the UK government by the European Commission. The amendment to the requirement to consult over proposed mass redundancies requires employers to consult 'with a view to reaching agreement'.[42] A reform to allow employers to escape the consequences of breaking any such agreement was perhaps predictable.

The simple fact that the government runs Parliament and Parliament determines the law does not mean that these legal changes can be described as lawful. The International Labour Organization[43] (the tripartite United Nations body which celebrated its 75th anniversary in 1995) has international conventions to which signatory states undertake adherence. The UK government has deratified a number of conventions to which it originally subscribed.[44] It remains signatory to the two most important of the conventions, nos 87 and 98, which protect union autonomy and activity from state interference. Unsurprisingly, the ILO committee of experts has each year since 1989 condemned aspects of the UK government's anti-union legislation. In 1992, the UK government tried to persuade the ILO general assembly to reject the committee of experts' report for that year. The general assembly was unmoved. The government was reminded that it had the right of appeal to the International Court of Justice in the Hague. It has not appealed.

The UK is also bound by the European Convention on Human Rights.[45] Article 11 protects freedom of association, and in particular a worker's right to join a trade union 'for the protection of his interest'. Unions are considering whether to take a case to the European Court of Human Rights in Luxembourg based on s. 12 of the Trade Union

Reform and Employment Rights Act 1993, which allows an employer to penalize workers for being members of a trade union where the object is union derecognition.[46]

The UK government has also fallen foul of the law emanating from the European Union.[47] Directives must be complied with and the government has had to alter much labour law to avoid infraction proceedings being brought against it.[48] Infraction proceedings were brought by the European Commission and upheld in the ECJ, condemning UK law for restricting consultation over transfer of undertakings and over collective dismissals to unions chosen to be recognized by the employer in question.[49] The government has fought to block[50] or water down every measure from Europe that might give protection to workers, even to the lengths of opting out of the Social Charter and the Maastricht Treaty.[51] It has not, however, fully managed to evade the Working Time Directive (93/104),[52] and it will be interesting to see how it will cope with the implementation of, for example, Article 4, which requires work breaks to be set by collective agreement![53]

Of course, rights and freedoms at work have been undermined and removed by means other than changes to the law.[54] Unemployment (rather than the total of those in receipt of unemployment benefit) at the end of 1994 stood at 3,665,300.[55] Mass unemployment is plainly a permanent feature of life under a Conservative government. As Mr Lamont put it with customary altruism, high unemployment is 'a price worth paying'. Unemployment in the traditional industries where union organization has historically been strong has had a devastating effect on trade union membership figures and income. Fear of unemployment has, without doubt, discouraged people from standing as safety representatives and shop stewards, and has undermined the ability to take industrial action to protect rights. And this fear is justified. While dismissal for trade union activities is relatively infrequent,[56] the more subtle use of redundancy to select activists (along with others) for dismissal is, in my experience, frequent.

The climate of industrial relations is soured by the fear induced by unemployment and the legal changes. No wonder there is no 'feel-good factor'. To this atmosphere the government has sought to add the bullying figure of the 'macho manager', representing a return to Victorian values. It has been the government which has, as an exemplar to the rest of industry, encouraged British Coal's appalling record of industrial relations over the past ten years: victimization, tearing up collective agreements, refusal of collective bargaining, encouragement of splinter unions, aggression and non-cooperation.

No one can seriously doubt that the decision to close Manton

Colliery (confirmed on 3 February 1994)[57] was made because it was a pit loyal to the National Union of Mineworkers (NUM). In the week prior to the closure announcement it was producing coal at 68 pence per gigajoule, making it the lowest-cost pit in Britain.[58] The savage attack on the coal industry with the announced closure of three more pits than the 31 announced by Mr Heseltine in October 1992 is the culmination of a policy described by Nigel Lawson in his autobiography: 'the need for diversification of energy sources, the argument I used to justify the PWR [pressurized water reactor] programme, was code for freedom from NUM blackmail'.[59]

The government's endless programme of privatization is another weapon that removes the rights of working people. Privatization is not merely pursued for the dogmatic preference of private over public ownership. It is not pursued simply so that private business (particularly the multinationals) can take the benefit and control of valuable assets and enterprises. It is not implemented solely as a means of syphoning off profit from the state into private pockets. Nor is it simply a means of government seizing capital in order to attempt to make good the lost revenue that the wealthy have been excused in tax. Let us charitably assume that the corruption and degradation of standards of public life revealed by the House of Commons Public Accounts Committee in 1994[60] was an unintended consequence of privatization and not a reason for it.

The Public Accounts Committee revealed that the corruption came not only from straight privatization but also from the displacement of elected institutions by the multitude of appointed quangos, which now manage £54,000,000,000 of public money, nearly a quarter of all government spending.[61] And this demonstrates another feature of privatization, namely the destruction of democracy, the removal of the right of ordinary citizens to have a say in the operation of these institutions. Not surprisingly, these unelected, undemocratic bodies are in the forefront of derecognizing unions and excluding the voice of their employees.

Privatization is a particularly effective tool in lowering pay, worsening conditions, creating redundancies and unemployment, breaking up collective bargaining structures and fragmenting the workforce. And these latter effects of privatization extend beyond the companies privatized. Privatization, with these objectives in mind, is a fundamentalist mania with this government.[62] Ministers give the impression of being willing to sell their own grandmothers along with the family silver. The Adam Smith Institute advised privatization of the Church of England in order to restore the 'market share' it has lost 'to better organized private-sector religious organizations'.[63]

The Home Secretary has instructed the police to draw up a list of their duties to be contracted out. It has been suggested that these might include traffic duties and the policing of neighbour disputes.[64] Prisons are already being contracted out.[65] Eight foreign but no UK firms tendered for the contract for the computerization of the Home Office criminal records.[66] In September 1993 the government published a consultation paper on contracting to a private firm the service of providing to prospective employers confidential criminal records on prospective employees.[67] The Inland Revenue has contracted out the running of its tax files to an American company, EDS, at a fee of £1000 million.[68] It now appears that the private sector is to be invited to bid for GCHQ.[69] This follows ten years of consistent refusal to restore the rights of the staff to join a trade union on the grounds that there was a conflict of interest between working for GCHQ and being a member of a British trade union. Presumably no such conflict arises between the nation's security and the profit motivation of a foreign subcontractor.

All these non-legal steps have added to the weight of the legal onslaught on the capabilities of wage earners to maintain or improve the condition of their working lives. As the Director General of the Institute of Personnel Management put it, we are on the verge of creating a 'permanently casualised industrial peasantry'.[70]

BRITAIN IS NOT ALONE

We tend to think that this barrage of legal gunfire is the product of a civil war unique to the islands of Britain. It is not. Trade union rights are under fire around the globe. And the bombardment is intensifying. Many countries have followed the lead of the UK by seeking to render trade unions ineffective by legislation.

- In Saudi Arabia, trade unions are totally prohibited. In China all strikes have been outlawed since 1982.

- In New Zealand, the Employment Contracts Act 1991 is devastating the union movement.

- In Bermuda, the Trade Disputes Act 1992 has drastically restricted the right to strike.

- In Ireland, the 1991 Industrial Relations Act has adopted some of the precise words of some of the UK law, resulting in injunctions against strikes.

- In Bulgaria, amendments to the Labour Code violate the right to organize, so as to exclude trade union representation in many workplaces and to undermine collective agreements.

In other countries the state has intervened increasingly to set aside the provisions of freely entered into collective agreements. Argentina and Canada provide examples. And in many others the legal apparatus of the state is abused by the imprisoning of trade unionists, usually on spurious criminal charges, as in the case of Noubir El-Ammoui in Morocco and Chafukwa Chihana in Malawi. Often trade union activists are imprisoned without charge under a euphemism such as 'administrative detention', as in Palestine.[71]

In Colombia, Guatemala, the Philippines and many other countries, trade union officials and active members are gunned down, hacked to death or just 'disappear'. Sometimes just to be an ordinary union member on a picket line is to face the risk of murder by unofficial organs of the state or by gangsters hired by companies.

Nor should we forget that October 1993 was the centenary of the occasion when the British army last fired upon British workers in an industrial dispute. Two miners were shot dead at Featherstone in Yorkshire in a miners' meeting protesting at the use of scab labour in a lockout. It was only 60 years ago that the British army was last used against the miners under the orders of Winston Churchill, though on that occasion they fixed bayonets but did not fire. Only 20 years have passed since the last trade unionists in Britain were imprisoned for no more than taking part in industrial action.[72]

It seems obvious that the choice of means (legal, quasi-legal or illegal) adopted in any particular state is a reflection of the degree of sophistication of society in that state. The intensity in each state of the attack, and the category of means selected, is (after the collapse of Stalinism) in linear relation to the commitment of the state to the free market. Such a commitment may originate from the dogma of the ruling party or from the intrusive power of the multinational corporations through their agents, the International Monetary Fund and the World Bank.

In looking at the abuse of trade union rights from a global perspective, we should not forget that the twin curses of mass unemployment and privatization are global and not just British phenomena. The ILO estimate in 1993 was that 30 per cent of the world's labour force, some 820,000,000 people, were unemployed.[73] In the European Union unemployment was just short of 18 million (just over 10 per cent) and estimated to rise to over 20 million by the end of 1994, and possibly 30 million by the end of the decade.[74] The

Third World, especially Latin America, looks forward to estimates of unemployment of between 40 and 50 per cent by the end of the century. In Eastern Europe and Russia, unemployment levels are climbing towards 20 per cent.[75] Poland already has 2,800,000 unemployed.[76] German unemployment has rocketed: from 3,700,000 at the end of December 1993 to 4,030,000 at the end of January 1994; in East Germany 700,000 jobs were lost in 1993 alone.[77] In France the unemployment rate in 1994 was 12 per cent, 3,300,000 people.[78]

Mass unemployment does not just restrain trade union action and tend to debase wages and conditions. In addition it increases public spending, creates an underclass and gives rise to conditions of social disorder leading to insurrection,[79] crime[80] and racism.

Privatization is a cancer spreading around Europe, with governments anxious to sell the family silver to pay for the costs of keeping so many men and women without work and to counter the loss of revenue caused by the recession. The German railways are to be sold.[81] The Swedish forests are to go.[82] The Italian government is selling its holdings in two of Italy's biggest banks.[83] Some months ago I received, unsolicited, an invitation to invest in the 'Kleinwort European Privatization Trust'. It attracts customers by pointing out that 'privatizations totalling at least £100 billion are possible over the next five years' and that they are priced 'attractively', i.e. they are being sold off cheap.

Privatization is, of course, the name of the game in Russia and Eastern Europe, with the multinationals getting stuck in fast. In the Third World privatization is part of the price often to be paid for assistance under the 'structural assistance programmes'. There is no reason to suppose that the effect of all this privatization will be anything other than job losses, worse conditions and derecognition.

AN INTERNATIONAL CAUSATION

If the intensification of repression of trade unions and workers is not merely a national phenomenon, neither is the cause of it. It is necessary for us to look wider than the small-minded and increasingly incoherent dogma of the Conservative Party.[84]

A first factor in the intensification of attack upon union rights is the acceleration in the growth of the world market. As the revolution in transport and communications technology spins yet faster, products and services are no longer in competition locally or nationally, but globally. It is the world price which sets the local price, not just of commodities but also, and especially, of labour.

The world market is the reason why, in October 1993, the Australian coal owners sought to slash the price of coal in order to win export orders to Turkey. They were met by a strike of 20,000 CFMEU members and, typically, the law was used against them. The world market in coal was the impetus behind the American coal owners' drive to smash the UMWA in 1993, to cut terms and conditions and so to reduce labour costs. Here, too, the law was used against the industrial action taken at Peabody's in order to defend union and worker rights. Though the destruction of the British national coal industry was fuelled by anti-unionism and pivots on the rigged energy market that makes the tax-payers prop up the nuclear industry, the fact remains that some British pits were being shut because coal can be supplied cheaper by pits in Poland, China, Colombia (where children work in the mines) and South Africa. What distinguishes the production of these countries is not their efficiency but the cheapness of their labour.

The global competition in labour is not just about wage costs; it is about labour costs. So in countries where the cost of accidents does not fall to any great extent on employers, and where replacement labour is in cheap and plentiful supply, the cost of safety protection may well be greater than the cost of accidents. Thus lower or absent safety protection legislation in such countries means lower labour costs than in countries where machines have to be guarded and overalls provided. In Thailand in 1992, 5000 workers were killed in industrial accidents and fires. No one knows how many died of long-term industrial diseases. But the cost of each death to the employer was only a fraction of the cost of a comparable death in the UK or USA, and that is a very valid element in the bookkeeping for the transnational corporations (TNCs).

Across the globe, worker is forced to compete with worker in a Dutch auction of diminishing wages and conditions. If workers refuse to accept cuts in terms and conditions, their work is simply moved to another country where workers will work on those worse terms.

This we see in every industry. In shipping, where Indian and Filipino seafarers fight for the opportunity to serve on the flagged-out ships registered in Panama and Liberia, the wage rates of British sailors, secured by the struggles of the ITF, have long since left them stranded 'on the beach': 100,000 British seafarers in 1970 had been reduced to 27,000 by 1994. The British merchant fleet (other than the fishing fleet, which is under a different threat) has all but disappeared. Our shores are now polluted by the wrecks of ships and cargoes lost because of ever-falling standards of vessels and crew conditions.

Seventy per cent of the 2000 vessels inspected at British ports in 1992 were found to be defective. The loss rate for British ships is five times less than for Liberian.[85] Some 125 years on, we will have to refight Samuel Plimsoll's struggle for the Merchant Shipping Acts – this time on an international basis.[86]

In textiles the low-paid workers in the cotton mills of Lancashire and the woollen mills of Yorkshire have been replaced by the yet lower-paid operators of the looms of South East Asia. In engineering, in shipbuilding, in iron and steel production and so on, the story of worldwide competition in wage rates is the same. Even clerical work is now contracted across the world to the cheapest labour supplier: British insurance companies have their computer records maintained in India.[87]

The world market has been facilitated by the astonishing development of technology. These technological changes to the way in which goods and services are created are equally evident in mineral extraction, in shipping, in agriculture, in information technology, indeed in every industry and service. But technology requires investment and investment requires a return, and a return requires maximization of the use of the equipment. This leads to pressure for longer hours and longer ·weeks. It leads to new forms of work organization and new kinds of 'flexible' worker. Production can be decentralized while control is centralized. The demarcation grows between the skilled in permanent jobs and the unskilled who alternate between work and unemployment. These new patterns of work replace the collective workforces of the 'Fordist' model. The very structure of employment, reinforced by modern management techniques, inhibits collectivism in favour of individualism.

Part cause and part effect of these changes, a dramatic feature of the global economy has been the increase in the holdings, operations and power of the TNCs. These corporations, as wealthy as many states, are self-perpetuating oligarchies not subject to democratic control by their workers, their consumers, the inhabitants of the countries in which they operate or even effectively by their shareholders. They employ global strategies and span rich and poor countries. They comb the world for cheap resources, cheap production and cheap transport costs. They open production here and close it there in accordance only with changes in the relative costs of production and access to consumers, indifferent to the needs and aspirations of their employees and the communities affected by their production sites.

One feature of the role of TNCs in the global market is the extent to which they control markets. Though workers must compete, corporations prefer to combine. The European Commission investigation of market rigging by a cartel of European steel producers, which resulted in a fine of £24.6 million for British Steel for its activities since privatization, is a classic example.[88]

In combination, the multinationals dominate their markets and pressurize governments. They lead the drive to deregulate workers' rights. They lead the campaign to privatize public services. They conduct about one-third or more of the world's trade. In Britain, 16 per cent of the workforce is employed by multinationals.[89]

These are some of the interacting factors that have changed the face of the world's economy. There are many others, such as financial and fiscal deregulation and the saturation of traditional consumer markets. Taken together, these interwoven elements in the economic revolution have accelerated the global pressure to compete in labour. These are the forces intensifying the drive against union and worker rights.

Nation states differ in their approach to these forces. The European Union plainly takes the line that (at least within its borders) it will restrain the pressures to undercut labour costs between one member state and its neighbour.[90] One reason for this (among many, including the prospect of increasing mass unemployment) is the fear of driving down consumer purchasing power in the most valuable market in the world.

The UK government has responded differently. Its strategy, outlined afresh in the Green Paper *Growth, Competitiveness and Employment in the European Community*,[91] is the same old policy we have had for the past 17 years – that which the Tory evangelists have preached throughout Eastern Europe and elsewhere. In particular, the 'upward trend in EU unemployment cycle since the late 1960s and an increasing number of long-term unemployed ... are evidence of inflexibility in, and over-regulation of, labour markets.'[92]

The UK government has taken virtually every measure conceivable to make its national labour market more flexible and deregulated, as we have seen. The result has been not merely mass unemployment (disguised by the fact that half the number of lost full-time jobs have been replaced by part-time jobs) but also the destruction of the manufacturing industry on which the country's wealth depends.[93] Far from winning work from the low-wage economies it seeks to emulate, Britain has continued to lose production to them. Britain slipped, for the first time since the industrial revolution, into a balance of payments deficit on manufactured goods in 1983, and is now the only country in Europe to run a deficit in manufactured goods.[94] And this disaster cannot be put down to the recession, since, as the Royal Society of Arts' devastating survey[95] in February 1994 showed, the UK has been outperformed on every count by those European states which have rejected the former's absurd policies. The blitz on union rights and

workers' terms and conditions has not improved productivity: Britain
has now achieved eighteenth place out of twenty two in terms of
productivity in the OECD and trails the inflexible and over-regulated
labour markets of France and Germany by 25 per cent.[96]

Yet the UK government boasts of its achievements. In a DTI
booklet to promote foreign investment in Britain the following is to be
found (written in American English):

> Labor costs in the UK continue to be low – significantly below
> other European countries. The UK has the least onerous labor
> regulations in Europe, with fewer restrictions on working time,
> overtime and holidays. Many companies setting up in the UK
> have negotiated single union agreements. However there is no
> legal requirement to recognize a trade union. Many industries
> operate shiftwork and 24 hour, 7 days-a-week production for both
> men and women. The UK government is committed to reducing
> regulatory and administrative burdens on business. No new laws
> or regulations may be introduced without ascertaining and
> minimizing the costs to business.[97]

One of the features of the globalization of the market and the
extension of the free market economy has been growing inequality.
Contrary to those who resist the imposition of international labour
standards on the grounds that the export of jobs from the developed to
the Third World equalizes wealth, the consequence is precisely the
reverse. Between 1960 and 1990, the richest one-fifth of the world's
population increased their share of the world's income from 58.3 to
64.6 per cent. The poorest one-fifth of the world's population had their
share of the world's income decreased from 5 to 3.4 per cent.[98] The
same trend may be observed in most, if not all, countries.

In the UK, the consequences of the Conservatives' policies since
they came to power are easily demonstrable. In 1979, 9 per cent of the
population lived on an income of less than half the average. By 1989,
this section of the population had risen to a staggering 22 per cent (12
million people). Meanwhile, the richest fifth of the population
increased their share of total income after tax and benefits from 37
to 43 per cent, and the poorest fifth decreased their share from 9.5 to
6.9 per cent.[99] In May 1992, five million people were in receipt of
benefit; by September the figure was 5.5 million; by February 1993, 5.7
million.[100] About 12 million people live in poverty.[101] In gross
domestic product per capita, Britain is now eighth out of the twelve
countries of the European Union.[102]

The relevance of this is that it disproves the thesis that lowering wages and benefits creates wealth and jobs, or that the increase in pay for the wealthy 'trickles down'. It shows that deregulation of labour laws does not create wealth for the poor but only for the rich.

The growth in economic inequality is not merely the product of the natural greed of the managers who ride the tide of economic change. It is also a necessity for capitalism, for the impoverishment of the majority of the world's population does nothing to create demand for the very goods and services produced by the lower wages. Increased purchasing power of the wealthy is necessary to stimulate demand.

Meanwhile the transformation of the world economy strides on. The year 1993 saw the signing of the North American Free Trade Agreement (NAFTA) and the conclusion of the Uruguay Round of the General Agreement on Tariffs and Trade (GATT). Ross Perot (no socialist) reckons that NAFTA will throw five million US workers out of a job in favour of lower-paid Mexican workers.[103] Half a million Canadian jobs have already gone.[104]

These developments are important stages in the accelerating development of world trade. They will be followed by further bilateral and multinational agreements designed to liberalize trade and remove tariff barriers.

STRATEGIES FOR THE FUTURE

It is neither necessary nor possible to sit back and let the described destructive processes continue unchallenged. The hundreds of millions of people in the world so prejudiced by what is happening to their rights, liberties and living standards need policies for change. What we need, in my view, is to get back to basics. I do not mean by this (as some Tories seem to) more fornication or refusing single mothers housing as a means of getting out of the recession. What I have in mind is an appeal to law and order, to democracy and to socialism.

Law and Order

First we must publicize the fact that the rights of workers and their trade unions are not mere self-interested privileges or pleas. They are matters of law. The right to organize, the right to strike, the right to associate, these are fundamental human rights enshrined in international law. We are entitled to demand them from the governments of the world. Next to the right to life itself they are among the most important legal rights in the world, for these are the rights that distinguish an employee from a serf. They are the only rights that enable the living standards of the world to be maintained or advanced. They are the rights that enable trade union leaders to organize to protect so many other rights and to fight against so many injustices outside the workplace.

The lawmaking of the ILO must itself be defended. There are forces at work who would seek to reduce it to 'a technical agency for human resource managers'.[105] The World Conference on Human Rights held in Vienna in 1993 did refer to trade union rights in its final communiqué, but it did not place them central to human rights and it did not refer to the vital role of the ILO. It also failed to develop any effective system of protection of human rights, in particular by failing to set up a High Commission on human rights. The task of defending the existing institution of the ILO and its role falls on all of us, but in particular on the trade union movement. Notwithstanding the ILO's inadequacies, as evidenced by the UK government's flouting of the conventions which bind it, the trade union movement must not lose patience with it.

Only insistence on international labour standards can halt the spiral of reducing rights and conditions of work. Consequently, pressure must be brought to bear to ensure that the international legal documents which facilitate international trade also uphold those labour standards.

This idea is not new,[106] and some progress has been made. The Tin Agreement 1975, the International Sugar Agreements 1977 and the International Natural Rubber Agreement 1979 all had clauses proclaiming that signatories would seek to ensure fair labour practices. They have not been effective.[107] The USA has several laws on international trade which link international labour rights, in particular the Omnibus Trade and Competitiveness Act 1988. The problem has been one of selective enforcement and non-enforcement depending on the stance of the USA to the country concerned. None the less, that legislation has been the focus of mounting pressure, including lawsuits.[108]

The NAFTA was concluded with a 'side deal' agreement on labour standards. It is weak and generally considered to be likely to be ineffective in levelling up labour rights rather than down.[109]

The European Union, of course, has social clauses as well as a clause on anti-dumping. Britain's opt-out of the former contained in the Maastricht Treaty (and the 1989 Social Charter) is reversible and requires continued pressure. For whatever may be the inadequacies of these provisions, it cannot be denied that they are steps in the right direction. British workers are unquestionably better served by the European directives on health and safety, on equal treatment, on transfer of undertakings, on working time and the like than if they had been left to the mercies of their own government. The trade union movement can support the propositions of the European Commission that:

> High social standards, which are a complex mix of working and living conditions, are a clear objective of the European Community.
>
> A key objective of European integration is that working and living standards in the community should converge.
>
> It is not in the interests of international economic cooperation that the exploitation of workers should become an instrument of international competition.[110]

However, the European Union opposed a labour rights clause in the GATT agreement, and Britain's voice in calling for unfettered labour competition is being heard within the Community. It is therefore necessary to continue to press the case in Europe.

President Clinton has supported the idea of a social clause in GATT to protect labour rights. But the reality is that the signatories to the GATT agreement have no enthusiasm for such a proposal. It still remains on the table but discussion of it has been adjourned.

The insistence on tying international trade to the international labour standards of the ILO is not a resurrection of protectionism. On the contrary, it gives no preference to the trade of the importing country. The purpose is to ensure fair trade and not just free trade.[111] It is designed to protect the workers and their unions, who are being ruthlessly exploited all over the world. The countries of the Commonwealth united on trade sanctions against South Africa because of its abuse of human rights in the form of apartheid. Why should not those countries which honour the conventions of the ILO refuse imports made or carried in breach of those conventions? The link could not be more direct. Unless the goods and services are certified as being produced by labour which enjoyed all the protections of international law and the ILO conventions, those goods and services should not be allowed in. This would protect home producers (both employers and employees) as well as the workers of foreign producers. Let competition be on a level playing field which respects international human rights.

The mechanism of enforcement needs attention. In my view we should press for the establishment of an international labour inspectorate. In the meantime, unions could usefully carry out audits of trading partners to ensure that they respect ILO conventions at home and abroad. On a national basis, too, pressure should build within the labour movement for governments to incorporate ILO conventions in national legislation. That was one of the demands of the 1993 Trades Union Congress. The trade union movement must press for the domestic legislation necessary to protect its rights and those of its members at work. And such legislative programmes must be founded on economic policies that respect the rights and dignity of working people: high wages, good conditions, adequate protections, full employment, efficiency, job security, high and appropriate investment, sustainable growth, competition on a level playing field, equality and justice.

This involves consideration of every field of the law as it affects work: a fair employment relationship, with terms and conditions no worse than established minima and collective agreements; fair discipline and dismissal procedures and adequate legal remedies; proper health and safety provision; equal opportunities and an end to discrimination; childcare provision; pension protection; the right to bargain collectively and to be represented; the right to industrial action and trade union autonomy; employers' duties to protect and involve workers; a tax and social security framework that protects conditions at work; education and training provision; fair courts and procedures.

It may be necessary, too, to embed fundamental trade union rights in a mechanism that prevents transient governments from interfering with them. If such rights are not to be in a Bill of Rights (a concept I find fraught with difficulties) then the parliamentary means of amending fundamental labour rights must be made procedurally difficult. In addition, all legislation not directly concerned with employment should be subject to a workers' audit to ensure that it does not indirectly diminish those rights.

Democracy

The tendency to exclude people from the important decisions that affect their lives must be reversed. We must insist on democracy in place of free trade as the essential institutional requirement, the dominant ideology of the world. Businesses run for profit must not be allowed to dictate our economic, political or social interests. Businesses are fundamentally undemocratic. Workers must have the right to a say through their unions in the decisions businesses take. Unions must have the right to represent their members' interests at work.

Democracy demands this. Furthermore, communities must have a say in the business decisions that affect them.

Socialism

It is time to reverse the process of privatization for the simple doctrinaire reason that placing such enterprises under public democratic control is a 'good thing'. I remind myself that the process of nationalization in Britain was not the product of socialists in the Labour Party, but was begun by a Conservative government, which nationalized the BBC and set the pattern for subsequent nationalizations, such as the railways and the coal industry.

But socialism implies more, in particular the construction of an economy that makes the poor less poor, and that irons out the hideous disparities of wealth we have become familiar with. We should again seek full employment, free education and the fulfilment of people's talents and aspirations. High productivity, high investment, good conditions of work: these are the way to an efficient economy and fulfilment of international labour standards.[112]

Finally, I include under this heading trade unionism. To counter the developments we have discussed clearly requires effective trade union internationalism. International cooperation and coordination is essential. It is the very spirit of trade unionism. And it is under way; for example, in the campaign against the Hanson empire.[113] The international trade union bodies, like the ICFTU, have a most important role to play, as do organizations intended to support them and international union rights, such as ICTUR.

CONCLUSION

The analysis points the way forward. There is a way forward, but it requires energy and commitment from all who are concerned about the rights at work of themselves and others.

NOTES

1. Following the opportunity provided by *Home Office* v *Evans* (1993, unreported, May J, 18 November 1993). See also *Boddington* v *Caton* (1994, unreported, 4 February 1994).

2. The Bill almost precisely coincided with the tenth anniversary of the date on which the staff of the Government Communications Headquarters (GCHQ) were deprived of their right even to belong to a trade union. But s. 22 of the Trade Union and Employment Rights Act 1993 shows that the government is actively pursuing public servants' rights to take industrial action (though the section extends beyond the public sector).

3. For example, the Teachers Pay and Conditions Act 1991 (virtual abolition of free collective bargaining for teachers); s. 6 Education Reform Act 1988 (industrial action by teachers in schools with delegated budgets unlawful if not confined to a dispute with their own governors).

4. S. 3(9) Employment Act 1980.

5. For example, the recommendation for six pickets only applied in *Thomas* v *NUM (South Wales Area)* [1985] ICR 886, *Newsgroup Newspapers* v *SOGAT 82* [1986] ICR 716.

6. Unfair Dismissal (Variation of Qualifying Period) Order (SI 1979, No. 959).

7. Unfair Dismissal (Variation of Qualifying Period) Order (SI 1985, No. 782).

8. See *Burdens on Business* (Department of Trade, 1985): 'the present one year period is too short for many smaller businesses, and is distorting dismissal decisions'.

9. S. 35 Trade Union Reform and Employment Rights Act 1993 (TURERA). Some 2,600,000 workers lost protection in consequence, a protection which only provided for minimum rates of between £2.59 to £3.10 per hour. A particular irony is that the UK is now the only country in the EU without minimum wage fixing machinery, yet has the highest percentage of the workforce earning low pay: *Guardian*, 31 August 1993.

10. See J. Hendy, *A Law unto Themselves* (London: Institute of Employment Rights, 3rd edn, 1993); P. Davies and M. Freedland, *Labour Legislation and Public Policy* (1993).

11. Ss. 10–11 Trade Union Act 1984, as amended by the Employment Act 1990, now in ss. 226–32 Trade Union and Labour Relations (Consolidation) Act 1992 (TULR(C)A).

12. Green Paper, *Democracy in Trade Unions*, Cmnd 8778, 1983.

13. P. Smith *et al.*, Ballots and union government in the 1980s (1993) 31(3) *British Journal of Industrial Relations* 356, p. 377.

14. S. 5 TURERA, creating a new s. 99(3A) of TULR(C)A. This applies absolutely regardless of the expressed wish or policy of the union, which may have been decided by the elected national executive committee, or by conference, or even by a prior ballot vote of the entire membership. Such an interference is not found in the law relating to companies or any other organization of capital or employer of labour. The purpose is plain: to attempt to restrain mergers which might strengthen the labour movement.

15. For example, s. 10 TURERA, creating new extensions to what is now s. 37 of TULR(C)A.

16. The significant embellishments to what was originally the Trade Union Act 1913 by Part III of the Trade Union Act 1984.

17. S. 8 Employment Act 1988, now s. 15 TULR(C)A.

18. S.15 TURERA, completely replacing s. 68 of TULR(C)A.

19. Exclusion and expulsion: ss. 4–5 Employment Act 1980, which became ss. 174–7 of TULR(C)A (completely replaced by s. 14 TURERA). Unjustifiable discipline: s. 3 Employment Act 1988, now ss. 64–5 of TULR(C)A (as amended by s. 16 TURERA).

20. Ss. 19–21 Employment Act 1988, amended by ss. 10–11 of the Employment Act 1990.

21. This is the latest figure available at the time of writing: see *Employment Gazette*, October 1994, p. 368. Claims for unpaid wages are now transferred from the courts, where costs are recoverable, to the industrial tribunal, where normally they are not. The absence of means testing by the CROTUM should be seen against the backdrop of changes which affect workers among the rest of the population. Legal Aid limits were reduced in 1993. Most litigation over accidents has been transferred from the High Court to the County Court, which is generally considered more administratively difficult for plaintiffs, and where awards of damages are smaller. It is now proposed that claims worth less than £1000 should be heard by a County Court procedure that awards no costs to the winner, so penalizing unions that back workers' accident claims.

22. Part II of the Trade Union Act 1984. In fact, the members themselves had no right to complain of a balloting failure until s. 1 of the Employment Act 1988! All these measures are now found in Part V of TULR(C)A.

23. S. 22 TURERA.

24. S. 11 of the Employment Act 1975, repealed by s. 19 of the Employment Act 1980.

25. See P. Smith and G. Morton, Union exclusion and the decollectivization of industrial relations (1993) 31 *British Journal of Industrial Relations* 97; and, by the same authors, Union exclusion – the next steps (1994) 25(1) *Industrial Relations Journal* 3.

26. N. Millward, *The New Industrial Relations* (London: Policy Studies Institute, 1994).

27. *R v British Coal Corporation ex parte Vardy* [1993] ICR 720 is probably a unique case and, in any event, judicial review is a common law remedy. It is doubtful whether the statutory remedies for non-consultation are adequate enough to survive challenge in the ECJ.

28. See below.

29. S. 35 TURERA. The Agricultural Wages Board continues.

30. White Paper, *People, Jobs and Opportunity*, Cm 1810, 1992; and see J. Hendy, *A Law unto Themselves, op. cit.*, pp. 56–7. The government has pursued a policy of de-unionizing public life as well. The tripartite National Economic Development Council was abolished in June 1992. The role of the tripartite ACAS has been significantly diminished: codes of practice were issued by the Department of Employment until its abolition and not by ACAS; ACAS's duty to promote collective bargaining (s. 209 TULR(C)A) is now abolished (s. 43 TURERA). The TUC no longer has the exclusive right to nominate worker representative members of the industrial and employment appeal tribunals or on the Health and Safety Commission. The government grant to TUC training courses (including health and safety) will have been phased out by 1996.

31. S. 18 Employment Act 1982, amending s. 29 Trade Union and Labour Relations Act 1974, now all in s. 244 TULR(C)A.

32. S. 15 Trade Union and Labour Relations Act 1974, amended by s. 16 Employment Act 1980 (now s. 220 TULR(C)A).

33. S. 17 Employment Act 1980 partly outlawed secondary action; s. 4 Employment Act 1990 (now s. 24 TULR(C)A) wholly outlawed it.

34. S. 10 Employment Act 1988, now s. 222 TULR(C)A.

35. S. 14 Employment Act 1982, now s. 225 TULR(C)A. And note, in abrogation of the doctrine of freedom of contract, that a recognition requirement in a commercial contract was made void by ss. 12–13 Employment Act 1982, now ss. 186–7 TULR(C)A.

36. Ss. 10–11 Employment Act 1984, s. 17 Employment Act 1988, ss. 5 and 7 Employment Act 1990, all now in ss. 226–34 TULR(C)A, further amended by ss. 17–21 TURERA.

37. S. 15 Employment Act 1982, s. 6 Employment Act 1990, all now in ss. 20–1 TULR(C)A.

38. S. 9 Employment Act 1990, amending s. 62 Employment Protection (Consolidation) Act 1978, now s. 237 TULR(C)A. By s. 9(2) of the Employment Act 1990 (now s. 223 TULR(C)A) industrial action to seek reinstatement of dismissed unofficial strikers is outlawed.

39. The original immunity given to employers against unfair dismissal proceedings except in the case of selective dismissal or re-engagement (s. 62 Employment Protection Act 1978) was extended by s. 9 Employment Act 1982, now s. 238 TULR(C)A.

40. S. 22 TURERA.

41. See Lord Wedderburn, The injunction and the sovereignty of Parliament (1989) 23(1) *Law Teacher* 4; and in Wedderburn, *Collected Essays* (London: Institute of Employment Rights, 1992).

42. The requirement to consult over mass redundancies arose from the European Directive on collective redundancies 75/129 and found form in s. 99 of the Employment Act 1975, which became s. 188 of the TULR(C)A. The with-a-view-to-agreement amendment came in s. 34 of TURERA. There is a parallel amendment to the Transfer of Undertakings (Protection of Employment) Regulations 1981 by s. 33(6) of TURERA, but there was never any special protection for any such agreement reached, so none needed removal by the Deregulation Act. In passing, it should be noted that such duties as there are to consult workers and their unions arise almost exclusively from European law.

43. On this subject matter, see K. Ewing, *Britain and the ILO* (London: Institute of Employment Rights, 1989); Lord Wedderburn, The right to strike: is there a European standard? In *Collected Essays, op. cit.*; J. Hendy, *A Law unto Themselves, op. cit.*, pp. 78–81.

44. For example, Conventions 26 – minimum wage fixing; 45, underground mine work by women; 95, public contractors to pay fair wages.

45. Britain is the worst law-breaker in Europe in this court, its government having collected 50 judgments against it by 1993.

46. This section was an amendment to the Bill introduced five working days after the Court of Appeal gave judgment (and before a transcript was available) in the case of *Wilson v Associated Newspapers* [1993] IRLR 336, in which it was held that such penalization was unlawful; though this was reversed in the House of Lords.

47. On this subject see Lord Wedderburn, *The Social Charter, European Company and Employment Rights* (London: Institute of Employment Rights, 1990); B. Hepple, *European Social Dialogue – Alibi or Opportunity* (London: Institute of Employment Rights, 1993); J. Hendy, *A Law unto Themselves, op. cit.*

48. The Equal Pay Act 1970 had to be amended in 1983, the Sex Discrimination Act 1976 had to be amended in 1986 and again in 1993, rights to maternity pay, employment particulars, consultation on redundancy and transfer of undertaking all had to be amended in 1993, though there are still doubts as to whether the changes are sufficient.

49. *European Commission v UK* [1994] ICR 664.

50. Amusingly, the European Employers Federation, relying on Britain's veto to block the directive on works councils, now finds that because of Britain's opt-out of the Maastricht Treaty it can no longer do so and has been forced to negotiate a compromise with the Commission and the European TUC: *Guardian, Financial Times*, 21 September 1993. However, the UK Government blocked a directive giving a right to paternity leave in November 1993: *Guardian*, 24 November 1993.

51. Though the European Commission has warned that it intends to review the opt-out in 1996, Commission lawyers have advised that British representatives will be asked to leave the room and 'stand in the corridor' while European legislation under the Maastricht Treaty is being discussed in the European Commission: *Guardian*, 8 October 1993.

52. It achieved an extension of time for compliance, as it did on the Directive protecting children and young persons at work.

53. See B. Bercusson, *Working Time in Britain: Towards a European Model* (London: Institute of Employment Rights, 1994).

54. See J. Elgar and R. Simpson, *Union Negotiators, Industrial Action and the Law: Report of a Survey of the Experience of Negotiators in 25 Unions, 1991–92* (London: London School of Economics, 1993).

55. Labour Research, *57*(25) *Fact Service*, p. 100.

56. Though note the instructive *Port of London Authority v Payne* [1993] ICR 30 (EAT), [1994] IRLR 9 (CA), where a large public authority was quite prepared to sack its shop stewards for trade union activity, lie about it in the witness box and refuse to comply with reinstatement orders.

57. *Guardian*, 4 February 1994.

58. Nuclear power costs around 350 per cent more. The *Guardian* of the same date carried an article pointing out that electricity consumers have paid £650 million more in electricity bills since privatization, at a time when the profits of the regional electricity companies have risen to over £1000 million.

59. N. Lawson, *The View From No. 11* (1992), p. 168.

60. *Financial Times*, 28 January 1994. The committee's report seemed to have passed Mr Portillo by when he claimed that 'Outside this country the standards of public life are way below what goes on in this country': *Guardian*, 5 February 1994. Indeed, Mr Portillo seems to not have been reading the daily reports on the arms for Iraq inquiry being held by Scott; or the £1 billion arms for aid Pergau Dam deal revelations. Perhaps he does not consider the acceptance of gifts like free holidays as unacceptable. Doubtless the holding of a directorship of a Group 4 company by the Chairman of the Conservative Party at a time when prisons were being privatized to the same group of companies was not regarded by Mr Portillo as below the acceptable standards of British public life. The history of ministers taking directorships of companies sold off cheap from the state is not to be regarded as impropriety, presumably. Lord Nolan's further report is awaited. I assume that Mr Portillo does not consider the placing of Tory supporters on to the quangos which supplant elected bodies as below the standard to be expected in public life, even though, unlike the elected representatives they replace, the placemen are exempt from surcharging by the district auditor in respect of their errors and defalcations. It would, of course, be unfair to suggest that the well-known

Tory contributor Asil Nadir was in 'public life' and so should be judged by its standards, likewise the £97 million tax fraudster Octav Botnar or Roger Levitt, who received 180 hours' community service for offences in connection with the £34 million debt left when his company collapsed. The same should doubtless be said of the 40,000 company directors, unfit to run a company, who have avoided disqualification by the Official Receivers since 1986 (The Insolvency Service Executive Agency, *Company Director Disqualification, Report of the Comptroller and Auditor General*, HMSO, October 1993). It would be unkind to mention Barlow Clowes, Blue Arrow, Guinness ...

61. *Guardian*, 19 November 1993. The 2200 quangos in existence in 1979 have been estimated to become 7700 by 1996.

62. The privatizations of the past decade are well known, with their history of profiteering, poor service and massive wage increases for their managers. The Employment Service's Skill Centres were sold to a convicted forger, Patrick Doyle, and are now in the hands of a receiver (*Guardian*, 20 October 1993). A Consumers' Association and National Consumer Council report in 1994 found that while the regional electricity companies' profits rose to over £1000 million, consumers' bills rose by £650 million (*Guardian*, 4 February 1994). The House of Commons Public Accounts Committee heard evidence that Medway Trust Port, privatized in 1992 for £15 million, was resold 19 months later for £104 million (*Guardian*, 10 February 1994). But the mania rages still. Michael Howard retreated in January 1994 on short-term contracts and performance-related pay for magistrates' clerks but it appears that John Selwyn Gummer still persists in his notion of privatizing the rent tribunals and other judicial functions. Perhaps the judges who opposed Mr Howard will be privatized next.

63. *Guardian*, 13 December 1993.

64. *Guardian*, 4 February 1994.

65. And will be extended by the Criminal Justice and Public Order Bill.

66. *Guardian*, 30 June 1993.

67. Green Paper, *Disclosure of Criminal Records for Employment Vetting Purposes*, Cm 2319, Home Office, 1993.

68. *Guardian*, 24 November 1993.

69. *Guardian*, 3 February 1994.

70. Quoted by K. Maguire in Sacking strikers: a British disease, *Tribune*, 28 January 1994.

71. See J. Hendy, *Palestinian Trade Unions and the Law* (London: International Centre for Trade Union Rights, 1989).

72. There are many other examples from this century, such as the picaresque case of the Betteshanger miners described in an appendix to the Donovan Commission on Trade Unions (1968, Cmnd 3623), pp. 340–1. Many have been imprisoned on criminal charges, often trumped up, in the course of industrial disputes, including the Shrewsbury building workers in 1974 and hundreds of the 10,000 miners arrested during the miners' strike of 1984–85.

73. Reuters, 3 February 1994.

74. *Guardian*, 14 October 1993.

75. K. Coates, *Unemployment and the Reform of Working Time* (European Labour Forum, summer 1993).

76. *Guardian*, 9 February 1994.

77. *Guardian*, 6 January 1994, 9 February 1994.

78. *Guardian*, 15 February 1994.

79. As graphically demonstrated in Mexico in 1993–84.

80. Plainly demonstrated, much to Mr Howard's discomfiture, by the study by David Dickinson of Cambridge: *Guardian*, 7 January 1994.

81. *Independent*, 3 December 1993.

82. *Financial Times*, 4 December 1994.

83. *Financial Times*, 18 November 1994.

84. The analysis that follows is a summary of Chapter 3 of J. Hendy, *A Law unto Themselves*, *op. cit.*

85. *Guardian*, 16 December 1993.

86. In *Sloman Neptun Schiffahrts AG* v *Bodo Ziesemer*, Conjoined Cases C-72 and C-73/91 [1993] *Official Journal* no. C 104/11 (15 April 1993), it was held that European Union member states did not offend against anti-dumping provisions by employing non-resident seafarers on worse terms than their own nationals.

87. Labour Research Department 52(46) *Factservice.*

88. *Guardian,* 17 February 1994.

89. Labour Research Department 55(10) *Factservice.*

90. See, *inter alia,* the European Green Paper, *European Social Policy: Options for the Union* (Luxembourg: Office for Official Publications of the European Communities, 1993), COM (93) 551.

91. In advance of the European White Paper, *Growth, Competitiveness and Employment* (Luxembourg: Office for Official Publications of the European Communities, 1993).

92. Summary, p. 1 (i).

93. The UK lost more jobs and manufacturing as a share of GDP dropped more than in any other OECD country between 1973 and 1989: OECD figures reproduced in Labour Research Department 55(40) *Factservice.*

94. See following note.

95. *Tomorrow's Company* (RSA, 1994) (Chair Sir Anthony Cleaver, head of IBM, UK). See also E. Balls and P. Gregg, *Work and Welfare, Tackling the Jobs Deficit Commission on Social Justice* (London: Institute for Public Policy Research, 1993); K. Coates *et al., Deregulation the Dismal Truth* (1994).

96. DTI survey quoted in *Guardian,* 11 February 1994.

97. *Britain the Preferred Location* (HMSO, 2nd edn, November 1994).

98. *Financial Times,* 15 June 1993.

99. C. Oppenheim, *Poverty: the Facts* (1993); *Guardian,* 3 June 1993.

100. DSS figures published in the *Guardian,* 27 August 1993, 26 November 1993.

101. Figures from the Centre for the Analysis of Social Poverty quoted in the *Guardian,* 1 September 1993. An Association of London Authorities' survey showed that more than half the children in London's poorest boroughs were so poor that they were entitled to free school meals; a quarter of all London's schoolchildren are so entitled. In 1991 only one-sixth were: *Guardian,* 31 January 1994. According to Shelter there are two million homeless people: *Guardian,* 31 January 1994.

102. European Commission Statistics published 24 January 1994, quoted *Guardian,* 25 January 1994.

103. *Guardian,* 18 September 1993.

104. See L. Compa, The act of ignoring impatient elephants; L. Kuehn, A social time bomb about to go off (1993) 1(4) *International Union Rights 5,* 9.

105. M. Malentacchi (General Secretary, International Metalworkers Federation, in a speech to the American Bar Association, 26 April 1993). See also P. Prior, ILO under bosses' attack (1993) 1(5) *International Union Rights* 18; B. Brett, *International Labour in the 21st Century* (1994).

106. See review of literature in G. van Liemt, Minimum labour standards and international trade: would a social clause work? (1989) 128(4) *International Labour Review* 433.

107. See previous reference for discussion of these.

108 See J. Brecher and T. Costello, *Global Village vs Global Pillage* (Washington, DC: International Labour Rights Education and Research Fund, 1991).

109. See I. Robinson, *North American Trade: As if Democracy Mattered* (Washington, DC: International Labour Rights Education and Research Fund; Ottowa: Canadian Centre for Policy Alternatives, 1993).

110. European Commission Green Paper, *European Social Policy: Options for the Union, op. cit.,* pp. 82–4.

111. See the speech of M. Ferguson (President of the Australian Council of Trade Unions) to the ICTUR Conference on International Trade Union Rights, Sydney, 28–29 October 1993; also J. Cavanagh *et al., Trade's Hidden Costs, Worker Rights in a Changing World Economy* (Washington, DC: International Labour Rights Education and Research Fund, 1988).

112. See S. Deakin and F. Wilkinson, *The Economics of Employment Rights* (London: Institute of Employment Rights, 1991); J. Michie and F. Wilkinson, *The Cost of Undermining Employment Rights* (London: Institute of Employment Rights, 1993).

113. See (1993) 1(5) International Union Rights, p. 6; *Financial Times,* 9 September 1993.

7

The Right to Strike: A Shift in Focus

Gwyneth Pitt

INTRODUCTION

What is to be done about strike law under a Labour government? Along with the difficulties inherent in any kind of law reform, in this particular case the issue also bristles with political problems. The opportunities for the media to have a field day with anything that can be misinterpreted as a 'return to union power' render the reform of strike law a delicate subject, and one which, perhaps, the leadership of the Labour Party might prefer to leave alone. But inaction should not be tolerated. The present law relating to industrial action is ludicrously unbalanced and ridiculously complex; workers and trade unions are entitled to expect that its reform should be a priority for a new Labour administration.

It will be argued here that the key to successful reform of industrial action law lies in focusing on the position of individual workers and establishing – for the first time in British history – a right to strike for individuals. If individual workers had the ability to engage in industrial action without losing their jobs and without incurring any legal liability, the potential legal liability for trade unions in organizing it would nearly disappear. And it seems likely that the public at large would be far more receptive to reforms based on protections for individuals; many people are quite unaware of how far the law is stacked against employees and are astonished to discover that people can be sacked without any redress even where industrial action is instigated by the employer![1]

This approach, it is submitted, is not only more realistic than calls for the total repeal of Conservative laws on strikes (which, it is clear, have not a snowball in hell's chance of being adopted as Labour Party policy in any case), but also fairer. The exposed position of workers who take action has always been the glaring defect in British law, and contrasts unfavourably with the position in most other countries. If this method of reform were adopted, there would still be a considerable battle to win over public opinion, and this is the fight in which activists should now be engaged. The key points, which will be developed here, are:

- to highlight the unfairness to individuals of the present position;

- to demonstrate that the UK is out of line with other successful industrial nations;

- to heighten awareness that the UK is also in breach of its international obligations;

- to show that reform is workable in practice;

- to link the protection of workers engaging in industrial action to the protection of employees taking part in trade union activities.

THE PRESENT POSITION

As is well known, official strikers who are dismissed have no redress unless the employer is selective in dismissal or re-engagement, and unofficial strikers have no redress if dismissed in any circumstances. This immediately makes a nonsense of any idea of a right to strike, but in fact it is worth taking a closer look at the provisions, so that their unfairness can be seen to be even more gross.

First, as a result of reform by the Employment Act 1982, provided an employer waits three months from the date of dismissal before re-engaging employees, other dismissed workers will have no claim based on discrimination.[2] Second, if the industrial action is provoked by a threatened or actual breach of contract by the employer, it makes no difference. For example in *Wilkins* v *Cantrell & Cochrane Ltd*,[3] employees argued that they had been compelled to take out overloaded lorries in fundamental breach of contract. They resorted to industrial action and were dismissed. The EAT held that, because they were on strike at the time of their dismissal, the industrial tribunal had no jurisdiction to hear their claims. Yet if they had resigned in such circumstances, it could have been constructive dismissal and held to be unfair.

Third, an employee can be acting within the terms of her contract and yet be lawfully dismissed if she is considered to be taking industrial action, as illustrated by *Power Packing Casemakers* v *Faust*,[4] where the employee was sacked for exercising his contractual right to refuse to do overtime. Because he had done so in pursuit of a pay claim, he could not claim unfair dismissal; if he had done so because he wanted to visit a friend or watch a football match (to use Stephenson LJ's examples), he could have brought his unfair dismissal claim and would probably have won it.

So if the employer commits a breach of contract and workers go on strike, they can be dismissed. If employees do not commit a breach of contract but are held to be taking industrial action, they can be dismissed. This is a bizarre state of affairs. When the law relating to lockouts is taken into account, the position looks even more peculiar. A lockout is not defined for the purposes of TULR(C)A s. 238, but the definition in Schedule 13 of the Employment Protection (Consolidation) Act 1978 (EP(C)A) was regarded as a good indicator by the Court of Appeal in *Express & Star Ltd* v *Bunday*:[5] 'the closing of a place of employment, or the suspension of work, or the refusal of an employer to continue to employ any number of persons employed by him in consequence of a dispute, done with a view to compelling those persons, *or to aid another employer in compelling persons employed by him*, to accept terms and conditions of or affecting employment' (emphasis added). (Note that sympathetic or secondary action by employers is all right, although it is unlawful for trade unions.)

Thus, if an employer wants to change terms and conditions, the state encourages it to do so without making serious attempts to reach agreement. Once it can be said that there is a dispute, all the employer needs to do is to issue an ultimatum, close the doors and then dismiss the workers! And there are no formalities for an employer to comply with before initiating industrial action in this way. The only possible remedy for an employee in these circumstances would be to claim wrongful dismissal at common law. But then she will only get a sum equivalent to notice pay, which the employer may be willing to pay in any case: it is unlikely to be a large sum.

This brings us to yet another striking illogicality. The Employment Act 1990, now TULR(C)A s. 237, provides that unofficial strikers cannot claim unfair dismissal in any circumstances: but 'unofficial' is taken to include workers who are not even union members, if it is the case that any of those taking part do belong to a union – something of which the non-members may be wholly unaware.

No doubt these illogical, unfair examples could be multiplied, but enough has surely been said to convince any dispassionate and reasonable observer that the law on dismissal is indefensible. Only unfair dismissal has been considered so far, but the position at common law is no better, as it is clear that engaging in industrial action justifies summary dismissal.[6]

The justification originally put forward when the equivalent of s. 238 was introduced by the Industrial Relations Act 1971 was that tribunals should not be drawn into pronouncing on the rights and wrongs of industrial disputes. If employees could claim unfair dismissal when sacked for taking part in industrial action, it was feared that tribunals would have to decide whether they were justified in taking the action in order to decide whether the employer acted reasonably in dismissing them.

Yet tribunals *do* have to make decisions about the validity of disputes as the law stands now. Deciding whether there has been a dismissal in connection with a lockout inevitably entails an evaluation of the events leading up to the employer's refusal to allow people to work.[7] Tribunals are also making similar judgments when deciding whether actions are protected union activities or duties or industrial action.[8] Again, where there has been selective dismissal or re-engagement of strikers, tribunals have to decide whether the selectivity was fair or whether compensation should be reduced,[9] as they have also done in cases where selection for redundancy has been on the basis of participation in industrial action.[10] The present position in relation to individual strikers and dismissal is therefore demonstrably indefensible.

COMPARATIVE AND INTERNATIONAL DIMENSION

By comparison with laws of other nations with economies that are at least as successful, British laws on strikes are among the most restrictive. As Wedderburn has pointed out, of the 12 countries constituting the EU until recently, all but Denmark and the UK treat the contract of employment as suspended during industrial action.[11]

In the USA, a distinction is drawn between unfair labour practice strikes and economic or organizational strikes. Where a strike is a response to an unfair labour practice by the employer, employees are entitled to their jobs back at the end of the strike, even if the employer has hired permanent replacements in the meantime.[12] In economic or organizational strikes, the strikers can be replaced[13] but remain entitled to vote in workplace elections for up to a year, and are entitled to their jobs when they next become available, provided that they are not themselves guilty of an unfair labour practice.[14] These rules are derived from the basic protection for union activities in the National Labor Relations Act s. 7.

In recent years, strong condemnation of British law on industrial action has come from the International Labour Organisation.[15] ILO Convention 87 on Freedom of Association and the Right to Organise (1948, ratified by the UK in 1949) contains two central provisions:

> Article 2
> Workers and employers, without distinction whatsoever, shall have the right to establish and, subject only to the rules of the organisation concerned, to join organisations of their own choosing without previous authorisation.
>
> Article 3
> 1 Workers' and employers' organizations shall have the right to draw up their constitutions and rules, to elect their representatives in full freedom, to organise their administration and activities and to formulate their programmes.
> 2 The public authorities shall refrain from any interference which would restrict this right or impede the lawful exercise thereof.

According to the ILO Committee of Experts, 'the Committee has always considered that the right to strike is one of the essential means available to workers and their organizations for the promotion and protection of their economic and social interests as guaranteed by Articles 3, 8 and 10 of the Convention'.[16] In 1989, the Committee's annual report, coming in the wake of the Employment Act 1988, considered that a number of aspects of the legislation were not compatible with the Convention, including 'the erosion of legislative protection against civil liability for industrial action and dismissals in connection with strikes and other industrial action'.[17] The particular contraventions noted were:

- the prohibition on unions disciplining members who refuse to take part in lawful industrial action;

- the total abolition of boycott activity and sympathy strikes;

- the requirement that disputes should be 'wholly or mainly' about trade dispute motives, ruling out the pursuit of mixed industrial and political/social objectives;

- the limitation to disputes between 'workers and their employer', which can be manipulated through the use of subsidiary companies with separate legal personality (as in *Dimbleby* v *NUJ*[18]);

- ruling out disputes about matters outside the UK unless the participants are likely to be affected by the outcome.

Here the Committee observed that it did not consider that 'purely political' strikes came within the protection of the Convention, but 'trade unions ought to have the possibility of recourse to protest strikes, in particular where aimed at criticising a government's economic and social policies'.[19] The overall complexity and uncertainty of the legislation was also regarded as incompatible with the Convention.

Most relevant for the present argument were the Committee's conclusions on unfair dismissal in relation to industrial action, seen as inadequate in three respects:

1 Because employees have no claim if the employer dismisses everyone.
2 Because selective re-engagement is permissible provided that there is a three-month gap.
3 Because there is no protection against detrimental action short of dismissal.

The Committee of Experts' request for reform was repeated in 1991, following consideration and rejection of points made by the UK government.[20] In 1992, the annual report noted that the Employment Act 1990 had removed protection from *all* kinds of sympathetic action and worsened the position of unofficial strikers. The British government argued that the position of individual workers was not covered by Convention 87 but rather by Convention 98, and also that UK law had always permitted employers to sack workers taking part in industrial action. The committee rejected these arguments and repeated its call for reform.[21]

The 1993 report effectively repeated the previous report, although the committee apparently conceded that some matters ought more properly to be considered under Convention 98. The 1994 report showed the stalemate continuing.[22]

It is thus abundantly clear that by the standards of the ILO the law of the UK on industrial action is in breach of Convention 87. The ILO Committee on Freedom of Association reached a similar conclusion in considering the claims arising out of the dispute between the National Union of Seamen and P & O Ferries in 1992. Convention 87 is one of the fundamental conventions of the ILO, ratified by the UK as long ago as 1949. The continuing breach of its treaty obligations is a source of shame for a country that was one of the prime movers in establishing the ILO.

REFORM IN PRACTICE

The suggestion that strikes should be treated as merely suspending the contract of employment was considered by the Donovan Committee in its 1968 report, but rejected on the grounds that there would be 'considerable technical difficulties' in introducing it.[23] However, it is submitted that the Donovan questions are not so difficult.

The first Donovan issue was: to what strikes should the doctrine of suspension apply? The original definition of 'trade dispute', still retained in TULR(C)A s. 218, but only in relation to the powers of ACAS to assist in trade disputes, worked without difficulty for over 70 years and accords with ILO guidance on Convention 87. There seems no reason to suspect that its reintroduction would cause technical difficulty, and if it were felt that the stipulation that the dispute should be merely 'connected with' one of the matters listed was too wide, it could be replaced with a formula like 'one of the main causes of which is . . .'.[24]

This points to the answer to the next Donovan questions: suspension should apply whether the strike is official or not and whether or not notice is given. This follows from the concept of the right to strike as an individual right. It would also be eminently sensible for it to apply to action short of a strike as well – although only if the action is in breach of contract. Otherwise, there would be an incentive for workers to react always by all-out strike action, rather than holding it in reserve as a weapon of last resort.

Should the same law apply to essential services? It is submitted that it should, subject to certain conditions. TULR(C)A s. 240 presently makes it a criminal offence to break a contract of employment where death, personal injury or danger to valuable property is a probable consequence. While I would not support the criminalization of industrial action, it would in my view be acceptable to require that in these circumstances at least, strikes would only be lawful if emergency cover was provided.

The Donovan Commission posed certain questions concerning termination: could an employee be dismissed for some other good cause, such as misconduct, while on strike? What if she took other employment during the strike? If there was no settlement, at what point would termination occur? As to the first, it would be reasonable and in accordance with present practice for a supervening reason for dismissal to override any suspension of the contract.[25] Taking temporary work for the duration of the strike should not be such a reason (subject to there being no breach of any obligations of confidence). In the absence of settlement, it is submitted that there are no technical difficulties precluding indefinite suspension of the contract unless and until the employee either indicates expressly that she is terminating the contract or does so impliedly (for example, by taking another permanent job).

The final Donovan question was whether contracting out of the law should be allowed. At present, a collective agreement prohibiting or restricting the right of workers to engage in industrial action is valid only if: the agreement is in writing; it contains an express term that it is capable of incorporation into individual contracts; it is reasonably accessible to the worker during working hours; and it is made with an independent trade union.[26] There is nothing to stop an employer insisting on such a term in an individual contract and, even if it is not an express term, it may be implied.[27] Here, the only restriction is that the employer will not be able to enforce performance of the obligation.[28]

It is submitted that it should remain open to independent trade unions to enter peace obligations, subject to the safeguards in TULR(C)A s. 180. However, it should not be possible to contract out of the right to strike on an individual basis, since inequality of bargaining power makes unfair exploitation of the worker's position likely.

BALLOTS AND NOTICE

In the consideration of workable reform, a final issue is whether requirements for strike ballots and notice to employers should be retained. One of the glaring anomalies of the present law is that there is an elaborate construction of complex rules that must be followed for a valid strike ballot but, even when they are complied with down to the last detail, workers can still be dismissed without redress.

There can be no justification for the present ballot and notice scheme, which is blatantly aimed at making it so difficult to hold a valid ballot that action will be discouraged or will be highly vulnerable to legal attack. However, the ILO committee of experts has indicated that the requirement for a secret ballot before industrial action *per se* is not a breach of the Convention,[29] and there can be no denying that, in the eyes of the general public, a secret ballot has a legitimating function. Hence, it is submitted that where industrial action is organized by trade unions, it should remain a requirement that there should be a secret ballot first, in order for the protection of individual workers to apply. Provided that the union can satisfy the basic conditions of an opportunity to vote in secret free from interference, there should be no further legal condition, e.g. that a ballot should be postal, subject to independent scrutiny, etc.: these should be matters for the union. Since a ballot is unlikely to take place without an employer's knowledge, it is submitted that there should be no further requirement of notice to the employer.

INDUSTRIAL ACTION AND UNION ACTIVITY

An efficient means of introducing the kinds of reforms outlined above would be to include industrial action within the concept of trade union activity, which is where it conceptually belongs. As noted already, the ILO has built the concept of the right to strike out of the Convention on Freedom of Association, thus implicitly accepting the argument that the ability to take strike action is essential if there is to be effective association in trade unions. The same is true of the USA, where the National Labor Relations Act s. 7 prohibits anti-union activity, which has been interpreted to include concerted industrial action in pursuit of legitimate objectives.

The difficulty of distinguishing union activity from industrial action under present English law has been noted in a number of cases.[30] We also saw above that the ILO has criticized the UK because British

taliatory action short of dismissal. luding industrial action within the Thus, from having no protection at n against action short of dismissal ed with attacks on union member- ally noted that there is an urgent union activities, given the recent *Associated Newspapers* v *Wilson*[32] missal does not cover omissions to provision outlawing unfavourable embership or activities or likely to ies.

NOTES

1. This is the case where an employer institutes a lockout: see the Trade Union and Labour Relations (Consolidation) Act 1992 (TULR(C)A) s. 238.

2. See now TULR(C)A s. 238(2)(b).

3. [1978] IRLR 483 (EAT).

4. [1983] ICR 282 (CA).

5. [1988] ICR 379 (CA).

6. See G. Pitt, *Employment Law* (2nd edn, 1995), pp. 293–9.

7. For example, *Fisher* v *York Trailer* [1979] IRLR 386 (EAT); *Express & Star Ltd* v *Bunday* [1988] ICR 379 (CA); *Campey* v *Bellwood* [1987] ICR 34 (EAT).

8. *Rasool* v *Hepworth Pipe (No. 2)* [1980] IRLR 88 (EAT); *Naylor* v *Orton* [1983] IRLR 233 (EAT); *Drew* v *St Edmundsbury DC* [1980] IRLR 137.

9. *TNT Express* v *Downes* [1993] IRLR 432 (EAT).

10. For example, *Laffin and Callaghan* v *Fashion Industries* [1978] IRLR 448, *Cruickshank* v *Hobbs* [1977] ICR 725 (EAT).

11. Lord Wedderburn, Laws about strikes. In McCarthy (ed.), *Legal Intervention in Industrial Relations* (1992).

12. *Arlan's Department Store* 133 NLRB 802 (1961).

13. *NLRB* v *Mackey Radio and Telegraph Co.* 304 US 333 (1938) (Sup. Ct).

14. *Laidlaw Corp* 171 NLRB 1366, enf. 414 F2d 99.

15. See K. D. Ewing, *Britain and the ILO* (London: Institute of Employment Rights, 2nd edn, 1994); D. Brown and A. McColgan, UK employment law and the ILO: the spirit of co-operation? (1992) 21 *Industrial Law Journal* 265.

16. ILO Committee of Experts, *Observations Concerning Ratified Conventions* (1989), p. 237 (reprinted also in Ewing, *op. cit.*, Appendix IV).

17. *Op. cit.*, p. 236.

18. [1984] ICR 386 (HL).

19. *Op. cit.*, p. 239.

20. Committee of Experts, *Annual Report 1991*, pp. 220–1.

21. *Annual Report 1992*, pp. 246–9.

22. *Annual Report 1993*, pp. 237–8; *Annual Report 1994*, p. 226.

23. Royal Commission on Trade Union and Employers' Associations, Cmnd 3623 (1968), paras 943–4.

24. See G. Pitt, *The Limits of Industrial Action* (London: Institute of Employment Rights, 1995), Chapter 5, for further development of these points.

25. Cf. *Simmons* v *Hoover* [1977] QB 284 (EAT).

26. TULR(C)A s. 180.

27. See *Ticehurst* v *British Telecom* [1992] IRLR 219 (CA).

28. TULR(C)A s. 236.

29. Ewing, *op. cit.*, p. 39.

30. See note 7 above and Pitt, *Limits of Industrial Action, op. cit.*

31. The definition would have to be solid enough to encompass union-like activity by non-union members too.

32. [1995] IRLR 258 (HL).

8

Re-establishing Trade Union Rights: For Positive Rights to Strike

Roger Welch

INTRODUCTION

The purpose of this chapter is to discuss what changes the trade union movement ought to be seeking to the legislation, enacted between 1980 and 1993, that restricts the ability of trade unions and their members to organize and participate in industrial action. The chapter does not analyse in depth the operation of the laws currently in force. Nor does it include a detailed comparison between British law and the law in the European and wider international context. However, discussing the practical consequences of the current legislation inevitably requires some reference to how the law actually works; and justifications for restoring and even extending 'rights to strike' can be strengthened by comparisons with the legal position internationally. The central propositions of the chapter will be: (a) that all legislation, passed from 1980 onwards, concerned with regulating industrial action should be repealed; and (b) that, rather than restoring the system of immunities which existed prior to 1980, new positive rights to take industrial action should be enacted.

THE RIGHT TO STRIKE

In 1979, within the framework of the system of immunities, it was legally permissible for trade unions and their members to organize and participate in industrial action if any group of employees had a 'trade dispute' with *any* employer. Moreover, the definition of 'trade dispute' was relatively wide, in that it included any dispute with a political and/ or international dimension, and disputes which might be perceived as disputes between workers in that they concerned issues such as demarcation or the use of non-union labour. It was for a trade union and its members to determine what procedures, if any, were to be followed before a union could declare that a dispute was official. Indeed, with respect to legal consequences no distinction was drawn between official and unofficial industrial action. Although rights to picket were controlled by the common law and public order legislation, it was nevertheless legally permissible for trade unionists to picket peacefully at any workplace in any numbers.

Today industrial action is lawful only if there is a trade dispute between a group of employees and their *own* employer, and a trade dispute is narrowly defined in that it must relate wholly or mainly to terms and conditions of the employment contracts of the workers involved, or to issues such as job losses, health and safety, discipline or collective bargaining matters. A trade union will lose immunity from legal liability even in these circumstances if detailed provisions requiring postal ballots and 'strike notices' to employers are not observed. If, in order to avoid such liability, a trade union repudiates action taken by its members, the action is then in law deemed unofficial and those involved may be dismissed on a selective and arbitrary basis. Workers in dispute may only picket their own workplace, and a picket in excess of six persons may incur legal difficulties.

The cumulative effect of this legislation, which combines a significant narrowing of statutory immunity with preconditions that trade unions must satisfy before immunity is conferred, is that any industrial action which falls outside of this statutory rubric will involve the organizer(s) in legal liability. The technical problem is that the organization of virtually all forms of industrial action constitutes the tort or civil wrong of interference with contracts of employment and/or commercial contracts. Interference with the latter has become very important in recent years, as it provides the basis of liability with respect to the organization of sympathetic industrial action.

If industrial action is outside the scope of the statutory immunities, adversely affected employers can obtain injunctions prohibiting the relevant union from supporting its members involved in the action. Defiance of an injunction by a union constitutes contempt of court and can result in the imposition of fines and, ultimately, sequestration (seizure) of a trade union's assets (as happened to the NUM in 1984).

RESTORING RIGHTS TO TAKE INDUSTRIAL ACTION

As established above, any trade union or individual trade unionist organizing sympathetic industrial action runs the risk of incurring legal liability in tort. This is so where the workers involved are in the same industry or profession, even where they work for the same person, but are employed in separate companies that person has established.[1] These controls on sympathetic action are a major factor in the current weakness of trade unions. Today a list of disputes could be cited which were long-running but ultimately unsuccessful from the perspective of the workers involved. The cause of failure was that the relevant union(s), constrained by the fear of the financial consequences of incurring legal liability, refused to countenance the organization of sympathetic action.

The defeat of the miners in 1984 can, to a significant extent, be attributed to this (although the NUM itself did of course seek support from other unions). The precedent set by this defeat was followed by News International, P & O, Timex and a host of smaller employers, such as Burnsalls and Middlebrook Mushrooms. Taking or threatening legal action proved sufficient to ensure trade union compliance with the law. Furthermore, employers have often combined the use or threat of litigation with the dismissal of workers on strike and the engagement of non-union labour.

Moreover, even if industrial action is relatively successful, controls on sympathetic action may still affect the course of a dispute by tempering the extent of any success and/or extending the dispute's duration. The dispute between Railtrack and its signal workers in 1994 provides a vivid illustration of this. All railworkers were affected by the dispute and its outcome, and Railtrack's use of supervisors to operate signals on strike days could have been neutralized if the RMT had been able to counter this by supporting members who, in such circumstances, would have been prepared to refuse to drive trains.

The other main restriction on a union's ability to support its members who are in dispute with their employer is where that dispute can be regarded as having a political dimension. Since 1982, a dispute can be defined as a 'trade dispute' only if it relates *wholly or mainly* to listed 'employment matters', such as the pay and conditions of the workers in dispute. This contrasts with the legal position which has existed for the best part of this century – that a 'trade dispute' need only have some connection with pay, conditions and the like. The practical consequence of this is that any dispute that arises at least in part as a result of government policy may be viewed by a court as being predominantly of a political nature, and therefore not a trade dispute.

Thus in a case, decided by the Court of Appeal,[2] which was concerned with industrial action organized in the context of the privatization of British Telecom, it was decided that the predominant motive behind the action was not fear of redundancies, as the unions claimed, but opposition on political grounds to the whole policy of privatization. Indeed, Lord Donaldson, the head of that court, went so far as to describe the unions' concern over job losses as a sham.

This approach can, of course, be extended to any dispute that takes place in the context of privatization. It is, therefore, a threat to all public sector workers who contemplate the use of industrial action to protect pay and, in particular, conditions from being worsened as a result of privatization. The boycott of school tests by the NUT and the National Association of Schoolmasters/Union of Women Teachers (NAS/UWT) was similarly made the subject of litigation, albeit in this case unsuccessfully because the unions were able to stress the increased workload that implementing the tests would bring.[3]

In Britain, it has always been a matter of some controversy whether workers should have the right to strike where a dispute can be perceived as political. The argument against 'political strikes' – an argument which can be heard from within as well as outside the labour movement – is that such strikes are undemocratic because they undermine elected governments. However, I argue that the distinction between a 'political' and a 'trade' dispute is generally artificial. In practice, virtually all strikes deemed 'political' have implications for workers' interests in an employment context. It is this type of so-called 'political' strike that should not be subject to legal restriction. Why should not teachers have the right to refuse to implement government policies that they believe to be harmful to the education of the children for whom they are responsible? Why should not workers threatened with the privatization or contracting-out of their work be able to take industrial action to resist changes that they believe (rightly) will ultimately result in worse services to the public; let alone in job losses and inferior conditions of employment?

The legislation that renders unlawful the organization of sympathetic action and action deemed 'political' has been condemned, at least in part, by the International Labour Organisation. It is also out of line with the positions in other member states of the European Union (such as France and Italy), whose constitutions permit workers to hold political strikes. The ILO committee has called for UK legislation to be amended to permit industrial action where there is a mixture of industrial and political objectives. It has also called for the legalization of sympathetic action where workers taking it have an economic or social interest in the outcome of the primary dispute.[4]

It would be in line with the ILO's requirements to restore the pre-1980 position as far as disputes with a political dimension are concerned. Implementing the ILO's proposals would also restore legality to sympathetic action where there is a commercial relationship between the employer in dispute and the employer whose employees are engaged in sympathetic action, or where the workers taking it are in the same industry or profession. Clearly, it would be impermissible for an employer to hide behind corporate legal identity as a device to make sympathy action unlawful. An employer would no longer be able to prevent one section of its workforce taking action in support of a different section by, for example, creating a different company to distribute the product to operate alongside the company established to make it.

Less clear-cut would be, for example, the legal position of trade unionists outside the National Health Service (NHS) who might be prepared to take sympathetic action in support of a pay claim by nurses. As consumers, trade unionists certainly have a 'social' interest in the efficiency of the health service, and this could be linked to pay claims by health workers. However, surely just as importantly, trade unionists may well wish to engage in sympathetic action to aid workers who are very reluctant to use what little industrial muscle they actually do have. This is irrespective of any interest, direct or indirect, that trade unionists involved in sympathetic action might have in the outcome of the dispute.

Similar doubts would exist with respect to the sort of solidarity action that the miners wanted and needed to win their dispute in 1984 (thus, in all probability, saving their industry and communities from the ravages which have been suffered in the years since). Could dockers, railway workers, power workers or steelworkers be viewed as having an occupational or social interest in the outcome of such a dispute? Certainly, it can be argued that there is a connection at the level of job security. However, the real connection of such groups is as trade unionists who do not want to see another group of trade unionists defeated. This is particularly so in contexts such as the miners' strike, given that it has since become clear that there was a pre-existing strategy on the part of the government, the National Coal Board and various organs of the state to break the NUM as an industrial force.

What cannot be emphasized enough is that workers need sympathetic action because they start from a position of weakness, and not strength, *vis-à-vis* their own employer and/or the government and/or the state. If this is accepted, it can be argued that sympathetic action is not something which is potentially illegitimate because it is too far removed from the actual essence of a dispute. Trade unionists are often accused (wrongly) of being greedy and selfish. But when they take sympathetic action they are, by definition, taking action that is primarily designed to help people other than themselves. This is the reality of sympathetic action. This is the reality that should be recognized in law. If workers wish to take industrial action not on their own behalf but on the behalf of others then surely they should have an unqualified legal right to do so.

The recommendations of the ILO should be used to substantiate how the existing legislation violates international law. Similarly, comparisons with the legal positions in other EU member states and the recognition of rights to strike accorded by the Social Charter can help to substantiate and emphasize the lack of rights possessed by trade unionists in Britain. However, the recommendations of the ILO and the general position in Europe should be regarded as no more than the base from which to argue for pro-union reform. Before 1979, and indeed for much of this century, British law as made by Parliament, as opposed to that developed by the judges, drew no distinction between primary and sympathetic industrial action. Moreover, the purposes for which industrial action could be taken lawfully were wide and varied.

It has been argued above that in the main there is no neat and genuine distinction between disputes which are 'political' and those which are concerned with 'employment matters'. It has also been argued that sympathetic action is both an honourable trade union tradition and often a vital necessity from the perspective of workers in dispute. If these arguments are accepted, it seems reasonable for trade unions and their members to seek to obtain the restoration of the rights which, in effect, existed until 1980. However, such a restoration should be in the form of rights, as against the traditional system of immunities, as, in my view, adopting a system of rights should make it more difficult than it has been in the past for judges to undermine pro-union laws (this argument will be developed below).

TRADE UNION DEMOCRACY

Until 1984 the procedures (if any) that a trade union was obliged to follow before it could organize industrial action, or officially support action its members were already taking, were determined by the constitution of the union concerned. Typically such a constitution reflected, or could be amended to reflect, the wishes of that union's membership.

The Trade Union Act 1984, under the guise of giving the unions back to their members, deprived union members of the ability to determine this major constitutional and democratic issue. The 1984 Act withdrew statutory immunity from a trade union (but not its officials or members) if the union authorized or endorsed industrial action without first holding a secret ballot. The detail of the 1984 Act, supplemented by complex provisions introduced in 1988, rendered the organization of a ballot a relatively complicated affair. However, until 1993 trade unions were allowed a choice between organizing a secret ballot wholly or partly at the workplace, or holding a fully postal ballot. Most unions preferred the former because it was simpler and less costly to organize. Most importantly, rates of participation were generally higher than was the case when ballot papers were sent to members' homes and posted on an individual basis.

Despite this, in 1993 the Trade Union Reform and Employment Rights Act (TURERA) required pre-strike ballots to be fully postal in nature. This has lengthened the time it takes to organize industrial action, and has effectively made it impossible for ballots to be organized at branch or workplace level without the support of the union's national administrative machinery. Moreover, the 1993 Act requires written notice to be given to employers at least seven days prior to the holding of the ballot. If the ballot produces a vote in favour of industrial action, similar notice must be given before the action may take place.

Before 1990, a trade union could always escape liability for industrial action not sanctioned by a secret ballot by repudiating, in writing, the actions of its officials (although it could not repudiate the acts of those who constituted the national leadership), officers or stewards. The 1990 Employment Act changed this by requiring a union to write to all members engaged in unofficial action to inform them that the union is repudiating their actions. This is likely to be perceived by many trade unionists as an instruction from the union to return to work. If they do not, they may be dismissed fairly on a selective basis (this is further considered below). If a trade union refuses to police its members in this way, the action is deemed official, and the union faces the risk of an employer securing a court order to compel it to repudiate or face proceedings for acting in contempt of court.

The government's justification for the balloting provisions is that union leaders should not be able to instruct their members to take strike action unless it is the clear democratic wish of the membership, as expressed through a secret ballot, to take such action. The clear implication of this is that ordinary trade unionists do not really wish to take strike action, and will be able to avoid being bullied into doing so by their leaders if they are able to express their real views in a ballot.

An examination of the history of British industrial relations would certainly provide examples of union leaders attempting to organize industrial action without having the real support of their members. However, such actions were likely to be short-lived and almost certainly doomed to failure. Any active trade unionist is aware that it is normally futile to try to organize a strike if the majority of relevant union members are not prepared to support it. More pertinently, the weight of history reveals that, if anything, union leaders tend to be more cautious than their members when it comes to the use of industrial action.

The controls on unofficial action introduced in 1990 were brought into being precisely to coerce union leaderships into pressurizing their members to end industrial action that the members concerned had taken on their own initiative, and without proper reference to the union's official machinery. Specifically, these provisions were the government's response to successful unofficial industrial action organized by rank-and-file workers employed by London Underground. Their strikes in 1989 were organized in a semi-clandestine manner following a decision to exclude union officials from knowledge of and control over when and what action was to take place.

The decision by the NUM not to hold a national ballot to ratify the 1984 strike is often given within the labour movement as justification for a future Labour government retaining balloting provisions. There can be no doubt there were members of the NUM who wanted a ballot. But the majority of the miners on strike took the position that they had already voted with their feet and, if anything, would have expressed anger if the strike had been called off by the national leadership until a ballot had been held. It is true that in Nottinghamshire the majority were against strike action, but they continued working, and many miners left the NUM altogether.

Whatever tactical assessments different members of the labour movement make of the refusal of the NUM to hold a ballot, I would argue that the real issue was not one of union democracy. The majority of NUM members (Nottinghamshire apart) did support the strike – were this not the case the strike could not have lasted the full year that it did. Moreover, the damaging court injunction that led to the sequestration of the assets of the NUM came not from litigation by working miners in Nottinghamshire, but from court action by two miners in Yorkshire. No one can argue that the court which granted that injunction was seeking to enforce the democratic wishes of the majority, given the passionate support for the strike by the Yorkshire miners and their communities.

The reality is that the legal requirement to hold a ballot if a union is to retain its immunity from legal liability is not a mechanism for making unions more accountable to their members. The object and effect of the balloting requirements, and of the pre-ballot and pre-strike notice requirements, is to impose a time-consuming process on to a union before it can organize industrial action. Moreover, a union will have to reveal its strategy to the employer, who can organize in advance both to influence the outcome of the ballot and to undermine any action that ultimately takes place.

That these provisions expose union members to the risk of victimization is shown in different ways by a case brought against the lecturers' union, NATFHE,[5] and the dismissal by Eastern National (a subsidiary of the Badgerline group) of bus drivers involved in a short one-shift strike in November 1994.

The effect of the NATFHE judgment is that notices to employers may be invalid unless they individually identify all members who are to receive ballot papers, and who are to be called on to take the action if there is an affirmative result in the ballot. This decision clearly breaches confidentiality, in that an employer is provided with a complete list of union members that the organization employs. Most importantly, it facilitates the identification of individual union members who can be targeted by managers (while the ballot is taking place) as candidates for pressure and/or intimidation into voting against the action. Similar pressure can be brought to bear on individuals not to participate in any action that the ballot result may sanction. What price the privacy of the secret ballot in these circumstances?

A common form of industrial action in the current climate of recession is the holding of a series of short strikes rather than the organization of indefinite strike action. Under the 1993 Act, a union must give seven days' notice before any specific short action can take place. The Eastern National dispute establishes how this requirement on a union to disclose its plan of campaign in advance is linked to the risk of victimization. It enables an employer to arrange secretly for alternative labour to be engaged, and then dismiss the union members who participate in the action in accordance with the strike notice.

As was the case with Eastern National, implementing such dismissals is particularly attractive to an employer whose employees are taking the action to resist the imposition of worse conditions of employment – a new workforce can then be engaged on new contracts. It matters not that the industrial action concerned is wholly lawful and of short duration. Providing the dismissals are implemented while the action is taking place, there are no legal repercussions for the employer. It is substantially more difficult for employers to use this tactic if they are unable to ascertain the precise date that industrial action is due to take place.

Any residual doubts that any trade unionists might have about the hollowness of the government's concern for trade union democracy ought to be dispelled by its provision of a right not to strike in the Employment Act of 1988. Most trade unionists who have participated in industrial action will have experienced a sense of outrage against other members who work through a strike. Not only is it necessary to work alongside such people once the strike has ended, but often they share any gains to the workforce that the strike has brought about. One consolation may be that the union will be prepared to discipline strike-breakers and either fine them or expel them from membership altogether.

As the law stands, strike-breakers have the right not to be 'subjected to unjustifiable discipline'. This includes any form of action against members who flout the democratic wishes of the majority by refusing to participate in industrial action, and it is a matter of complete irrelevance that the action was sanctioned by a secret ballot. The general practical consequence of these provisions is that union members will no longer be disciplined for strike-breaking, because of the expense this may cause to a union through claims for compensation. Strike-breakers who have been expelled from the union can oblige a union to take them back into membership (with full access to the services and time of its officials and workplace representatives) or pay, at the very least, £2770 per person by way of compensation (this is the minimum award the EAT must currently make in such circumstances).

It should be noted that these provisions were opposed even by the CBI and the Conservative Trade Unionists Group. They have also been held by the ILO to be in contravention of Article 3 of the Freedom of Association Convention, which is intended to control strictly the circumstances in which the state may interfere with the internal life of a trade union. These provisions are now supplemented by the 1993 Act, which prevents any union from excluding individuals from membership (except on limited grounds, such as occupational relevance or being in arrears with union subscriptions). Therefore, strike-breakers who resigned from the union now have the statutory right to be readmitted into membership.

RESTORING TRADE UNION DEMOCRACY

It is common currency within the trade union movement that, in line with traditional practice in this country and with international law, pro-union reform should return to trade unions powers to discipline, expel and exclude from membership individuals who have been guilty of strike-breaking. Additionally, there is almost certainly general support for the abolition of the technical restrictions that ballots currently must conform to if they are to be considered valid. Similarly, it is generally agreed that the current notice provisions should be repealed.

On the other hand, there is certainly some support within both the trade union movement and the Labour Party for the retention of some legal requirement for pre-strike ballots. But it has also been suggested that 'post-strike' ballots may be permitted to ratify and enable a union to support spontaneous walkouts. Furthermore, many would argue that the right of employers to take legal action if ballots are not held should be removed.

However, granting a right to a union member to secure a court order, if a strike ballot has not taken place, may still have adverse and unjustifiable repercussions for the right to strike. As stated above, the legal action which resulted in the seizure of the assets of the NUM was brought by two Yorkshire miners. It is also well known that shadowy organizations were behind such litigation. In other words, giving union members the right to court orders if strike ballots are not held can amount, in practice, to giving employers the ability to create the situation where such orders are obtained to prevent a union from supporting a strike. This can happen even where the facts clearly establish that a strike is in accordance with the wishes of the overwhelming majority of the relevant union members.

It also seems to me to be impractical (even illogical and bizarre) to allow trade unionists to engage in a spontaneous walkout and then require them, presumably, to return to work while a secret ballot is held to permit their union to support their action. As during the miners' strike, the argument must be that the union members have already voted with their feet. The dynamics of industrial action are such that it is often advantageous, indeed essential, to 'strike while the iron is hot'. Any advantage gained by trade unionists through spontaneous action will be lost if they cannot receive the support of their union until a ballot has been completed.

Debate concerning the merits and demerits of pre-strike ballots should also take account of the dynamics of sympathy action, if it is accepted that rights to take such action should be restored. Arguably, a trade union should not be able to compel members to take sympathy action if they are opposed to doing so. However, in such a situation it will often be the case that some union members wish to take sympathy action and/or refuse to cross picket lines. The absence of a ballot, or a positive vote if one has been held, should not deprive union members of the official support of their union if, as individuals, they choose to act in solidarity with other trade unionists engaged in an industrial dispute. Very pertinent to this argument is the legal position in some European countries that the right to strike is not possessed by a trade union as an organization but by a trade unionist as an individual (this is discussed further below).

It is my view that trade unionists ought to be able to organize industrial action without first holding a secret ballot. This enables decisions to be taken quickly, and permits flexibility with respect to further actions to be taken by way of escalation. However, it is accepted that there are a variety of views within the trade union movement (and within all unions) as to whether ballots are more or less democratic than mass meetings and as to whether, tactically, the holding of a ballot is useful or unduly restrictive.

The fundamental argument is that trade union democracy means allowing the members to determine the contents of the constitution of the union to which they belong. If the membership of a given union wish to prohibit industrial action unless there has been a secret ballot, then that is their right. Equally, if members of a different union believe that they or their union ought to be able to organize industrial action without first being obliged to hold a secret ballot, then they should be entitled to a constitution that reflects this position. The central principle is that, whatever the outcome of a debate on this issue within a particular union, a union's constitution must be the genuine product of the preferences of the majority of that union's members, rather than the consequence of state interference.

PROTECTING TRADE UNIONISTS FROM DISMISSAL AND VICTIMIZATION

Reference has been made above to the dismissals of bus drivers employed by Eastern National while they were participating in a short strike. The statutory provisions that permit this were incorporated into the Labour Party's trade union legislation of the 1970s. Under these provisions, industrial tribunals had no jurisdiction to hear claims for unfair dismissal if an employer dismissed all employees participating in industrial action while that action was taking place. That such provisions in practice gave employers the right to sack workers exercising their 'right' to strike was exposed by the famous Grunwick dispute in 1977. George Ward, the owner of Grunwick, dismissed an entire workforce for striking to secure union recognition, and replaced it with alternative labour.

At the time it appeared to be the case that only a limited number of employers were able to use this tactic to break a strike and/or avoid unionization of the workforce. Legislative amendments, introduced by the Conservatives in 1982, along with conditions of mass unemployment, have resulted in the increasingly frequent use of this tactic. The effects of the amendments are that: (a) an employer may dismiss a section of the workforce that continues to take industrial action after some union members who initially participated in it have been pressurized or induced to return to work; (b) an employer may re-engage selectively once three months have expired from the date of the original dismissals. A condition of re-engagement may be that employees accept different conditions of employment. This is particularly useful to an employer if the dispute was caused by proposals to introduce new contracts.

In recent years the use of these rights of dismissal has intensified among the 'Grunwick-type' of employer. For example, there were clear parallels between the Grunwick dispute and the year-long Burnsalls dispute in Birmingham. Both disputes involved workforces, composed predominantly of women of Asian origin employed in 'sweatshop' conditions, who were dismissed for striking to secure trade union rights. Moreover, the climate of fear produced by such cases has been reinforced by the fact that highly skilled workers, once safe from such strike-breaking tactics, have also been dismissed for taking strike action. Notable examples include the printers at Wapping, the seafarers at Dover and the locked-out Timex engineering workers. It is argued below that the substantial decline in union membership over the past 15 years has some connection with the vulnerability of the individual trade unionist to dismissal if she or he engages in industrial action.

The above position is compounded by the current controls on unofficial action. As stated above, the 1990 Act was designed primarily to coerce trade unions into repudiating unofficial action by their members. Once such repudiation occurs, as it almost inevitably will, any union members who continue with the action may be dismissed on a selective basis. Obviously, an employer will generally decide to dismiss first those who are leading the strike. In practice, such individuals will tend to be the union activists and/or workplace representatives, and their dismissals will seriously weaken, or even destroy, union organization at that workplace. Indeed, it is not beyond the bounds of possibility that an employer might provoke unofficial industrial action precisely in order to engineer such an outcome.

Further legal controls on individual trade unionists organizing unofficial action have been provided by the 1993 Act. The Act gives individuals (but not companies) the right to restrain unofficial action that might result in a delay in the supply of goods or services to them. The applicant does not have to establish the presence of tortious liability, as the absence of a ballot is sufficient to enable a court to grant an order. These provisions are aimed most directly at public sector workers, although their utility is limited if the identity of those organizing unofficial action cannot be ascertained. On the other hand, judicial development of tortious liability might expose individual workers taking unofficial action to the risk of civil actions for damages.[6]

The fact that these developments are most significant in the public sector is particularly important because in that sector trade union membership is at its strongest. While, in the private sector, trade union membership and density has fallen consistently throughout the 1980s and 1990s, the position for the public sector is relatively similar to that in the 1970s. The decline of trade unionism in the private sector can, to a significant extent, be attributed to legal curbs on industrial action – those taking it risk losing their jobs and joining the ranks of the unemployed. The law has both undermined the ability of trade unionists to resist redundancies and closures (including wholesale closures of particular industries that were heavily unionized) and prevented workers in the traditionally non-unionized service sector from securing trade union representation.

The current plight of trade unions is exacerbated by the growing trend for derecognition that has emerged in the past few years. However, the incidence of derecognition must not be exaggerated. Research with which I have been involved has not revealed any major movement to derecognize trade unions by employers in the East Anglian region. When derecognition does occur it tends to be partial rather than total, with only employees at managerial or supervisory level being removed from collective bargaining.[7]

Nevertheless, derecognition of trade unions in both private and public sectors is today facilitated by statutory provisions included in the 1993 Act. Derecognition does not in itself terminate contracts of employment derived from collective agreements. But since the 1993 changes, an employer may restrict pay increases to employees who accept new contracts of employment. This is in accordance with the government's preference, revealed in its 1991 White Paper *People, Jobs and Opportunities*, for replacing supposedly outdated methods of collective bargaining with the use of personal contracts and performance-related pay.

These provisions were introduced as last-minute amendments to the 1993 Act in order to nullify a Court of Appeal decision that such tactics by an employer constitute an unlawful action short of dismissal against an employee because of his or her union membership. The provisions have been rendered virtually superfluous by the decision of the Law Lords, in March 1995, to overturn the Court of Appeal's ruling.[8] According to their Lordships, withholding a pay rise (or other contractual benefits) constitutes an *omission*, rather than a *positive act*, and therefore is not prohibited by current legislation. The majority of the Law Lords went so far as to suggest that this is so even though the evidence shows the employer consciously intended to discriminate against trade union members.

Workers thus have no legal protection against the derecognition of their union, or consequent pressure by an employer to accept new employment contracts. It is, of course, lawful to take industrial action in these circumstances, but the ability of workers to resist such employer offensives is clearly undermined by the high risk of dismissals if industrial action takes place.

PROTECTING THE RIGHT OF THE INDIVIDUAL TO 'STRIKE'

The ability of employers to dismiss employees for taking lawful industrial action has its origins in the law of contract. Refusing to work constitutes a repudiatory breach of contract that entitles the employer to treat the contract as at an end. The rules of contract law are superseded by the statutory provisions outlined above, although it should be noted that these provisions apply to permit dismissals even if industrial action does not involve workers breaking their employment contract.[9]

The overwhelming majority of trade unionists argue that a right to strike does not exist unless it is possible to withdraw one's labour, in whole or part, without incurring the risk of dismissal and (perhaps permanent) unemployment. Indeed, the author's research[10] indicates that a significant number of trade unionists (wrongly) believe that this is the current legal position, at least if the industrial action takes place in accordance with a majority vote in a secret ballot.

The research (which was conducted in the autumn of 1987, more than a year after Rupert Murdoch had successfully used the tactic of dismissing all his employees who objected to the move to Wapping) established that almost 45 per cent of the sample believed that employers could not dismiss employees participating in a lawful strike. This proportion was increased to 70 per cent if the industrial action involved was short of a strike (the specified action being an overtime ban). This research remains relevant today – many trade unionists assumed that the dismissals by Eastern National occurred because there had not been a valid ballot. In fact, it was the strikers' compliance with the detailed statutory provisions that enabled the company to draw up plans to use other Badgerline employees to drive their buses until new drivers, on new contracts, could be recruited.

If a right to strike is to be meaningful, workers must be able to exercise it in the knowledge that, when the strike ends, they have a right to return to work. This right could be implemented by giving employees the right to reinstatement on termination of the strike. It would be necessary for provision to be made to enable employees to enforce this right by obtaining court orders requiring the employer to reinstate. Indeed, a procedure should be developed to enable a trade union to obtain such orders on behalf of its members. A legally enforceable right to reinstatement contradicts the normal principle in British law that an individual cannot be compelled to employ (or work for) another. However, if a right to strike is to be provided, there has to be a concomitant right to reinstatement.

Pro-union reform should also remove the law of contract from industrial disputes by providing that the effect of industrial action is to suspend the operation of the employment contract. This would mean that industrial action could not amount to a breach of the employment contract by the individual employee. This would reinforce protection against dismissal or suspension, and would prevent employees from being sued for damages to recover the employer's loss caused by the action. Suspension of the employment contract would have the additional major advantage of eliminating the relevance of the main torts that organizers of industrial action currently commit – these torts revolve around acts that threaten to or do break or interfere with the employment contract.

If such proposals appear radical then this is only in comparison to the wretched legal position of strikers, as individuals, in British law. In the majority of the member states of the European Union, employers do not have the right to dismiss workers engaged in lawful strike action. The ILO has condemned the legal position in the UK as yet another violation of international law and has recommended that strikers should be protected from dismissal. Furthermore, in light of the experience of the workers at Timex, it should be noted that the use of lockouts by employers is tightly regulated in other EU member states – in some countries they are prohibited altogether.

There are those who support the above but argue that employers should be permitted to dismiss unofficial strikers. It is my view that the distinction between official and unofficial industrial action should have no significance with respect to the individual's right to job security. It is often lost sight of that any worker on strike is making a sacrifice. Unofficial strikers, by definition, have to bear the additional burden of not being able to claim strike pay or any other form of material assistance from their unions. Surely there is no good reason why they should have to fear for their livelihoods as well.

Comparison with the legal positions in other European countries is again useful in this context. It is generally the case, in Europe, that no-strike agreements in collective agreements are legally enforceable. However, this does not have the same legal significance in all countries. In Germany and the Scandinavian countries (where the systems of industrial relations are highly centralized), the right to strike is possessed by the union rather than the union member, and unofficial strikers may incur legal penalties. By way of contrast, in Italy, France and Spain the right to strike belongs to the individual and cannot be taken away by the union entering into a no-strike agreement.

This concept of a right to strike as a democratic individual right should be used by trade unionists in the UK to call for the current controls on unofficial action – including employers' rights of dismissal – to be removed. The government has reintroduced the notion, dead since the days of the Industrial Relations Act, that unofficial strikers should be subjected to special legal penalties. It is a notion that the labour movement should reject in its entirety.

Another consideration relates to the employment of alternative labour. It is interesting to note that in Greece, Portugal and Spain, employers are not generally permitted to use alternative labour to replace strikers. It could be argued that a similar legal position should be adopted in the UK. However, assuming that such a proposition would not be adopted, it will be necessary to give an employer the right fairly to dismiss alternative labour that it has employed during a dispute.

One problem area that would still need to be tackled is the situation where the action is short of a strike, in that the employee is still prepared to carry out some, but not all, of the normal contractual duties. In such circumstances, recent case law suggests that the employer has a choice between making deductions from pay to cover the work not performed or refusing to make any payment of wages whatsoever, until the employee agrees to resume normal working. In effect, the latter option amounts to suspending the employee.

Many trade unionists would not accept that employers should have a right to suspend if the employee is prepared to carry out at least some of the duties specified in the contract. Two situations can be identified and distinguished. (a) The employee is refusing only to carry out genuinely voluntary duties. Here, the employer should have no right of punitive or retaliatory action. (b) The employee is refusing to carry out particular duties, but is prepared to fulfil part of the contract. Here, the employer should have no right of suspension, but should be able to make appropriate deductions from pay. Such changes might also facilitate the securing of sympathetic action, as this often involves workers refusing to carry out some, but not all, of their contractual duties.

ESTABLISHING A RIGHT TO PICKET

The Employment Act of 1980, the first piece of legislation designed by the then new Conservative government to control industrial action, made important changes to the immunities protecting pickets from legal liability. Pickets and their trade unions were exposed to liability in tort if they picketed any workplace other than their own. Immunity was lost even if workers in dispute picketed other workplaces of their or an associated employer, or of other employers who were suppliers or customers of their own employer. An accompanying code of practice, while not having the status or force of law, cast doubt on the legality of mass picketing by proposing that pickets at an entrance to a workplace should not exceed six in number.

These controls have been important: a number of injunctions have been secured by employers to prevent picketing that was intended to close down the operations of the employer in dispute, or to make the industrial action more effective through the securing of sympathetic action. A particular sting in the tail was revealed by the dispute between News International and its printers, which led to the former transferring its operations to 'Fortress Wapping'. Any picketing (even token picketing) of the Wapping plant potentially incurred legal liability simply because the sacked printers had never worked there. In law, they were only permitted to picket the empty Fleet Street premises at which they had been employed.

However, arguably the most important long-term consequence of the 1980 changes has been their use to justify police operations against pickets (including the abuses of police powers during the miners' strike and at Wapping) and to justify the extension of those powers by the Police and Criminal Evidence Act 1984, the Public Order Act 1986 and, most recently, the Criminal Justice Act 1994. There is an erroneous but general view in society that any form of mass, flying or so-called secondary picketing is inherently contrary to the criminal law. In fact, such picketing is not automatically tortious, let alone criminal in nature.[11] My research demonstrates that these misconceptions are shared by trade union activists: 70 per cent of the sample believed that mass picketing was a criminal offence, and 78 per cent took the same view of flying picketing.

The use of picketing is often an important tactic if trade unionists are to win an industrial dispute. This is particularly so in the current economic climate, where whole workforces are dismissed and replaced with alternative labour, or workers on strike simply do not have sufficient economic power to succeed unless they can spread industrial action to other workplaces or organizations. Letters and leaflets from unions' head and regional offices, although useful, are generally not enough to win strikes if employers and/or governments are prepared to engage in what amount to 'wars of attrition'. Moreover, as a matter of human psychology, workers are more likely to make the sacrifices involved in taking sympathetic action if they receive direct appeals from the workers primarily involved in a dispute. The most traditional, speedy and effective way of making such appeals is through picketing.

In short, if it is accepted that the right to strike is an essential feature of collective bargaining (and a fundamental democratic and civil right), it must be accepted that there should be a concomitant right to organize picketing that can be effective in achieving legally permitted purposes. It is contradictory to recognize a right to strike, or to express support for workers when they take strike action, without also supporting their right to use tactics that increase the odds of a strike being successful. This is the essential justification for recognizing both that the right to strike must include the right to organize and participate in sympathetic action, and the relevance of picketing in bringing such action about. Therefore, there should be no *a priori* controls on the numbers involved in picketing, or on the workplaces where it may lawfully take place.

It could be argued that the extensions of police powers to control picketing have increased the ability of the police to ensure that violent picketing does not occur. However, a brief survey of police operations during the National Graphical Association (NGA) dispute at Warrington, throughout the miners' strike and at Wapping will establish that 'strong' policing of picket lines (particularly when the use of convoys of strike-breaking lorries and coaches is accompanied by militarized police operations, including cavalry charges) is more likely to promote rather than prevent public disorder.

The increase in violent picketing has been the product of changes to public policy and the law, rather than an activity that has been curtailed by increased police and legal controls on picketing. Violence has occurred because trade unionists have felt frustrated and outraged by policing that has prevented them from even talking to workers contemplating crossing picket lines.

It is in the interests of trade unionists to join with other groups whose civil liberties have been infringed by the above-mentioned increases in police powers, to secure the repeal of the relevant statutory provisions. However, it is also important to address an essential problem that is not the product of current legislation, but of decisions by judges in the 1960s and 1970s concerned with the interpretation of 'peaceful picketing'. Typical of these is a statement by Lord Reid, in a case that arose out of the building workers' strike of 1974, that a picket is analogous to a hitchhiker: 'One is familiar with persons at the side of the road signalling a driver to stop. It is for the driver to decide whether he will stop or not. That, in my view, a picket is entitled to do.'[12]

The law has long failed to take account of the fact that many people drive to work, and that effective picketing must allow pickets to stop vehicles in order to speak to the driver and any passengers. Thus rights to picket should not just be restored, but should be extended to include a limited right to stop. There may be logistical problems with defining the scope of such a right, but granting it is more likely to result in peaceful picketing than in the scenes of police-provoked disorder that have become more and more commonplace in recent years.

RESTORE THE IMMUNITIES OR ESTABLISH POSITIVE RIGHTS?

Implementing the proposals contained in this chapter would require a total repeal of the legislation passed by the current government.

Securing this must be the priority for the trade union movement. The form into which new rights are put is of secondary importance to this. However, it is argued that the traditional system of immunities, although designed to protect trade unions, contains inherent drawbacks which could be at least partly overcome by movement to a system of positive rights.

One practical problem with the immunities is that judges can circumvent them without resorting to restrictive interpretations (although in fact they often do). Immunities provide protection from pre-existing liability and, although attempts can be made to predict and cover liabilities that they may invent in the future, judges have proved very adept at creating new torts. Having done so, they can then claim that they are not acting contrary to the democratic will of Parliament, but implementing it by imposing liability for which Parliament did not intend to grant immunity.

This method was used at the turn of the century to render all forms of industrial action potentially unlawful by the creation of the tort of conspiracy to injure (thus completely nullifying the reforms of the 1870s which were designed to legalize industrial action). In the 1960s, when the judges decided they needed to intervene to control a resurgence of rank-and-file trade union militancy, they did so by deciding that a threat to break a contract of employment constituted intimidation, and by extending the tortious concept of unlawful means to render the organization of sympathetic action a tort without immunity. (It is my view that the timings of these judicial interventions were not coincidental.[13]) Even today, when the scope of the immunities has been substantially reduced, judges have signalled, in a number of cases, the availability of new forms of liability, such as procuring breaches of statutory duties, using duress or even redefining acting in breach of contract as the use of unlawful means.[14]

Most fundamentally, the drawback with the system of immunities is the ideological advantage it gives to judges, the media, employers, politicians and anyone else who wishes to attack the legitimacy of industrial action. This is because a system of immunities leaves the common or judge-made law intact. The language used by judges to identify the liabilities they impose results in the use of industrial action being depicted in the worst possible light. Worse still, it means that the organizing of any strike, or virtually any other form of industrial action, can be castigated as law-breaking. The immunities are then not perceived as rights, but as privileges to break the law. There are a number of statements by judges that employ this sleight of hand. One of the most unambiguous is the following, by Lord Denning:

> When parliament granted immunities to the leaders of trade
> unions, it did not give them any *rights*, it did not give them a *right*
> to break the law or to do wrong by inducing people to break
> contracts. It only gave them immunity if they did ... the words of
> the statute are not to be construed widely so as to give unlimited
> immunity to lawbreakers.[15]

The system of immunities has facilitated what I describe as a process
of legal mystification: rights to take industrial action are labelled as
privileges to break the law; the language of the common law is used to
determine the nature of the liabilities that organizing industrial action
involves. This process has provided a potent ideological weapon to the
opponents of trade unionism. To the ordinary public, 'law-breaking' is
likely to be taken to mean 'criminal'. The question then becomes: why
should unions be above the law? The problem is compounded by the
fact that many trade unionists suffer the same confusion and
misconceptions as to the legal nature of what they are doing when
they take industrial action, even if they feel that their actions are
justified. What is forgotten is that organizing industrial action is 'law-
breaking' only in the sense of being a judge-made tort.

It is not being argued that a system of positive rights would provide
trade unions and members with fail-safe rights, perpetually immune
from judicial attack. Leading pro-union lawyers such as Lord
Wedderburn remain, at the very least, agnostic as to the utility of
replacing immunities with rights. As Lord Wedderburn has consistently warned, trade unionists could be misled into thinking that positive
rights could provide a panacea (or magic formula) to prevent judges
from ignoring democratically passed pro-union laws, and imposing
their own controls on rights to strike. Judges, through restrictive
interpretations, will always possess the ability to weaken the content of
rights to which they are hostile.

It is acknowledged that in those countries where rights to strike do
exist the judges have engaged in restrictive interpretations. For
example, French courts have ruled that 'go slows' are not lawful
because the right to strike guaranteed by the French Constitution
requires a total stoppage of work. Nevertheless, the general experience
in continental Europe has been that the existence of rights has
contributed to a political culture which has prevented trade unions, and
the use of industrial action, from ideological attacks that question their
very legitimacy. This is in stark contrast to the castigation to which
British trade unions have been subjected by forces hostile to effective
trade unionism (be they judges, government ministers or sections of the
media).

Opposition to the adoption of positive rights has come from some in the trade union movement, who appear to believe that immunities secure the independence of trade unions from state control, whereas rights would be conferred by the state and would mean increased legal regulation. In fact, the system of immunities was favoured historically by British liberalism as the means of introducing pro-union reform in a way that would seem consistent with prevailing *laissez-faire* philosophies. The history of the relationship between the law and the use of industrial action reveals that immunities have not led to less legal regulation, let alone independence from the state. Anyone who fears that a system of positive rights would bring more law into industrial relations need lose no sleep on that score. The judges will not let a system of rights get in their way, if they are given a chance to intervene, but nor has the system of immunities kept out the law, although it has permitted it to be developed in a number of confusing and ideologically damaging ways.

CONCLUSIONS

Implementing the recommendations of the International Labour Organisation, and thus abiding with international law, would require a government in the UK to allow trade unionists to take industrial action in a variety of contexts. These would include, in certain circumstances, the display of solidarity with other trade unionists, and the opposing of political policies perceived as contrary to trade unionists' economic and social interests. Complying with ILO conventions would similarly necessitate restoring to trade unions rights to discipline strike-breakers, and giving individual trade unionists the right to take industrial action free from threats of dismissal. All the above is consistent with norms throughout continental Europe and could form the basis of a trade union campaign throughout the EU to secure minimum irreducible rights.[16]

However, this chapter has argued for and sought to justify rights that are wider than the above. These include: unqualified rights to organize and participate in sympathetic industrial action; allowing union members to control the contents of a trade union's constitution with respect to the procedures to be followed prior to industrial action taking place; rights to engage in non-violent picketing in any numbers at any workplace; and, in order to increase the effectiveness of picketing, the provision of the right to stop individuals and vehicles in order that pickets have some genuine opportunity to persuade other trade unionists not to cross a picket line and/or to take sympathetic action. The final part of the chapter has stressed the utility of adopting a system of positive rights using other European countries as a model. Such a system has distinct advantages over the traditional British system of immunities, in that it would: override the definitions given to various forms of industrial action by judge-made law; inhibit the ability of judges to circumvent pro-union legislation by creating new liabilities; prevent the organization of industrial action being castigated as law-breaking. Positive rights would thus deprive judges, governments, the media and employers of the significant ideological ammunition they have always possessed through condemning rights to strike as privileges to break the law.

It is reiterated that positive rights will not act as an impenetrable barrier against judicial and ideological attacks on trade unionism, but nor will such a system provide quite the ideological hostage to fortune that has been presented by the system of immunities. Moreover, the unravelling of the process of legal mystification, which for over a century has fundamentally distorted the nature of trade unionism and industrial action, could be used by trade unionists to expose the nature of judicial intervention and the way in which the current legislation operates. This would help to strengthen arguments in favour of establishing rights to strike, and help to gain momentum for trade union campaigns in Britain and throughout Europe for the securing of such rights.

NOTES

This chapter is based significantly on a paper I wrote in 1991 for the Institute of Employment Rights: *The Right to Strike: a Trade Union View* (London: Institute of Employment Rights, 1991). A number of members and associates of the institute contributed ideas and comments that helped in the writing of that paper, although the views and any errors it contained were solely my responsibility. This chapter has enabled me to incorporate a number of events and changes in the law that have occurred since 1991. In particular, references are made to a number of provisions in the Trade Union Reform and Employment Rights Act 1993, which, despite its title, is the most recent piece of Conservative legislation designed to impose shackles on effective trade unionism.

1. See *Dimbleby* v *NUJ* [1984] IRLR 160 (HL). In this case the Law Lords applied orthodox company law to a situation where a newspaper proprietor (who was notoriously anti-union) established one company to produce his newspaper and a separate company to print it. This meant that the two companies had separate legal identities and were separate employers, although they were owned by the same person and operated from the same premises. In such a situation, if there is a dispute between Company A and its employees, those employed by Company B may not lawfully

take industrial action unless they have a dispute of their own with the company that employs them. That the employees of both companies are employed by the same human being is not of significance to the law. Rupert Murdoch used this legal position during the Wapping dispute to prevent employees involved in distributing News International newspapers taking industrial action in support of the sacked printers.

2. *Mercury Communications* v *Scott-Garner and POEU* [1983] IRLR 485 (CA).

3. *Mayor and Burgesses of the London Borough of Wandsworth* v *NAS/UWT* [1993] IRLR 344 (CA).

4. For a full discussion of the ILO's reports and recommendations, see K. Ewing, *Britain and the ILO* (London: Institute of Employment Rights, 1994).

5. *Blackpool and Fylde College* v *NATFHE* [1994] IRLR 227 (CA).

6. See *Barretts & Baird (Wholesale)* v *IPCS* [1987] IRLR 3. In this case a high court judge, Henry J, suggested that breaking a contract of employment might constitute unlawful means as far as injured third parties were concerned. This may give businesses, and even members of the public, the right to sue unofficial strikers for damages if tortious interference with commercial contracts or trade can be established.

7. R. Welch, P. Leighton, and N. Whatley, *Collectivism or Individualism in Employment Contracts? Evidence from a Second East Anglian Survey* (Chelmsford: Anglia Polytechnic University Employment Relations Research and Development Centre, 1995). This research examines the extent of trade union derecognition and the use of personal contracts in East Anglia. The sample consists of 505 employers from Cambridgeshire, Essex, Norfolk and Suffolk. Forty-seven per cent of the employers surveyed recognize trade unions for the purposes of collective bargaining on pay and conditions, although only 18 per cent so recognize a union for *all* of their employees. Five per cent reported total derecognition in the past five years; a further 7 per cent had derecognized for managers only. Although 80 per cent use personal contracts for at least some of their employees, there is no evidence that, in recent years, employers have implemented the government's preference for terminating collective bargaining arrangements and replacing collective agreements with personal contracts.

These findings are consistent with research that we carried out in the region in 1991, which established that many employers using new management techniques, such as quality circles and performance-related pay, continued to recognize trade unions. The trend would not appear to be for full derecognition, but for collective bargaining to be conducted very much on the employer's terms. The current weakness of trade unions in this context can be clearly attributed (at least in part) to the legal controls on industrial action.

For discussion of the 1991 research, see P. Leighton, R. Welch, and C. Brady, *Employee Involvement: the East Anglian Experience* (Chelmsford: Anglia Polytechnic University Employment Relations Research and Development Centre, 1992); and R. Welch, European works councils and their implications: the potential impact on employer practices and trade unions (1994) 16 *Employee Relations* 48.

8. *Associated Newspapers Ltd* v *Wilson (2) Associated British Ports* v *Palmer & others* [1995] ICR 406 (HL). As a result of the rather dubious reasoning that a decision to withhold contractual benefits is not a positive action, the 1993 statutory provisions now act as a safety net for employers who, having derecognized, positively and intentionally discriminate against trade union members. Such employers will only commit an unlawful act short of dismissal in the (unlikely) event that a tribunal or court views their behaviour as beyond what a reasonable employer might do.

9. *Power Packing Casemakers* v *Faust* [1983] IRLR 117 (CA).

10. This research was based on a survey of rank-and-file trade union activists who were branch secretaries, stewards and/or delegates to trades councils. This research is discussed in R. Welch, The behavioural impact on trade unionists of the trade union legislation of the 1980s (1993) 24 *Industrial Relations Journal* 236.

11. For a discussion of the view that mass and 'flying' picketing are not automatically criminal in nature, see P. Wallington, Policing the miners' strike (1985) 14 *Industrial Law Journal* 145.

12. *Broome* v *DPP* [1974] IRLR 26 (HL).

13. My analysis is that judges cautiously withdrew from intervention in industrial disputes after the First World War, as part of a strategy by the state to incorporate trade union leaders into the management of the economic system. This strategy broke down with the onset of economic crisis and trade union militancy in the 1960s. Consequently, and albeit cautiously, judges began, once

again, to develop torts to restrain industrial action in certain contexts – particularly where the action was unofficial or sympathetic in nature. There was a similar flurry of judicial activity, particularly by the Court of Appeal, once the Social Contract broke down in the late 1970s. I have sought to substantiate this thesis in R. Welch, *The Case for Positive Trade Union Rights* (Chelmsford: Anglia Higher Education College Employment Relations Research Centre, 1989); and R. Welch, Judges and the law in British industrial relations: towards a European right to strike (1995) 4(2) *Social and Legal Studies* 175.

14. For example, *Barrett & Bairds, op. cit.*, and the Court of Appeal's judgment in *Associated Ports* v *TGWU* [1989] IRLR 305. Although the decision of the Court of Appeal in this case was reversed by the House of Lords, their Lordships did not comment on the Court of Appeal's reasoning that inducing a breach of statutory duty could constitute unlawful means, which could result in tortious interference with trade. There is no immunity with respect to such a tort, even where there is a lawful trade dispute and a valid ballot. The judgment poses a particular threat for public sector trade unionists engaged in industrial action that results in the non-performance of statutory duties (for example, by local councils).

15. *BBC* v *Hearn* [1977] 273 (CA).

16. While I argue strongly for legislation in the UK that restores rights to take industrial action as they existed prior to 1980, it is also my belief that a Europe-wide trade union campaign for the Social Chapter to incorporate common rights to strike would be advantageous – particularly as a mechanism for building links between trade unionists throughout the EU, and helping to overcome the traditional insularity of British trade unions. I have developed this argument in Welch (1995), *op. cit.*

9

Trade Unions, Productivity and Unemployment

Jonathan Michie and Frank Wilkinson

INTRODUCTION

The growth of unemployment and the erosion of employment rights are closely linked. Unemployment encourages employers to worsen the terms and conditions of employment and this has been deliberately encouraged by government policy, which has seen employment rights as costly impediments to the workings of the labour market. The promise is more employment: the reduction and increased variability of wages will, it is proposed, encourage firms to hire more workers and any loss to those with jobs will be compensated by a reduction in unemployment. But the key economic variable is not employment costs alone but employment costs per unit of output, so attention also has to be focused on what is happening to productivity. The problem with wage cutting is that it develops a dependency on cheap labour on the part of employers and reduces pressure for improved managerial efficiency, better training, new investment and other means of enhancing productivity. There are no limits to the reduction of unit labour costs by these means, but they are actively discouraged when firms have opportunities for low wage and poor working conditions.

Moreover, in a world where competitive success increasingly requires cooperation in production to make the best use of new technologies and to achieve the required product standards, employment policies that have a complete contempt for basic rights have the opposite effect by alienating workers. Such effects are well illustrated by the Citizens Advice Bureaux evidence on employment problems in the recession.[1] In 1991–2 the Citizens Advice Bureaux dealt with 856,855 employment rights enquiries, up more than 10 per cent on the previous year's figure. There is increasing concern over the frequency with which employers are unilaterally changing their employees' terms and conditions of employment, most commonly cuts in pay and/or increased hours. Even with a written statement of their terms and conditions, as required by the Employment Protection (Consolidation) Act 1978, many workers will feel unable to oppose changes in their terms and conditions for fear that such opposition would lead to dismissal. Existing employment legislation requires employees to accumulate two years' continuous service before they qualify for employment protection; until recently, those working between eight and sixteen hours required five years' service, and those who worked for under eight hours could never qualify. The evidence presented in the Citizens Advice Bureaux report demonstrates that dismissals frequently have nothing to do with employees' failure to perform their jobs adequately and that people are losing their jobs because their employers want to prevent them from getting employment protection. Even those with more than two years' service often feel vulnerable to redundancy, with selection for redundancy frequently based on highly questionable criteria.[2]

On the basis of this evidence the National Association of Citizens Advice Bureaux (NACAB) makes recommendations for action, advocating the restoration of employment rights eroded over the past 17 years. What is perhaps surprising is that the demands are coming from a group mainly concerned with the rights of *citizens* to reasonable terms and conditions of employment. This leads to the questions. First, why is it that capitalist prosperity requires the sacrifice of citizens' rights by the poorest sections of society? Second, why should a democratically elected government give the denial of such rights such high priority? J. K. Galbraith's answer to the question is to argue that the most disadvantaged in society are effectively disenfranchised, so that governments can manipulate their welfare in the interests of the affluent 'contented' classes upon whose electoral support they depend. But political opportunism does not guarantee economic efficiency, even though it may be expedient for politicians to engage the support of economists who would make it appear so.

DEINDUSTRIALIZATION

The second half of the 1980s was taken by the supporters of deregulation as proof of its economic benefits. Economic growth was relatively rapid, with some fall in unemployment, although this remained high. But at the end of the 1980s the revival came to an end, with global recession and a return to mass unemployment, with the early 1990s witnessing recession and unemployment comparable to the 1930s. Yet any suggestion that fiscal and monetary policies should be used to combat unemployment immediately raises the spectre of high inflation in the minds of policy-makers.

This threat receives its support in the economics literature from the idea that there is a unique 'non-accelerating inflation rate of unemployment' (NAIRU): in other words, the assertion that there is one particular level of equilibrium unemployment at which inflation stabilizes. We have argued elsewhere[3] that this NAIRU framework is unhelpful, since it rests on the implicit assumption of unchanged and unspecified policies and practices; we have also elsewhere[4] plotted the relationship between unemployment and changes in earnings variously measured for Britain in the 1980s, and the results could not be more at variance with the notion of a predictable relationship between the two variables. The historical evidence for any credible relationship between the level of joblessness and the rate of inflation is thus fragile at best.[5]

This NAIRU theory is a version of Milton Friedman's 'natural rate of unemployment' developed by the economists Richard Layard and Stephen Nickell. They argue that as unemployment falls the 'bargaining wage' demanded by workers rises, while the 'feasible wage' that employers can afford to pay does not rise with output. This failure to rise of the wage that employers can afford to pay as output rises is based on one or both of two seriously flawed arguments. First, it is supposed that as firms increase their level of output productivity fails to rise and may fall. But in fact the opposite is usually the case: in economic expansions output per head generally rises (it increased by 20 per cent between 1984 and 1990). This increase in productivity is explained by the fact that old, less efficient plant is scrapped in recessions, capital is operated at a higher level of utilization as demand increases and firms invest in more modern equipment with renewed prosperity. The more reasonable assumption that productivity and hence the 'feasible wage' increases with output destroys one of the bases for the NAIRU law. If increased capacity utilization and, over the longer term, an increased and more technologically advanced capacity allows a growth of the feasible wage then there may be no unique 'equilibrium' point (NAIRU) with only that one level of unemployment associated with non-accelerating inflation. Thus, even if the bargaining and feasible wages happened to coincide at a given level of unemployment, if unemployment falls with the feasible wage increasing (owing to increased productivity) more than the increase in the bargaining wage, then such a model would actually predict that the reduction in unemployment would result in inflation falling rather than rising.

The second string to the NAIRU bow is the argument that firms have to cut prices to sell more. By enabling firms to lower prices, cuts in wages and other employment costs allow them to sell more and increase employment. But this argument is also fatally flawed. The size of the market of a firm (and hence the employment it can offer) is determined by its price *and* the price of its competitors. If the workers employed by that firm accept a lower wage so that the firm can retain its monopoly profits at a lower price, it will be able to increase its output and its market share, but only at the expense of other firms and the employment they offer. But, of course, if all firms lower their wages there will be no change in relative prices and no increase in demand. In fact, if this happens, the chances are that demand will decline because a general fall in wages relative to prices will have reduced the purchasing power of wage income.

The rise of unemployment can thus be more usefully analysed by ignoring such economic orthodoxy and referring instead to the interrelation between macro-economic policy, balance of payments constraints and deindustrialization. European unemployment has been accompanied by a relatively rapid decline in manufacturing employment, and in this process Britain has shown the lead. The share of employment in manufacturing fell in the decade 1976 to 1986 from 22.8 to 19.1 per cent in the USA, from 25.5 to 24.7 per cent in Japan, and from 28.9 to 24.4 per cent for the EU. This relative decline represented an absolute fall for Europe of almost 5.5 million jobs. Of the 12 member states, only Portugal and Greece avoided a fall in manufacturing employment, with the UK experiencing the most extreme cut (of 16 per cent, representing more than two million jobs). The UK, whose government trumpets the success of deregulating the labour market as a route to competitiveness, was responsible for more than 40 per cent of the EU's loss of manufacturing employment. So with well under two in ten of the EU population, the UK managed to account for more than four in ten of Europe's loss of manufacturing jobs.

There has been considerable debate over the causes of such 'deindustrialization'.[6] A shift in employment from manufacturing to other sectors could simply be the result of a shift in consumption patterns away from manufactured goods and towards services and/or differential productivity growth between the industrial and service sectors. However, two important points are clear. First, the decline in manufacturing employment in the EU – and, in particular, in the UK – has *not* been caused by shifts in consumption patterns, or by other sectors' requirements for labour. The loss of manufacturing jobs has been accompanied by an increasing deficit in manufacturing trade and by a rise in unemployment. And in the UK most dramatically, manufacturing has not experienced rapidly rising output as a result of productivity growth, but, on the contrary, a stagnant trend in output, with the productivity growth hence translating not into output growth but into falling employment. Second, an economy's distribution of output (and employment) between sectors can lead to balance of payments constraints, and hence can impact not just on relative shares of output and employment but also on absolute levels. It is this danger of a balance of payments constraint on economic recovery and the achievement of full employment that should be of concern for the EU in the 1990s.

GOVERNMENT POLICY AND LOW PAY

The switch in macro-economic policy towards the belief that direct government intervention is counterproductive and that the economy can only be effectively regulated by monetary means has as its micro-economic corollary the assertion that joblessness results from impediments to the working of the invisible hand in the labour market. As a result, the policy response to the growth of unemployment resulting from restrictive monetary policy and balance of payments constraints has been labour market deregulation. A consequence of such liberalization is that inequality has increased in most EU countries over the 1980s; but it was in the UK that inequality was most deliberately pursued through the government's labour market policies.

Post-1979 British governments have attributed much of the blame for unemployment to 'market rigidities'. In particular, ministers have argued that 'artificial' constraints on the labour market have prevented wages falling to adjust to changed conditions, and that for many groups wages are being held above their true market level, thereby 'pricing' workers from jobs. To cure these supposed rigidities a large number of measures have been implemented, designed to reduce wages and enable the 'market to work more freely'. Employment rights such as unfair dismissal protection and maternity provisions have been watered down and had their coverage reduced; public services have been contracted out to private firms, often with wages and conditions much poorer than in the public sector itself; other government services have been privatized, which has removed the low paid from the coverage of collectively negotiated agreements; wage-protecting conventions such as the fair wage resolution and Schedule 11 have been abolished; and the Wages Councils, introduced to set legally binding minimum wages in low-wage sectors, had their scope and powers drastically reduced in 1986 and were abolished in 1993. Concurrently, the rolling programme of trade union legislation has seriously impeded trade union organization and the ability to gain bargaining rights – to the particular disadvantage of low-pay sectors.

The effects of government policy on relative pay are demonstrated in Table 9.1, which shows that while real earnings for some sections of the population rose fairly rapidly, this masks a huge increase in inequality, with the pay of the higher paid growing more rapidly than that of the lower paid. This is reflected in the more rapid increase in non-manual earnings and the higher increase in pay at successively higher points of the earnings distribution. Thus, at the lowest decile for manual males, the increase in real pay from 1979 to 1992 was only 4 per cent, while at the highest decile for non-manual males it was 53 per cent; for females these increases were 10 and 60 per cent respectively. However, when one considers the relative performance of female earnings, account should be taken of the increase in part-time from 40 to 46 per cent of female workers, and the fact that hourly pay for part-time work is on average less – and has increased at a slower pace – than hourly pay for full-time work.

Table 9.1 *Percentage increase in UK real earnings at different points in the income distribution, 1979–1992*

	Males		Females	
	Manual	Non-manual	Manual	Non-manual
Lowest decile	4.0	21.8	9.6	28.6
Lower quartile	8.1	30.7	12.5	36.7
Median	11.4	38.1	15.5	46.1
Upper quartile	15.2	45.1	21.4	60.5
Highest decile	18.3	53.2	31.1	60.3
Mean	13.3	44.1	19.9	51.6

Source: Department of Employment, *New Earnings Survey*. London: HMSO.

This change in the structure of earnings can be explained by three main factors. First, the decline in employment in manufacturing and in other non-service sectors has been concentrated mainly in the middle range of the earnings distribution. Second, the increase in employment was concentrated in sectors such as banking, insurance, finance and business, where earnings are relatively high, and in hotel, catering and other such services, where earnings tend to be low. The disappearance of jobs from the middle of the earnings distribution and the increase at each end would explain at least part of the widening of the earnings distribution. The third factor explaining the changed distribution of earnings is the tendency for the earnings of the relatively higher paid to grow rapidly and those of the low paid to increase relatively slowly since 1979. This is indicated by the fact that earnings in manufacturing grew by 5 percentage points more than in services. But the main differences between the rates of increase in earnings between different industrial sectors were within the service sector itself, with earnings in the highly paid banking, insurance and finance sector growing 2.5 times more than those in the low-paid distribution and hotels and catering sectors. Moreover, it is in the low-paid service sectors that the growth in part-time female employment has been located.[7]

UK governments have added to the regressive effects of their labour market policies on the distribution of income by their tax and social welfare policies. The elimination of higher tax brackets, the switch to indirect taxation and increases in National Insurance contributions have favoured the rich. Meanwhile, the least well off have been hit by the elimination of the earnings related elements and dependants' benefits from unemployment and sickness pay; by the break in the link between social welfare and earnings, and in some cases inflation;[8] and by the restrictions on eligibility for out-of-work benefits, and the coercion of the unemployed into accepting poorly paid jobs by the redefinition and more rigorous enforcement of availability-for-work rules.[9]

As a consequence, in 1989 social benefits were a smaller proportion of GDP than in 1979, despite an increase in the number of pensioners of around one million, a similar increase in those without work and claiming benefits, and an increase in the recipients of family credit of some 250,000. Redistribution has therefore been from the poor to the rich and within the different categories of the poor.

The overall effect of the increase in unemployment, differential rates of pay increase, the growth of part-time work and the government's tax and welfare policy is that between 1979 and 1991 the share of household income of the bottom half fell from 33 to 27 per cent and by even more – from 32 to 25 per cent – after deducting housing costs.[10]

While the average household saw its real income rise by a total of 36 per cent over the 12 years after 1979 (itself not a huge annual increase), the poorest families suffered a *cut* of 14 per cent. In 1979, five million people were living on less than half the average income – the nearest thing in Britain to an official poverty line. The latest figures show this to have increased to 13.5 million people, almost a quarter of the entire population. Many of these people are having to work excessive overtime just to make up their poverty wages. Figures published in June 1993 show that more overtime is worked in Britain than in any other EU country except Portugal. Around four million British workers are having to work more than 48 hours a week.

The objective of labour market deregulation – rooted as it is in the notion that social welfare and labour standards, imposed by trade unions and government, seriously impede the effective working of the labour market – is to generate a higher level of employment by securing equilibrium between supply and demand. However, the evidence is that the labour market is in unstable equilibrium, only held in balance by high levels of unemployment, and that low pay is a major cause of labour market instability. For example, almost 40 per cent of the vacancies notified to the Department of Employment Job Centres[11] are in the low-paid distribution, hotels and catering and repairs sector, although this sector accounts for only 20 per cent of total employment. As a percentage of employment, notified vacancies in distribution, hotels, catering and repairs were 23 per cent in 1988, the peak of the boom, declining to 14 per cent in the first half of 1991. Comparable figures for all other industries and services are 10 and 7 per cent respectively. This suggests that except, possibly, in periods of exceptionally high unemployment, in the low-pay segments of the labour market there is a substantially greater degree of unsatisfied demand for labour, meaning that compared with other sectors wages are too low. Recession brings supply more into line with demand by destroying alternative job opportunities. Thus, rather than low pay being an answer to unemployment, high levels of joblessness are a precondition for many people accepting low-paid jobs, which they soon quit when job prospects improve.

Low pay and the resulting labour force instability also prove to be major obstacles to effective training and personnel policy. When unemployment is high the pressure on management is relaxed and when the labour market tightens firms are reluctant to train because labour turnover is high and potential recruits are reluctant to take training seriously because of the poor job prospects. Entry to low-paying trades is often a last resort and quitting is done at the first opportunity. Consequently, investment in training shows a poor return to both employer and employees.

These problems became increasingly pressing in the low-paying sectors of British industry in the late 1980s, as the labour market tightened with economic recovery, as the declining birth-rate threatened the supply of cheap labour and as employers faced the implications of equal value legislation. This led to a spate of new company policies and collective agreements designed to improve the relative position of low-paid and part-time workers, to extend fringe benefits to part-timers, to introduce job evaluation and more effectively to train, motivate and involve workers at the lower end of the job hierarchy.[12]

But these necessary reforms were confined to the leading firms and sectors, where unions were well organized. The vast majority of undervalued workers were not included. Moreover, with the growth of unemployment the threat of the 'demographic' time bomb has receded, and with it the pressure on firms to improve their personnel policies so as to increase pay and to improve productivity and quality of service. In fact, quite the opposite has happened. Major employers, such as the Burton Group of retailers, have taken advantage of high levels of unemployment to casualize jobs, cut pay and worsen conditions of work.[13] Elsewhere there has been widespread use of new legal powers and other more legally dubious devices to intensify the exploitation and intimidation of an increasingly vulnerable workforce. Reporting on the increasing levels of enquiries about employment problems, the NACAB concluded that 'Numbers of employees are faced with impossible choices – accepting a severe deterioration in their working conditions; or losing their jobs. With unemployment standing at over 3 million, the implications of this dilemma are obvious.'[14]

Thus the aim of social security legislation has increasingly been to sharpen 'work incentives', on the assumption that the unemployed are made reluctant to take up available paid work by the receipt of benefits and by poverty and unemployment traps. Simultaneously, paid work at the lower end of the labour market has been made more and more unattractive, both to the unemployed and to those in employment, by the dilution of social and employment protection and the consequent decline in job quality. It is a matter of fine judgement whether the net effect of this policy of making the receipt of out-of-work income increasingly unattractive, while at the same time reducing the range of decent jobs available within employment, has been to induce greater labour market participation among the unemployed. But there can be little doubt of the degenerative effect of these employment practices and intensified exploitation on economic efficiency.

LABOUR UNDERVALUATION AND WORKER EFFICIENCY

Orthodox economists argue that low pay reflects low levels of productivity. When, as is the more usual case, low pay and poor working conditions result from the undervaluation of labour owing to the imbalance of power in the labour market, the direction of causation runs in precisely the opposite direction. Such circumstances are not conducive to worker cooperation, and workers might use the power they derive from their ability to withhold labour and from the additional skill and information they acquire from work experience by, for example, keeping effort within prescribed limits, working closely to the 'rules' so as to resist any flexible use of their time and keeping managers uninformed of improvements to technology and working methods learned on the job. The consequence of this is an adjustment of work effort and cooperation (which might require more ingenuity and effort than the work itself) to match employers' perception of workers' worth as represented by the pay and conditions on offer. But in these cases the direction of causation runs from low pay to low effort, rather than the reverse.

Another way by which the undervaluation of labour leads to its dissipation can be accounted for by the relationship between low pay and poor working conditions on the one hand and skill and training on the other. The orthodox explanation is that low pay is the result of a lack of training and skill, and that an increase in pay will further discourage employers from providing training. But a closer examination reveals a quite different direction of causation. First, low-paying employers are the least likely to train. Inefficient low payers require undervalued labour to subsidize poor management or keep obsolete equipment in production, and cannot afford to train except in the narrowest sense. The interests of predatory low payers are in exploiting human capital rather than creating it.

Second, skill is to an important degree a social category, and jobs with poor terms and conditions of employment are unlikely to be afforded high status, whatever their skill level. Moreover, status as well as the content of jobs will determine the willingness of individuals to acquire the necessary entry qualifications by undertaking education and training. The identification of particular jobs with socially deprived groups lowers their skill status and the training routes by which they are acquired. One of the effects of the process of deindustrialization in the UK and elsewhere has been a decline in levels of pay and conditions of work in the industries directly affected, as well as in those industries into which the redundant workers have been crowded.

Deindustrialization creates conditions for social deskilling in four closely related ways, which add to the spiral of decline. First, rapid increases in unemployment weaken workers' resistance to employers' offensives against the terms and condition of employment and traditional forms of control of skilled work. Second, a common response by firms to their declining fortunes is to cut back on training. This may take the form of a reduction of in-house training and/or a decline in support for external provision by training agencies, so that the local infrastructure for skill generation is weakened. This, and the migration from the trade of workers in a position to generate skill, creates a skill shortage. The response to this, in the face of the decline in formal training, is, third, the replacement of on-the-job instruction with a focus on a narrow range of specific skills to meet the firms' immediate needs, often accompanied by the exclusion of worker representatives from the training design and implementation processes. Consequently, the skill content of jobs is diluted, and this interacts with the deterioration of the terms and conditions of employment and the increasing pessimism about future prospects of the industry to discourage new entrants from traditional areas of recruitment.[15] Fourth, any subsequent relaxation of hiring standards to meet the labour shortage serves further to reinforce the social downgrading of the job, the dissipation of skills, the loss of competitiveness and industrial decline.

The response of governments to the twin problems of increasing unemployment and a growing skill shortage has been to institute new training schemes. Whatever the original intention, or, indeed, the quality of much of the training, these schemes tend to acquire a reputation for disguising unemployment, for creating new forms of cheap labour and for failing to provide adequate training. The general effect is therefore a downgrading, in labour market terms, of the participants and the job areas at which the schemes are targeted. Individuals then become increasingly unwilling to take part in training programmes because of the knowledge that the time and effort spent is wasted and individuals who have so trained tend to quit the resulting job at the earliest opportunity.

A related problem is that the practice of targeting training at the unemployed to get them into jobs with low-paying firms, which are in need of undervalued labour to keep obsolete equipment in operation and outdated product lines profitable, is a waste of training resources. Such firms need skills that are specific to outdated technology and are therefore effectively obsolete. The cumulative effect of low pay, poor working conditions and the policy responses of employers and the state is therefore to weaken the skill base (in both technical and social terms), discourage individuals from undertaking training and misallocate training resources. In these circumstances, lack of demand for training rather than paucity of supply explains skill shortages and reinforces deindustrializing processes.

THREE CASE STUDIES

The links between labour undervaluation and productive inefficiencies are illustrated in three case studies of US industries that have gone down the deregulatory route, only to find that firms have been driven to compete not by upgrading their products, processes and productive systems, but rather by abandoning standards of health and safety, training and other aspects of the industries' productive infrastructure that become too costly for individual firms to maintain when their competitors can seek short-term advantage by opting out.

The US Meat–packing Industry

In the post-war period the US meat-packing industry benefited from effective collective bargaining, with self-sufficient earnings, steady jobs, an experienced and reliable workforce and stable communities. This productive system was broken up by competition from new entrants, who were innovative in product, process and labour organization. Processes were changed by the introduction of fully integrated disassembly plants, where cattle were converted into boxed beef by semi-skilled workers; union busting, wage cutting and speed-up followed. Poor wages and working conditions drove out good, and increasingly the stable workforce was replaced by a workforce that was low paid and transient: one to which the industry today has no commitment and which has no particular commitment to the industry.

The combination of hard-driven, inexperienced workers, insufficient training and poor health and labour standards rapidly increased the sickness and accident rate, so that meat-packing became the most dangerous industry in the USA. The meat-packing companies put communities in competition with each other for jobs, and divided communities from organized labour because resistance to concessions on wages and working conditions was perceived as a threat to job creation. But meat-packing jobs proved a mixed blessing for communities, because of the social costs imposed by the companies' recruitment and labour management policies and the environmental problems of heavily concentrated slaughtering and meat processing. Consumers benefited from improved and possibly cheaper products, and corporations initially earned high profits, although these were driven down as the new competitive strategies became widely emulated. The cost was borne by the communities, the workers who lost their jobs and the incumbent low-paid workforce faced with poor and hazardous working conditions and employment instability.

In more recent years the industry has become increasingly concentrated in few hands. Progress has been made in re-unionization, and the appalling health and safety record of the industry has resulted in more effective regulation. In this latter respect, union involvement in health and safety has been decisive and, in turn, health and safety regulation has been an important lever used by unions to achieve bargaining rights.

The US Trucking Industry

Until the late 1970s, competition in the US road haulage industry was regulated by the 1935 Motor Carriers Act. This was designed to prevent destructive price competition by encouraging collective rate setting, controlling entry, guaranteeing standards of service and security, and encouraging adequate investment, thereby improving road safety. The granting of quantity discounts and other forms of price discrimination by large companies was outlawed to protect small operators. Subsequently, the industry was further stabilized as wages were increasingly taken out of competition by high levels of unionization and well-established and increasingly multi-employer collective bargaining.

Deregulation of the industry began in 1977 when, under pressure from the Carter administration, a dramatic increase of new entrants into the industry was allowed, and limitations were placed on the collective determination of rates – a reduced degree of economic regulation which was codified in the Motor Carriers Act of 1980. The consequence of deregulation was a significant change in the structure of the industry. Road transport can be divided into truckload carriage (TL) and less-than-truckload carriage (LTL). TL assignments are picked up from the sender and delivered directly to the receiver. LTL assignments are collected from the sender, unloaded and sorted at docks and reloaded into trucks according to final destination;

consequently, they require a docking infrastructure for unloading, sorting and reloading that is not required for full-load carrying. Prior to deregulation, operators usually carried both TL and LTL, but after deregulation the extra terminal infrastructure costs of LTL resulted in a segmentation between TL and LTL. New TL carriers quickly emerged without a developed pick-up and delivery framework. These formed and folded quickly; they were non-union and their low wages, low capitalization and low rates forced many existing carriers out of business.

Wages and conditions were thrown into destructive competition. Firms relocated or went 'double breasted' (that is, set up or acquired non-union subsidiaries to compete with unionized parts of their own organizations) in order to de-unionize and/or enforce concession bargaining. A two-tier wage structure emerged, with new hires (usually skilled and experienced drivers) paid rates 32 per cent lower than the existing workforce, and the pay of casuals cut. Firms forced their workforces into wage cuts, many under-the-table and some disguised as loans or bogus Employee Stock Option Programmes from which they later defaulted. Real wages declined by 24 per cent from 1978 to 1993. Reorganization of working hours to the detriment of drivers was encouraged by the exclusion of motor carriers from the maximum hours and overtime provisions of the Fair Labor Standards Acts, on the grounds that 80 per cent of the workforce were covered by union contracts, a judgement based on pre-deregulation estimates of coverage.

Deregulation has been followed by increases in concentration in some segments of the industry, but easier entry and unregulated competition in others. The ability of carriers to give quantity discounts discriminates against small carriers and small shippers. The costs of deregulation have fallen on the workforce in the form of declining terms and conditions of employment. At the same time, the demands on drivers have been increasing. Downward pressure on costs has intensified, trucks and trailers have increased in size and load weight, and the requirements of just-in-time delivery have increased demands on drivers, while making the quality of their service pivotal in the improvement of economic performance. Moreover, as a response to the increasing safety problems associated with deregulation, driving tests are now more stringent and the standards required of truck drivers more exacting. Non-union firms are increasingly complaining of a shortage of skilled and responsible employees at the wages they pay. Clearly, if the industry is to attract and retain a stable, literate, careful workforce, it must improve wages and working conditions.

The US Construction Industry

A high proportion of the US construction workforce is skilled and productivity and quality in building depend on effective training. But employment in construction is insecure. Construction sites have short duration, job changes are frequent and employment is made even more unstable by the boom/bust cycles to which the industry is prone. Apprenticeships provide the continuity necessary for training, and are closely linked to trade unionism. Apprenticeship training is broadly based and includes a combination of classroom and on-the-job training. Its provision, administration and costs are shared by trade union members, the tax-payer, the employers and the trainees, who during part of their training receive wages below the rate for the job. Apprentice training is central to trade union interests because it enhances skill and hence wages, serves to prevent the use of trainees as substitutes for skilled labour and helps to control the labour supply, improving the bargaining power of skilled workers. But in addition, the unions as representatives of skilled workers have a long-term perspective on skill and its orderly reproduction, unlike that of individual employers, whose demands for skilled workers are short-term and uncertain. Alternative forms of training to multifaceted apprenticeships include helpers and labourers picking up a degree of skill on-site or on narrowly focused task training schemes. Most workers in the non-union sector receive their training on the job, although small apprentice programmes are administered by the employers' association. However, whereas, in the early 1980s, 60 per cent of the construction market was open-shop, these contributed only 10 per cent of total expenditure on training.

Construction workers have traditionally been well organized in separate and often competing trade unions and a substantial union/non-union differential existed, although this was offset by the greater productivity of apprenticed union labour. However, from the late 1960s, unions came under increasing attack from employers' organizations, government and the courts. Between 1970 and 1992, union membership fell from 42 to 22 per cent, wages lagged behind prices in the 1970s and, between 1980 and 1992, real wages fell by 17 per cent and unions were forced to make concessions on overtime and weekend premia. The Construction Users Anti-inflation Roundtable (later the Business Roundtable) was formed to orchestrate anti-unionism and to lobby for legal changes, and to facilitate this the Republican administration tilted the National Labor Relations Board (NLRB) in favour of the employers. It became easier legally for employers to repudiate pre-hire agreements unilaterally and to 'double breast'. These moves reduced the costs of terminating collective bargaining and spawned a new market for legal and strategic advice on union busting. Some employers seized the opportunity to de-unionize, while others were forced into such actions to meet the low-wage competition from open shops. The industrial relations environment was further soured as unions countered by granting contractors rebates to reduce the difference between union and non-union pay, mounted campaigns to discredit corporations and infiltrated non-union shops with union members to organize or to disrupt.

In the unionized sector the need to remain competitive while maintaining labour and training standards has led to increasing cooperation between unions and between unions and management. Local joint worker–management committees have been set up and joint efforts have been made to standardize working conditions across trades, to change work rules and to make other improvements in operating efficiencies. This, together with the superior training capabilities of the unionized sector, can be regarded as the high road to competitive success.

Lessons

In each of these three industry case studies it was found that for firms to benefit from having a trained, healthy and motivated workforce they need assurances that their competitor firms will also be committing equivalent resources to the training, health and safety and other measures involved. This assurance can be, and in the past has been, maintained through a combination of government regulation setting certain standards and trade union organization capable of enforcing these standards and building upon them. Deregulatory processes have had a doubly negative impact. First, the reduction or elimination of statutory requirements on firms means that each firm has had to fear the worst in terms of its competitors taking advantage of short-term cost-cutting opportunities, and hence they have all felt compelled to go down this road. Second, by the increase in both the motivation and opportunity for de-unionization, the stage has been set for each firm – by escaping from trade union pressure on itself to maintain standards – to contribute to the industry-wide move to de-unionize, and this in turn has increased the pressure that all firms then put on each other.

It would be in the best long-term interest of each firm if they were all to invest in adequate training of their workforce and in the various other aspects of their productive operations. But in the absence of any mechanism for ensuring this behaviour from other firms, it becomes in the individual firm's own short-term interests to cut costs and standards. This inability of individual firms to act in their own best long-term interest has become more acute with the trend towards less stable workforces – there is an even greater danger that the benefits from training the firm's workers will be transferred to a rival firm. It is ironic that in the face of such industrial trends, which intensify the scope for market failures resulting from divergent private and social costs and benefits, the mechanisms whereby these market failures have in the past been alleviated have themselves been weakened.

It is the workforce that has a private interest – in training, skills, health and safety – to match the public interest in economic development. Individual firms have less and less scope for acting in line with this public interest. The public benefits that would follow from trade unions being in a position to enforce the upgrading of standards therefore promises to be greater than ever.

COSTS OF INEQUALITY

In addition to the above effects of deregulation-inspired wage cutting leading to industrial inefficiencies and short-termism, the growth in inequality and poverty has detrimental effects on the economy's macro-economic balance of payments constraint, with a transfer of resources to the better-off, who import more,[16] on the government's own fiscal deficit (the public sector borrowing requirement or PSBR) and on the real economy as consumer spending is depressed and the pressure on firms to upgrade their production processes is thereby also weakened.

With regard to the PSBR, rising inequality and poverty means that the costs of welfare, benefits and income support grow. A growing share of the income of the working poor is met not by their employers but by the tax-payers. This not only increases both the spread and the grip of the poverty trap (whereby any increase in pay by employers is matched by an equivalent loss of benefits from government), it also increases the burden on public expenditure. And if total government spending is constrained – for example, by the Maastricht 3 per cent formula – then this burden has to be met by public spending cuts imposed elsewhere, cuts which may well exacerbate unemployment. An alternative response is to cut per capita income to the poor, as was done in Britain in the 1980s.[17] A further possibility that is increasingly being touted is a direct subsidy to employers to provide jobs for the out-of-work.

This increasing use by private capital of low-paid workers, requiring public funds to raise their income to a living wage, is in essence a return to the 'Speenhamland system' of Poor Law used in Britain in the eighteenth and nineteenth centuries.[18] The 'Poor Law' ceased to be something to fall back on, and became the general framework of the rural labourer's life. 'The distinction between worker and pauper vanished.'[19] There are parallels with the currently fashionable 'basic income' schemes; indeed, the following description sounds uncannily like an advocacy of the present 'basic income' ideas:

> No measure was ever more universally popular. Parents were free of the care of their children, and children were no more dependent on their parents; employers could reduce wages at will and labourers were safe from hunger whether they were busy or slack; humanitarians applauded the measure as an act of mercy even though not of justice and the selfish gladly consoled themselves with the thought that though it was merciful at least it was not liberal; and even the ratepayers were slow to realise what would happen to the rates under a system which proclaimed the 'right to live' whether a man earned a living wage or not.[20]

It is therefore perhaps particularly important to remember that 'It was at bottom an attempt to maintain the ancient ideal of a stable though unequal society',[21] 'setting its face against the only thing which could have at least provided some defence against the fall in wages, the combination of the workers'.[22] Given the danger of the EU seeking to tackle unemployment by cutting employment taxes on firms – and in particular through subsidizing low-paid sectors[23] – it is worth quoting at length the implications for the productive system of the Speenhamland system:

> The traditional social order degenerated into a universal pauperism of demoralised men who could not fall below the relief scale whatever they did, who could not rise above it, who had not even the nominal guarantee of a living income since the 'scale' could be – and with increasing expense of rates was – reduced to as little as the village rich thought fit for a labourer. Agrarian capitalism degenerated into a general lunacy, in which farmers were encouraged to pay as little as they could (since wages would be supplemented by the parish) and used the mass of pauper labour as an excuse for not raising their productivity; while

their most rational calculations would be, how to get the maximum subsidy for their wage-bill from the rest of the ratepayers. Labourers, conversely, were encouraged to do as little work as they possibly could, since nothing would get them more than the official minimum of subsistence.

Nobody can measure the dehumanization or, in economic terms, the fall in productivity that resulted.[24]

SUBSIDIZING JOBS – THE SOLUTION OR A DIVERSION?

The key to a return to full employment is, then, to shift the emphasis of policy, to concentrate on employment creation rather than unemployment treatment. The current orthodoxy among policy-makers is that further deregulation is still the way to more jobs and that there is no macro-economic policy route to higher employment (although the orthodox economists never make clear why; they just build the assumption into their models). The recommended cures that follow seem to be either to get the low skilled to accept low-paid jobs or to train them so they can compete more effectively for the high-paid ones. It is not obvious how such an increase in the supply of people willing and/or able to take jobs can affect the overall level of employment unless there is an increase in demand for goods and services and hence an increase in the number of jobs available. Although it might be argued that either higher skills or lower pay will increase the competitiveness of Europe and increase the number of jobs there, this is unlikely to do any more than reshuffle world employment unless there is an easing of macro-economic policy.

The high level of overall unemployment at the European level can be explained by the deflationary bias in the macro-economic policy of Germany. Even so, there can be little doubt that there is no easy route to full employment in the UK through demand management alone, whatever happens at the European level, because the UK economy is balance of payments constrained. The historically progressive deindustrialization of the UK economy exacerbated by the Thatcherite experiment means that even with a prolonged recession and unprecedented unemployment the current account of the balance of payment remains stubbornly in deficit. This growth of the current account deficit has important deflationary consequences and also indicates the extent to which full employment of the industrial capacity of Britain is progressively lower than the level necessary fully to employ the workforce. It should be further noted that the erosion of the industrial base has gone furthest in the capital goods sector, so that the re-equipping of industry to remove the balance of payments constraint has serious implications for the balance of payments.[25]

The policy-makers are reassured that the balance of payments does not matter by the argument that the international capital markets' willingness to lend money to Britain – so that the capital account surplus offsets the current account deficit – is a measure of confidence in the British economy. This ignores completely the importance of short-term speculative gains in triggering international capital flows, the destabilizing effects of these movements and the consequences for interest rates of being obliged to attract hot money to offset current account deficits. In 1979, world trade stood at $1500 billion and foreign exchange trading at $17,500 billion. By 1992, trade had tripled to $4700 billion, yet foreign exchange trading had increased almost fifteen-fold, to $252,000 billion.[26]

Thus, in 1978 to 1981 the commercial bank interest rates adjusted for producer prices averaged 1.9 per cent but in 1989 to 1992 they averaged 7.3 per cent. This almost four-fold increase in real interest rates has serious implications for industrial costs and investment and consequently has made – and continues to make – its own contribution to the erosion of the industrial base and the lowering of the sustainable level of employment.

The explanation given by the British policy-makers for the lack of competitiveness and high unemployment is the inflexibility of the labour market. To remedy this they have followed the USA down the route of reducing labour and social standards. But in neither country has this reversed economic decline; rather, both countries have become increasingly uncompetitive, generating larger and larger balance of payment deficits. Both countries have a growing proportion of their population in primary poverty and have larger and larger budget deficits as the costs to society of deindustrialization and unemployment mount. The consequence has been an interrelated downward spiral of social and labour market standards and a growth in the number of casualized, part-time and low-paid jobs with bad working conditions.

The increasing number of takers for these jobs can be explained by the increase in poverty, a decline in the ability of labour to defend employment labour standards against the combined efforts of employers and the government to reduce them, the pressure on families to throw more of their members on the labour market in an attempt to maintain customary living standards and an increasing tendency to subsidize employment by various means, including the topping up of low wages by social welfare. These effects have combined both to increase the number of jobs and to reduce meaningful employment. Despite this and the warnings from other economic indicators, the ability of the USA and UK to increase the job count has, in the minds of many commentators, made the labour market and social welfare policies of these countries models for effective full-employment strategies elsewhere. Various measures are being proposed for increasing labour market flexibility in Europe to increase employment.

The European Commission is currently considering two different but related policy programmes for reducing indirect employment costs as a way of gaining international competitiveness and reducing unemployment. First is the idea of a general reduction in the employment taxes and other charges that fall on employers for each worker employed. The argument is that such indirect costs (that is, in addition to the direct wage costs) are higher on average in the EU than in the USA or Japan, and that a reduction would allow a concomitant reduction in prices, boosting international competitiveness, world market shares, output and employment. However, there are a number of questions begged by this hoped-for virtuous circle. First, would the entire reduction in employment costs feed directly through into lower output prices, or might some go in higher profit margins? Or, by reducing market pressure on the firms to pursue international competitiveness through productivity gains and quality improvements, might these tax reductions be accompanied by lower gains in productivity than might otherwise have occurred, resulting in no net gain in unit costs? Second, from where would the lost tax revenue be recouped? There are, of course, arguments against increasing income tax, VAT or any of the other possible candidates. And if the lost revenue is not to be made good, then what would the implications be for the government budget deficits, which are already greater than allowed by Maastricht's convergence criteria? If the fall in employer taxes is to be matched by government spending cuts, then the potential harm that such cuts might do, including to the functioning of the productive system and hence to international productivity and world market share, would also need to be considered. Indeed, in the present economic and political climate where there is pressure to reduce government deficits yet resistance to increasing income tax, it may be that raising money to pay for public services from insurance-type charges, such as employers' national insurance contributions in Britain, will have to play a greater rather than a reduced role. That these and

166 Jonathan Michie and Frank Wilkinson

other questions should be researched in more detail is suggested by the fact that one of the few EU countries with employer charges already down to the US and Japanese levels is the UK, and there is not the correlation with market shares and employment success on which the Commission's policy is predicated.

The second policy programme for reducing indirect employment costs being considered by the European Commission is to reduce these particularly on low-paid employment (or, as this employment is usually described when such proposals are being advocated, low-skilled). The idea is to encourage the sort of employment creation witnessed in the USA in the 1980s, through a combination of expanding the sectors of the economy in which such labour is employed and encouraging the further substitution of labour for capital in such sectors. However, again there are other possible consequences that need to be investigated, first to have a clearer picture of what the likely impact of such a policy would be, and second to consider if there are any additional or alternative measures that would allow the employment gain without the associated loss of productivity pain. Specifically, the idea that labour–capital substitution follows changes in relative prices does not, at that general level, enjoy any empirical (or indeed theoretical) support. More generally, the idea of differential cuts in indirect employment costs is a type of labour subsidy towards that type of labour, and as such there are various associated dangers: first, there may be a disincentive to upgrade the productive system if this would involve the associated labour losing its subsidy; second, there is the risk that the economy is diverted towards the low-skill, low-investment sectors that are subsidized.

A POLICY AGENDA

The industrial world is in the grip of an unemployment crisis of historic proportions, which bears striking resemblance to its 1930s predecessor. In the 1920s, the world economy was highly volatile, with unprecedented stock market and currency speculation. Organized labour was on the retreat and wage cutting and labour market deregulation was the order of the day, especially in the USA and the UK. The consequent underconsumptionist tendencies were exacerbated by the collapse of commodity prices in the early 1920s which benefited industrial profits but ruined agriculture. This unstable economic base collapsed in 1929, when the world financial system was completely disrupted by the Wall Street crash and industry was undermined by the Great Depression, against which national governments proved individually and collectively powerless. Economic orthodoxy, then as now, held trade unions, state labour market regulation and social welfare payments responsible for unemployment, and preached balanced budgets, opposing state intervention to counter joblessness. When translated into policies, these notions, by deepening the recession and multiplying social deprivation, had the opposite to the predicted effect, and the consequent widening of the credibility gap led to weak and vacillating governments. In Britain, the Labour government split over policies that cut pay, reduced unemployment benefit levels and introduced means testing, policies which were insisted on by international bankers and finally implemented by the National Government led by Ramsay MacDonald. In Germany, six million unemployed, widespread poverty and cuts in unemployment pay paved the way to fascism and ultimately to the Second World War.

The lessons learned from this débâcle, at the level of economic theory and public policy, laid the groundwork for the post-war prosperity. National governments committed themselves to full employment and a welfare state policy that included health, social security, education and housing. In the labour market, collective bargaining was encouraged, minimum employment rights were guaranteed and industrial training was strengthened. At the international level agreements on finance and trade were concluded that were designed to encourage international commerce but were targeted at currency speculation and the problems of chronic surplus countries. These were reinforced at the national level by controls on international capital movements. Contingency plans were made for the stabilization of commodity prices, but these made little headway after the end of the Korean War crisis, when the collapse of raw material prices turned the terms of trade in favour of industrial countries. The purpose of these policies was to create a framework of rules for encouraging free enterprise creativity, while prohibiting the strong predatory and exploitative tendencies in capitalism.

This national and international collectivist effort created the promise that for some small proportion of the world's working class, poverty would at last be lifted. This promise was most fully realized in those countries of Northern Europe that most completely adopted the cooperative state model; no more so than in Sweden, where the Social Democratic Party embraced the 'wage solidarity' with 'active labour market' policies formulated by the trade unions, so that labour effectively managed capitalism. The real failure of the post-war period was at the international level. This can be explained by the dominant economic power of the USA and that country's continued adherence to the notion that capitalism operates at its best when completely unrestricted. This philosophy came to pervade the workings of the international agencies (the IMF, World Bank and GATT) and subverted their role as agents working for world economic stability. The cost to the USA itself was great. Its own unrestricted capital moved the production base of the US economy offshore and came increasingly to be dominated more by short-term speculation on the stock market than long-term industrial investment. This, and the fact that the degenerating industrial relations and labour market conditions in the USA made it incapable of meeting the quality competition from abroad, undermined American competitiveness so that it joined the UK as a newly deindustrializing economy.

This combination of, first, the lack of any effective stabilizing international institutions and, second, the progressive decline in the economic power of the USA played a major part in re-creating the sort of financial and trade volatility last seen in the inter-war years. This undermined the ability of national governments to exercise control and destroyed the credibility of the policies that formed the basis for post-war economic prosperity. The return to pre-Keynesian orthodoxy in macro-economic management completed the circle. Restrictive monetary policies, intensified competition for shares in markets that were growing more slowly than productive potential and unrestricted currency speculation interacted to re-create world recession.

Unemployment today is not, therefore, the result of the working of mystical economic laws regulating wages. There is no substance to the claim that if the worst off in society accept a cut in their living standards, long-term prospects will be magically restored; the opposite is more likely to be the case. Nor is unemployment the result of there being too little work needing doing to employ fully all those who seek employment. Both private need and public squalor are on the increase. The physical environment needs to be improved; more work should go into education, health and public services generally; housing and other infrastructure work would in almost all countries be welcome. The problem is not a shortage of things that need doing. It is a shortage of political will to do them.

The lessons of history have to be relearned. Just as today's economic orthodoxy, political commentators and ruling elites have all retreated back to repeating the free-market dogmas of the 1920s, so we need to remember the lessons learned at such enormous costs from the resulting Great Depression and the rise of fascism. At the international level those lessons included the need for really effective international agreements – not to 'set free' capital but rather to stabilize trade flows and restrict speculative activities. At the national level there was not only a commitment in principle to full employment and a welfare state, there was also a recognition of the need for generally applicable effective labour market and social conditions, including meaningful employment rights.

NOTES

1. National Association of Citizens Advice Bureaux (NACAB), *Job Insecurity* (London: NACAB, March 1993).

2. See *ibid.* for further evidence, the key points of which are summarized in this paragraph.

3. J. Michie and F. Wilkinson, The growth of unemployment in the 1980s. In J. Michie and J. Grieve Smith (eds), *Unemployment in Europe* (1994).

4. J. Michie and F. Wilkinson, Inflation policy and the restructuring of labour markets. In J. Michie (ed.) *The Economic Legacy: 1979–1992* (1992).

5. An incorrect theory can still have a powerful impact, of course, if for no other reason than that it is held to be true and hence influences people's actions. For this reason the NAIRU theory is certainly important, as illustrated by the reaction to what would ordinarily be thought to be good news on the economic front, of a fall in unemployment; if central bankers interpret this to mean that unemployment has fallen below the NAIRU then, in order to prevent accelerating inflation, unemployment has to be increased again and interest rates will be raised to bring about this state of affairs.

6. See, for example, A. Singh, De-industrialization. In J. Eatwell, M. Milgate and P. Newman (eds), *The New Palgrave Dictionary of Economics* (1987); B. Rowthorn and J. Wells, *Deindustrialisation and Foreign Trade* (1987); M. Kitson and J. Mitchie, Britain's Industrial Performance since 1960: Underinvestment and relative decline (1996) *Economic Journal.*

7. The impact of labour market policy on relative earnings, including the unequal growth in earnings between different sectors of the economy, is analysed in greater detail in S. Deakin, J. Michie and F. Wilkinson, *Inflation, Employment, Wage-bargaining and the Law* (London: Institute of Employment Rights, 1992).

8. See B. Rowthorn, Government spending and taxation in the Thatcher era. In Michie (1992), *op. cit.,* for an analysis of government spending and taxation in the Thatcher era.

9. For a detailed analysis of the Conservative government's labour market policies, see S. Deakin and F. Wilkinson, *The Economics of Employment Rights* (London: Institute of Employment Rights, 1990).

10. *Households below Average Income 1979–1990/91* (London: HMSO, 1993).

11. The Department of Employment estimates that it is notified of approximately one-third of all job vacancies.

12. Firms involved include Tesco, Sainsbury's and Safeway in retailing, Coats Viyella and Courtaulds in textiles and clothing and a range of leading firms in hotels, catering and leisure.

13. IDS, *Report 639* (London: Incomes Data Services Ltd, April 1993).

14. March 1993, p. 49.

15. This is argued in more detail in F. Wilkinson, *Why Britain Needs a Minimum Wage* (London: Institute for Public Policy Research, 1992).

16. See V. Borooah, Income distribution, consumption patterns and economic outcomes in the United Kingdom (1988) 7 *Contributions to Political Economy* 49.

17. In 1982, the 'earnings related supplement' to the standard unemployment benefit was abolished; in 1984, the allowance for dependent children of those on unemployment benefit went. The maternity grant that used to be available for all mothers giving birth was abolished in 1987. The industrial disablement benefit was abolished in 1986 for all those whose disability is assessed at less

than 14 per cent. In 1987, the death grant was abolished. And the automatic link of pensions with earnings was broken by the Tories. For the financial implications of such policies, see Rowthorn (1992) *op. cit.*

18. During the depressed years of the mid-1790s the rulers of the countryside, following the example of Berkshire magistrates meeting at Speenhamland, decided to subsidize low wages out of local rates where the labourers' family income fell below subsistence. See E. J. Hobsbawm and G. Rudé, *Captain Swing* (1969), for a description and discussion of the system, from which this section draws.

19. *Ibid.*, p. 47.
20. Cited in *ibid.*, pp. 48–9.
21. *Ibid.*, p. 48.
22. *Ibid.*, p. 50.

23. A May 1993 EC document on tackling unemployment proposed reducing employers' social security contributions for unskilled workers (see the *Guardian*, 14 May 1993). The dangers associated with such arrangements, whereby private sector wages are subsidized from the public purse, are also relevant for considering the relative merits of government employment creation policies of, on the one hand, expanding public sector employment and, on the other, subsidizing employment in the private sector, as discussed by A. Glyn and B. Rowthorn (European employment policies. In Michie and Smith (1994), *op. cit.*), who find in any case that subsidizing private sector employment is less desirable in terms of balance of payments and inflation constraints.

24. Hobsbawm and Rudé, *op. cit.*, pp. 50–1.
25. See J. Michie and J. Grieve Smith (eds), *Creating Industrial Capacity: Towards Full Employment* (1996).
26. See J. Michie and J. Grieve Smith (eds), *Managing the Global Economy* (1995).

10

Deregulation: The Contemporary Politics of Health and Safety

Charles Woolfson and Matthias Beck

INTRODUCTION

In a recently published article, Laureen Snider has stated that many of the most serious, anti-social and predatory acts committed in modern industrial countries are corporate crimes; in particular those resulting from the neglect of workers' safety.[1] Corporate crime is a major killer. The USA reports an average of 20,000 murders a year. Industrial accidents, which stem from violations of safety codes, cause 14,000 deaths per annum, while 30,000 deaths result from unsafe and illegal consumer products.

The number of deaths in the UK from accidents at work has declined. Yet, during each of the past five years, an average of approximately 500 persons died in work-related incidents. Much of the recent decline in the rate of fatalities can simply be seen as a result of changing patterns of employment, with the shift away from the high-risk extractive and manufacturing industries towards the service sector. By contrast, there has been no significant improvement in the reported non-fatal major injury rate. This has remained approximately the same, at above 30,000, since the start of the current series of Health and Safety Commission reports in 1986-87. Altogether, there were about half a million accidents at work in 1993-94.[2]

In the hostile industrial relations climate that currently exists, management has the upper hand and employees are under greater than ever pressure to 'get the job done'. The temptation to cut corners on safety is strong. The penalties for employees who raise safety concerns and are deemed to be 'uncooperative' can be severe, as North Sea oil workers have found to their cost over many years. By contrast, the penalties for employers who flout the law on safety are generally derisory. However, there is extensive health and safety law in the UK, in particular the Health and Safety at Work Act (1974) and, more recently, the transposing into domestic legislation of important European directives. There is also a regulatory agency, the Health and Safety Executive (HSE), which is supposed to enforce the legislation, and which is itself responsible to the overseeing body, the Health and Safety Commission (HSC). This chapter seeks to examine the question of how far the UK system of health and safety protection for employees at work is now threatened by the government's deregulation programme.

THE DEREGULATION INITIATIVE

The government's deregulation initiative was announced in the spring of 1993. Eight business-led government-appointed deregulation 'task forces' were appointed to re-examine regulations across the board. They included, as chairmen, some of the government's most rabid supporters in the ranks of big business. Altogether, members from ten such firms have between them contributed about £3.5 million to the Conservative Party and affiliated organizations. The task forces produced a report recommending wide-ranging deregulation of measures, from those establishing the size of head on a pint of beer to redundancy procedures. In the context of a broad deregulation assault on nearly every major government department, this report also made over 70 recommendations which directly affected the work of the HSC and the HSE.[3] The task forces were led by Lord Sainsbury, appointed by Michael Heseltine MP (then Minister in charge of the Department of Trade and Industry) to act as advisor on deregulation. The remit was to produce proposals for 'reducing the burden of regulation', while securing a 'strong business voice' in the review of regulations that departments had been asked to undertake. Although each task force had representatives on it of the major firms, particular attention was paid to representing and articulating the interests of small firms in each group. These small firms collectively tabled their own proposals to ensure that 'sufficient weight' was given to their views. The assumptions that guided the work of the task forces were therefore explicit: regulators should 'think small', and make sure small firms could cope with the regulation; avoid regulations that were out of proportion to benefits obtained; make regulations goal-based, not over-prescriptive. Among the small business group proposals, the following give the flavour of their recommendations:

Proposal 4   Regulate only if the answers dictate the need. Stop knee-jerk reactions to specific one-off incidents/accidents.

Proposal 5   Make regulators and enforcers into 'enablers', not 'threateners'.

Proposal 9   Permit flexibility in the achievement of objectives. Encourage positive response from 'enablers' by referring all negative judgements to a higher authority.

Proposal 10   When drafting regulations, assume all businesses are small. Use the 'small business litmus test'.

So deep was the hostility towards and mistrust of the regulatory authorities that, besides calling for 'easy channels of complaint' and the appointment of an 'independent arbitrator', the small businesses group, instancing fear of 'recrimination' by the regulators, even proposed an anonymous complaints telephone 'hot-line'.

The task forces' proposals were extensively incorporated into a separate Department of Trade and Industry publication, *Deregulation: Cutting Red Tape*.[4] Of 600 recommendations, only 70 were explicitly rejected, while 440 were to be implemented or were under active consideration for inclusion within the scope of the subsequent Deregulation and Contracting Out Bill.[5] This Bill, introduced in January 1994, had its second reading in February and became law in the autumn. The Deregulation and Contracting Out Act sets out sweeping delegated powers for ministerial repeal of literally hundreds of regulations, with only abbreviated procedures of parliamentary scrutiny. Henceforth, under s. 37 of the Act, regulations could simply be revoked by ministerial order without the requirement for primary legislation. Certainly, some consultation with the 'appropriate authority' might occur before regulations are revoked. But ministers are now able to repeal full Acts of Parliament by statutory instrument – the so-called Henry VIII clause. In so doing, ministers are in the position of effectively arrogating the regulatory function to themselves. In a recent article, Kevin Williams comments:

> The minister will then have become the regulator (*de facto* as well as *de jure*) and, having cut himself off from expert understanding of the way industry and private regulation work, will not be well placed to propose optimal public regulation. Moreover, the minister will be operating on the basis of social and other values which will not be apparent and for which there is no method of accounting.[6]

Yet for Michael Heseltine MP (then President of the Board of Trade) the Deregulation Act, which he described as 'the biggest bonfire of controls that has taken place in modern times in this country', is to be only 'the first stage' of an ongoing deregulation initiative.[7] A permanent deregulation task force has been put in place to advise the minister and publish an annual report. Altogether, the government has identified 1000 regulations it wishes to remove.

The chief impediment facing the government in implementing changes in health and safety law is not a procedural one. It is the fact that the existing framework of health and safety law is not only well entrenched but, disconcertingly, commands a wide measure of support in industry itself, particularly among more responsible employers. But there are also real legal obstacles to a fundamental dismantling of health and safety regulation.

The Deregulation Act, while promoting extensive deregulation throughout industry and commerce, does not, as some in the trade union movement had expected, seek to revoke s. 1(2) of the Health and Safety at Work Act 1974. This key section of the Act requires any new legislation to 'maintain or improve the standards of health, safety and welfare'. Michael Forsyth, then Minister for Employment, had specifically asked the new and now only part-time Chairman of the HSC, Frank Davies, for his 'definitive advice' on whether s. 1(2) might 'impinge on the Government's deregulation exercise'.[8] It would seem that advice was given to the minister against any interference with this section of the Act. This meant, in other words, that new legislation such as the Deregulation Act could not weaken existing health and safety law.

This is a principle also enshrined in Article 118A of the Single European Act, under which EC safety directives are proposed. Whether this is to be more than a temporary set-back in the tide of deregulation remains to be seen. Any direct attempt to dismantle the Health and Safety at Work Act would inevitably have brought the British government into conflict with Europe, and at a time when the Conservative administration was still licking its self-inflicted wounds over the Maastricht Treaty. Indeed, the deregulation initiative was intended precisely to rekindle ideological unity in a badly divided Conservative administration.

What is crucial to understand, however, is that the system of regulation put in place through the Health and Safety at Work Act by the Robens Committee itself contains elements of permeability. The notion of self-regulation and goal-setting, which are key innovations of the Health and Safety at Work Act, permit a latent deregulation within the existing system. Such deregulation does not require the explicit elimination of existing legislation. The seeds of the destruction of the Health and Safety at Work Act were planted at its inception by faulty assumptions and misconceived regulatory practices, which the current deregulation initiative exploits.

ROBENS AND THE CREATION OF PERMEABLE REGULATION

The key strength of the Robens Committee's approach to health and safety was that it sought to replace the inherited mass of detailed, prescriptive regulation, much of it dating back many years, with a more rational goal-based regulatory framework. Instead of narrowly conceived regulations, the Committee proposed general goal-setting regulations that state the objectives of safety policy while allowing more flexible ways to attain these objectives.[9] In some respects, what the Robens Committee proposed was an advance on the previous regulatory regime.

The Committee also provided the rationale for a single piece of comprehensive unifying and enabling legislation, which laid out the duty of the employer to provide a safe working environment, and of the employee to observe health and safety provisions. Health and safety was intended to become the concern of those who created risk, namely everyone at work. Safety, therefore, became more a matter of self-regulation than prohibitory, or negative, external regulatory control. The contention on which the Robens Committee's whole approach was based was that there was 'too much law'. The existing system, it was said 'encourages too much reliance on state regulation, and rather too little on personal responsibility and voluntary self-generating effort'.[10] The conclusion was most clearly put: 'There are several practical limits on the extent to which progressively better health and safety at work can be brought about through negative regulation by external agencies. We need a more effectively self-regulating system.'[11]

The Robens Committee accepted the prevailing view that the threat of prosecution by external regulatory agencies should only be a last resort. Rather, non-judicial administrative techniques for ensuring compliance were recommended, with minimum set standards for safety and health at work. Advice and persuasion, rather than a punitive approach, were seen as the best means of securing improvements in safety. This view was based on a fundamentally flawed and simplistic view of accident causation. The dubious evidence of the Factory

Inspectorate, that only a small proportion of accidents resulted from wilful breaches of regulations, was unquestioningly accepted. This, according to Woolf,[12] was despite substantial available evidence which suggested that nearly all accidents at work resulted from employers' breaches of their existing common law duty of care. Woolf reports the conclusions of the 1972, 42-month study of '2000 accidents' by the National Institute of Industrial Psychology, actually commissioned by the Robens Committee but ignored in the final report. These results are described as 'a blinding glimpse of the obvious'. They suggest: 'that nearly all accidents are the inevitable result of unsafe working systems which could themselves be made safe by employers, by a combination of hazard analysis, planning, training and supervision'.[13] Yet the majority (four-fifths) of accidents, it was asserted by the Factory Inspectorate, were caused by 'apathy'. It was this simplistic view of accident causation that led Robens to reject the applicability of 'the traditional concepts of criminal law'. Robens states:

> Relatively few offences are clear-cut, few arise from reckless indifference to the possibility of causing injury, few can be laid at the door of a particular individual. The typical infringement arises rather through carelessness, oversight, lack of knowledge or means, inadequate supervision or sheer inefficiency. In such circumstances the process of prosecution and punishment ... is largely an irrelevancy.[14]

Merely because the dangerous consequences of 'carelessness' and 'oversight' were not foreseen is hardly sufficient reason for dangerous offences not to be subject to prosecution. As Woolf queries, are not employers, like other citizens, 'deemed to intend the natural and probable consequences of their actions?'[15] It is precisely for failing to plan and supervise efficiently the safety of their operations that employers should be prosecuted. This issue still resonates in current debates over legal reform, particularly in the area of corporate responsibility as discussed below.

The Robens Committee proposed a general statutory duty of care, on the one hand, while simultaneously displaying (according to Woolf) 'an almost total misunderstanding of, and indifference to, the nature and function of the criminal law as it affects the liability of corporations and applies to regulatory offences.[16] The function of the criminal law, says Woolf, should be precisely to 'establish minimum standards in such a way that it is both unattractive and unprofitable to fall below them'.[17] Without prosecutions as the 'normal consequences of discovery', where penalties are derisory in relation to potential gain, the effect is therefore to remove any voluntary inclination to prioritize safety performance.

The fundamental flaw with Roben's self-regulation approach was that it presupposed a natural consensus between management and workforce. The Committee, in essence, dramatically overestimated what Robens claimed to be a 'natural identity' of interests on the part of 'the two sides' of industry.[18] In the words of Nichols and Armstrong:

> the real safety and health problem is to protect workers against the inherent 'unnatural' excesses of a society dominated by the market; a society in which some men are paid to squeeze as much production as possible out of others ... they [the Robens Committee] never saw that what lies behind so many accidents is not an apathetic state of mind but a preoccupation with the concrete reality of getting the job out.[19]

ECONOMIC DETERRENCE

If self-regulation is flawed in its assumptions, what alternative approaches are available? Phillips, a critic of the Robens Committee report, pointed to the neglect of 'economic deterrence' by the Committee.[20] Economic deterrence seeks to reinstate consideration of 'the potential effectiveness of economic sanctions in the promotion of safety'.[21] Its proponents argue that, where such sanctions are not deployed, companies do not bear the true costs of accidents arising out of employment and externalities are created. If companies are not made liable for damages and, at the same time, medical services are free or subsidized, distortions in the national distribution of resources will arise. As Phillips argues, 'Misallocation of accident costs prevents the achievement of efficient allocation of productive resources. Not only is the allocation between industries affected: so, within a particular industry, is the allocation between safety and other inputs.'[22] The absence of economic deterrence can result in output being too high and price too low with respect to other industries with which a company competes. This misallocation of resources is particularly important in very dangerous industries, says Phillips:

> The distortion in dangerous industries is likely to have substantial repercussions in the field of safety, for the high level of output implies a higher level of employment and therefore a greater number of accidents than would occur if the industry were

bearing its full accident costs.[23]

Misallocation of resources, then, leads to over-employment in dangerous industries and results in insufficient expenditure on accident prevention.

As Codrington and Henley suggest in their study of fatalities in the construction industry, most of the costs of accidents do not fall upon employers.[24] The primary costs are borne by insurance, injured employees' families and, to a large degree, the welfare state. Thus, although employers bear the costs of prevention, they do not incur the full costs of failing to provide safe working conditions. Consequently, in a competitive market system, dominated by the profit motive, firms cannot necessarily be expected to incur the costs of prevention on a voluntary basis.[25]

The Robens Committee purported to promote safety as a 'balance' between 'regulation and supervision by the state and self-regulation and self-help' by industry.[26] In reality, it tilted the scales firmly in favour of the latter, to the almost total neglect of the former. In so doing, it continued the approach to enforcement that had characterized the previous Factory Inspectorate, who 'regarded themselves more as educators and persuaders than as enforcers or prosecutors'.[27] Evidence from the Inspectorate to the Robens Committee had emphasized the 'last resort' nature of prosecution.

PROSECUTIONS UNDER THE HEALTH AND SAFETY AT WORK ACT

In a desire to discourage the punitive approach, the Robens Committee recommended 'non-judicial administrative techniques for ensuring compliance with minimum standards of safety and health at work'.[28] In 1974, HSE inspectors were given powers to issue 'improvement' and 'prohibition' notices. In effect, a regulatory regime was established in which, as Carson said, non-compliance with the law on health and safety tended to be a matter of routine acceptance.[29]

Prohibition notices are tied to the risk of 'serious personal injury' and can require that an activity cease. For both types of notice – improvement and prohibition – there is a right of appeal to an industrial tribunal, although a prohibition notice would remain in force in the interim. Normally, only in the event of a serious injury or a fatality would actual prosecution be contemplated, and even then, as will be argued, this may not necessarily be the case.

As against 6432 improvement notices and 4026 prohibition notices issued by the HSE in 1992-3, about 1800 prosecutions were undertaken, an overall ratio of notices to prosecutions of about five to one.[30] While over 86 per cent of prosecutions undertaken were successful, court proceedings are seen as both costly and time-consuming by the HSE, taking inspectors away from their primary role as persuaders. In terms of the distribution of inspectors' effort between various aspects of their work, a breakdown of their time confirms the above emphasis. Only 11 per cent of time is spent on investigations and a mere 4 per cent on court activity, as against some 60 to 70 per cent on preventative inspections.

In general, only a sixth of workplace deaths lead to a company being prosecuted by the HSE, and then generally only on lesser charges in the lower courts. The average fine following a successful prosecution for a health and safety offence was just over £2735 in 1993-4.[31] The average fine following a conviction involving a fatality is about £11,000. This is dramatically less than in the USA and most industrialized countries, with the exception of Japan. Currently, owing to the expense of prosecuting companies in the higher courts, most prosecutions initiated by the HSE take place in magistrates' courts in England and Wales and sheriff courts in Scotland. Here the maximum fine available has historically been low. From 1 October 1992 the maximum fine in the magistrates' courts rose from £2000 to £5000 for 'other offences' under the Health and Safety at Work Act. With the passing of the Offshore Safety Act, the level of fines rose to an exemplary £20,000 maximum for the more serious offences (breaches of ss. 2-6 of the Health and Safety at Work Act). Higher courts remain free to impose unlimited fines and up to two years' imprisonment. The HSE now claims to be referring more cases to the Director of Public Prosecutions in England for consideration by the Crown Prosecution Service of possible manslaughter charges. [32] However, as detailed research by the West Midlands Health and Safety Advice Centre has recently shown, in that area at least there have been no referrals whatsoever.[33] The HSE has not revealed whether, nationally, it has a formal referral policy. Although the Executive more recently has referred 20 workplace deaths to the Crown Prosecution Service, only three of these have resulted in any prosecution action.[34]

Prosecution activity should in turn be weighed against the wide-spread under-reporting of notifiable accidents. The HSE supplement to the 1990 Labour Force Survey, which was based on interviews with members of about 40,000 households in England and Wales, sought to establish the true (as against the reported) level of workplace injuries and work-related ill-health. The gross figures estimate that, during 1989–90, some 1,430,000 injuries were suffered at the workplace in England and Wales. Taking a crude uprating of 10 per cent for Scotland, this suggests a figure of 1,573,000 injuries at work.[35] This works out at an annual level of injury of about one in sixteen of the workforce, resulting in 21.1 million days off, an average of 15 days per person (over double that for reportable injuries, i.e. injuries involving over three days' absence from work). The figures from the Labour Force Survey suggest that employers overall are reporting less than a third of reportable injuries. Reporting rates varied from around 80 per cent in the energy industries and 40 per cent in manufacture and construction, to around 20 per cent in both services and agriculture. Among the self-employed a mere 5 per cent of notifiable accidents were reported.[36] These levels of under-reporting have led the HSC to review the existing Reporting of Injuries, Diseases and Dangerous Occurrences Regulations (RIDDOR) 1985.

Pressure is growing, particularly from the relatives of disaster victims, through groups such as Disaster Action and the Piper Alpha Families and Survivors Association, to reform the law to permit a wider use of custodial sentencing, the bringing of criminal proceedings against companies and the introduction of a form of strict liability focusing on the senior executive with health and safety responsibility. The Law Commission, in examining this issue, is considering the awarding of exemplary damages against companies. This last is a response to the failure, in 1991, of the prosecution for corporate manslaughter of the directors of P & O after the *Herald of Free Enterprise* Zeebrugge disaster. There have been only three such attempted prosecutions this century and all have failed.

Exemplary damages are now seen by the Law Commission as a 'superior enforcement technique to criminal law prosecutions'.[37] This is an indication that the principle of economic deterrence is being actively reconsidered by the legal community in the face of growing public outrage at corporate recklessness. The Law Commission's more recent recommendations have been to reform the manslaughter laws so as to make it easier to prosecute company directors for acts of gross negligence under a charge of involuntary manslaughter.[38] For many, this is a long-overdue step in the right direction. The jailing of the director of a leisure company in December 1994 for three years (reduced on appeal to 18 months), on a manslaughter charge following the deaths of four students, is a significant development. The trial judge was explicit in his recommendation that the safety of children should not be left 'to the inadequate vagaries of self-regulation'.[39]

Even where the courts are willing to impose stiffer penalties, they face barriers to making employers accountable before the law. Large companies, which increasingly employ contractors to carry out maintenance or specialist work rather than directly employ such workers themselves, can avoid taking full responsibility for their safety and welfare. In the case of an accident at BP Grangemouth, where one worker was killed and three others suffered serious burns, the client company was fined £200,000, whereas one of the employing contractors, a Belgium-based concern with no registered UK address, escaped prosecution.[40] This is a situation likely to be encountered with increasing frequency as European integration gathers pace, and it calls for early legal remedy.

Issues of criminal justice and deterrence after workplace death and injury significantly fail to feature in the rhetoric of a government supposedly committed to law and order. Whether the law will be strengthened must remain in doubt, given the business-friendly nature of the current administration as exemplified by the deregulation exercise.

THE REJECTION OF THE POST-WAR SETTLEMENT

The Robens Committee's assumptions surrounding self-regulation and its neglect of economic deterrence had been shaped in the broadly consensual approach characteristic of the post-war social era (with government embracing a degree of societal responsibility for the welfare of its citizens). The Conservative administrations of the 1980s and 1990s rejected this wider consensus in favour of explicitly free-market philosophies of political and economic deregulation. Put another way, the new social value judgement was based on the elevation of the interests of individuals, more particularly the interests of the individual employer above the social good.

The economic recession of the early 1980s created an imperative to limit the cost impact of new health and safety legislation on businesses. The recession of the late 1980s and early 1990s accelerated this imperative. Not simply new but existing health and safety provision was to be re-examined as part of an intensified political drive towards wholesale societal deregulation. The increasingly residual regulatory functions of the state were to be severely circumscribed.

This can be seen most obviously in the budgetary curtailment of the regulatory agency for safety and health. After the few years in the late 1980s during which the HSE's budget had been temporarily stabilized, a 2.6 per cent cut was imposed in 1994–95 to be followed by a 5 per cent cut in 1995–96, with the grant frozen thereafter. Over the two years 1994 to 1996, this will amount to a £15 million reduction in the HSE's budget and the loss of up to 230 out of about 4800 staff.[41] Not only are experienced inspectors increasingly encouraged to take early retirement,[42] but restrictions on recruitment during the 1980s have resulted in a less experienced inspectorate, with over one-third of its staff having less than five years' experience.[43] In one month alone (March 1995), a total of 85 inspectors, medical staff and managers had already left the HSE under the early retirement programme. The HSE's ability to meet its responsibilities has, according to trade unions, increasingly been undermined.[44]

Over 24,000 accidents and complaints were dealt with by the HSE in 1992–93. The National Audit Office[45] noted in its examination of HSE inspection work that most (but not all) fatal injuries were investigated. However, the proportion of major injuries (such as fractures) investigated varied between area offices from 8.5 to 20.8 per cent. In the case of non-major injuries leading to three or more days off work, the proportion of accidents investigated ranged from 2.4 to 7.6 per cent.[46] An average of 6.4 per cent of the reported workplace injuries were investigated by the HSE in 1992–93.[47] Dawson had already noted in the mid-1980s that, overall, the number of visits by HSE inspectors had 'declined markedly' over the previous decade.[48] The fall in the number of visits has been linked to increasing reliance on a priority system, whereby the 'more responsible' establishments are visited less than before and a more 'targeted' inspection approach is adopted.[49]

The actual assault on the HSE as a regulatory institution had been preceded by imposed budgetary cuts, reduced inspections and a staff recruitment freeze. Now even the 'reluctant enforcement' strategy of the HSE is under direct attack. First, in 1993, the Department of Trade and Industry issued a new 'code' for 'enforcers', which emphasizes the need for inspectors to adopt an approach more sympathetic to business problems.[50] The HSE was also enjoined to advise local authority inspectors to adopt a 'softly, softly' approach to enforcement of health and safety legislation. Environmental Health Officers who enforce health and safety at local level, primarily in the service industries, were encouraged to offer 'guidance' to employers rather than take 'immediate enforcement action'.[51]

In addition, various branches and functions of the HSE have been directly subject to 'market testing'. This provoked even the normally restrained John Rimington, then Director General of the HSE, to warn: 'although there was no technical impediment to market testing any activity other than policy making, there would be important risks and drawbacks to set against any advantages of market testing the main operational arms of HSE'. [52] The civil service union (the Institute of Professionals, Managers and Specialists) was more forthright, arguing that 'the real impact of market testing will be to fragment the organisation and destroy the morale of staff'.[53] Since April 1992, £199,000 has been spent in five market tests, which have cut 92 posts. Key among the specialist branches of the HSE to undergo this process has been the Employment Medical Advisory Service.[54] While in-house teams have already won contracts for typing and messenger services (although not security), the Employment Medical Advisory Service was specifically prohibited from producing a competitive tender.

Contracting out is now under way for in-house training, the HSE helpline and scientific support work. It is not inconceivable, therefore, that such core regulatory functions as those of inspection itself may be contracted out. A confidential CBI document has already partially anticipated a move in this direction. The Deregulation Act enables ministers to make orders for some of the responsibilities carried out on their behalf to be privatized. The CBI document notes: 'It may be possible under this power to designate health and safety inspection by local authorities as a function which could be delegated to outside contractors.'[55]

THE HSE UNDER REVIEW

In addition to these externally imposed constraints on regulatory activity, the HSE has begun the more far-reaching process of redefining the basic assumptions that govern its regulatory oversight. In December 1992, the Health and Safety Commission, under ministerial prompting, announced a comprehensive review of existing health and safety law. Its aim was to propose 'the removal of provisions not making a contribution proportionate to the costs they inflict'.[56] It also examined the issue of enforcement of regulations and the means by which information and advice on regulations is communicated to business, especially small businesses. The HSC and the internal review's support team in the HSE 'kept in close touch with developments on the wider deregulation scene', especially the DTI's deregulation task forces.[57] Even at the stage of interim review in November 1993, it had been noted that there was 'a great deal of common ground between the perspectives emerging from the two exercises'.[58] The HSC task groups conducting the internal review had, as their priority, the scrutiny of those sets of regulations which in their judgement had the biggest impact on business. Like the DTI task forces, the business interest was strongly represented in the task groups, which were led by chairmen and dominated by CBI representatives from major firms, although on each task group there was also a small firm representative and two TUC nominees.

HSE Director General Rimington, in an effort to put a gloss on the exercise, had welcomed the HSC internal review as a way of removing 'fussy' or 'unnecessary detail'.[59] This review, of approximately 200 existing pieces of health and safety legislation, was completed by April 1994. The review process revealed many of the strengths and weaknesses of the HSC. The major strength of the HSC is the tripartite nature of that body, in which the trade union movement, through the TUC, is directly represented by three trade union officials (Paul Gallagher, AEEU; Alan Grant, TUC; Alan Tuffin, UCW). Another member of the Commission with a trade union background is Councillor Eddie Carrick, who represents the local authorities. Despite this, however, doubts existed about the ability of the individual TUC representatives on each of the seven HSC's internal review task groups to mount any real resistance to the business-dominated membership and agenda.

Nevertheless, the interim report of the task groups noted that none of the existing safety legislation it had reviewed was the source of undue costs for business.[60] The main report of the HSC internal review confirmed this, noting that 'there is little evidence that, despite the costs of compliance, the system as a whole is unduly burdensome for business'.[61] Nor was there any compelling evidence of a high level of concern among businesses in general, or small firms in particular, about the overall arrangements for securing health and safety at work. The main report observed: 'There is very widespread support for the framework of health and safety legislation established in 1974. The standards set out in current legislation are almost universally seen as reasonable.'[62]

Moreover, on the basis of the internal review, the HSC has explicitly recommended that s. 1(2) of the Health and Safety at Work Act – which requires that new legislation should not result in the diminution of safety standards – remain unchanged. It would appear that the Commission is unwilling to surrender this primary legislative lever which safeguards health and safety standards from erosion. These were hardly the sort of conclusions designed to gladden the hearts of the root and branch ideologues of deregulation currently occupying government. In particular, the imposition of further large-scale legislative change was specifically identified by the HSC review as being 'unwelcome to business'. It was not the substance of the regulations that was causing concern, but how to apply them at the level of the individual business or firm.

The bulk of the HSC's recommendations arising out of the main report of the task groups are aimed at reducing the volume, simplifying the various reporting procedures and clarifying aspects of enforcement of the legislation. In his minister's foreword to the main report, Michael Forsyth makes the claim that the review exercise will, 'in time', lead to a reduction of 40 per cent in the volume of health and safety law 'covering the generality of businesses'.[63] Almost all pre-1974 legislation will be removed. But so far, only some seven out of a total of 28 pieces of primary legislation (including the remaining provisions of the Factories Act 1961 and the Offices Shops and Railway Premises Act 1963), and some 100 (out of a total of 367) sets of regulations, have been identified for removal or replacement by more modern regulations. Even these proposals are more in the nature of an overdue administrative tidying-up process than a wholesale clear-out. Most of the Commission's detailed recommendations relate to a perceived 'information gap' requiring more streamlined 'practical guidance', consultation exercises and simplified explanations of actual requirements and procedures, rather than major legislative repeal.

To identify the main thrust of future 'deregulation' attempts as they are likely to affect health and safety, it is necessary to be alert to more subtle stratagems that are taking advantage of the existing weaknesses within the current regulatory regime. First of all, the HSE itself is currently endorsing a philosophy of enforcement that offers to business the promise of maximum discretion. Systematic non-compliance with legislative requirements is often treated as an acceptable practice. Jenny Bacon (the Deputy General Director of HSE) for example, in a paper to local authority enforcement officers, has stated: 'Overall, very few regulations have been identified as having an adverse impact on business – partly because many firms simply give up on trying to comply with everything at senior level.'[64]

The new view is that compliance with the law is not necessarily desirable; instead, whatever compliance can be achieved is to be considered as legally adequate. As Bacon puts it, it is 'acceptance' that gives law validity: 'In other words, if you have got most of the punters with you, you can kick the rest. If you have got most against you, you need to change tactics.'[65] This 'lowest common denominator' approach to enforcement implies an institutionalized tolerance of routine violation. It is close to what criminologists have identified as effective decriminalization, which is typical among white-collar criminal activities.[66] Above all, it withdraws responsibility from the employer and, with that, reduces the protection of the individual worker. As John Hendy QC has commented, 'If a health and safety law continues to put a burden on the employer, the likelihood is that it is continuing to provide protection to the employee.'[67]

FEATURES OF THE NEW REGIME

Safety as a Business

Modern health and safety regulations require firms not merely to address prescriptive requirements, but to think through actively the overall management of health and safety as a system to assess risk and carry out the functions of audit. These requirements have been a source of discontent on the part of business. The HSE's internal review found no support for the view that enforcement practices were overly harsh. The complaints that the main report considered focused primarily on the need for a greater 'consistency of enforcement', for making more explicit the expectations and criteria for enforcement, and for including a clearer statement of the HSE's principles. This reflects unease about the current spate of regulation, in which uncertainty about regulatory requirements of new European-derived regulations introduced in 1992, as well as UK legislation such as the Electricity at Work Regulations 1989, have created considerable confusion as well as resistance. According to Bacon, just such legislation 'comes out tops in unpopularity and burdensomeness'.[68]

The HSE has reacted with embarrassment to the complaints of business that additional 'burdens' of paperwork will be required to comply with new sets of legislation.[69] The Commission's recommendations to reduce the amount of form-filling and to utilize electronic media, in complying with reporting requirements, are no doubt worthy but essentially cosmetic suggestions.

The HSE is also concerned that health and safety 'consultants', to whom businesses may have turned for advice on complying with the new regulations, may have overstated the legal requirements that need to be met. In so doing, consultants have secured unwarranted fees for themselves as well as creating unnecessary outlays, particularly for smaller firms, as far as the real legal requirements of risk assessment are concerned. Rimington, in his Director General's foreword to the most recent HSC report, states:

that there had been an over-implementation of the law ... due to the activity of a minority of consultants and contractors who, with an eye to business ... had been exaggerating to their clients the legal requirements to be imposed. In the course of the year we published an advisory booklet, *Selecting a health and safety consultancy*, and we also made clear our willingness to take legal action in flagrant cases of misrepresentation.[70]

Here we face an amazing paradox, in which regulatory changes have created the space for an opportunistic safety advice business, effectively a new layer of 'regulatory interpreters'. These, in turn, now require a new level of control which, incredibly, includes the explicit threat of legal sanction for those recommending 'over-implementation'.

Making Regulation Palatable

One area the internal review addressed closely, therefore, was the 'architecture' of health and safety legislation. This concerns the comprehensibility, transparency and consistency of the overall structure of health and safety regulations. The HSC has issued a discussion document, since the completion of the internal review of regulations, which effectively seeks to re-open the debate about general guidance principles versus more legally based requirements. 'One of the views' emerging from the review, we are reminded, is that health and safety law has become 'too complex and fragmented' and needs to be 'simplified', so that its main principles are 'easier to grasp'.[71] The principal target would appear to be all legislation in which risk assessment is a feature, which the HSE is seeking to simplify by creating 'a common set of legal requirements'.[72]

Currently, the HSC distinguishes between three levels of regulation: the mandatory; the less binding approved code of practice (ACoP); and the more general and non-legally binding 'guidance notes'. The major concern among some business organizations is ACoPs, because they require an employer to demonstrate in law that it either has fulfilled legislative requirements or has devised a system which is demonstrably equally effective. Today, there is concern in the trade union movement that the proposed redefinition of regulatory requirements in the direction of guidance, together with the weakening of ACoPs, could place too much discretion and flexibility in the hands of employers. As it is, for the first time, a proposed ACoP (on measures to prevent asthma) has now been reduced to guidance status following employer objections. The HSC has issued a consultative document, which questions the necessity for ACoPs in the future.[73]

'Clarification' and 'simplification' of legislation should not lead to a backdoor downgrading of mandatory health and safety requirements. In fact, modern non-prescriptive goal-setting legislation can actually make it easier for employers to avoid compliance by providing them with greater discretion over how to meet regulatory demands. In the absence of specific legal requirements, it also makes it harder for safety representatives at the place of work to challenge employers when they feel that corners are being cut over safety.

Reducing the Cost of Compliance?

A purported complaint of business that has provided a key rationale in the deregulation initiative has been the supposedly 'arbitrary and idiosyncratic way' in which 'over-zealous' officials were enforcing health and safety law.[74] This rationale has also formed a continuing thread in the deliberations of the HSC internal review. Regulation *per se* has been seen as 'red tape'. The complaint of over-zealousness proved to be largely unfounded in an investigation by the National Audit Office.[75] This has not deflected the government from its preoccupation with 'educating inspectors'. As the DTI has put it, 'We want to do what we can to soften the impact of a visit from an enforcement official. In line with the Citizen's Charter principles we aim to make inspectors more sensitive to business realities.'[76] This philosophy is now being applied to newly introduced regulations. The announcement by the HSE of the long-awaited Construction (Design and Management) Regulations and ACoP (which came into effect on 31 March 1995) was accompanied by the soothing reassurance that, 'While we expect duty holders to comply, enforcement will be carried out sympathetically, especially during the first nine months after the regulations take effect.'[77]

The application the 'small business litmus test' to all legislation means that small business has come to serve as a screen for big business interests in securing comprehensive deregulation. The HSE's internal review, however, specifically rejected proposals, mooted by the DTI task forces, that there could be exemptions from health and safety law for small firms or self-employed people. Many of these firms operate in areas of high risk, a point that the internal review also observed. A number of researchers have pointed out that, precisely in the smaller firms where managerial commitment to health and safety of employees is often low and union organization generally too weak to exert pressure for change, the need is for greater external enforcement.[78]

However, as Barrett and James have observed, the adoption of a more rigorous enforcement policy *per se* is unlikely to improve safety standards, unless the resources for the HSE and local authority inspectorates are increased to meet the considerable proliferation in the number of workplaces, mainly small, that has occurred in the 1980s.[79] It has already been suggested that such resources are unlikely to be forthcoming in the immediate future.

A priority for 1995/96 for the HSC was to issue a consultation document on 'new approaches' to helping small firms comply with the law, which was to concentrate on 'problems of communication' and advice on health and safety. Problems of compliance are not confined to the small business sector. The current economic climate has directly exposed intrinsic weaknesses of the self-regulatory philosophy of the Health and Safety at Work Act, which, even in its original formulation, took insufficient account of poor compliance. It is now manifestly inadequate in a period when, along with the widespread growth of subcontracting and self-employment, the small business sector has undergone expansion while large-scale employment in manufacturing has substantially contracted. The change to a more fragmented industrial structure in itself makes safety more difficult to manage, an issue that the HSC is also to examine further in a discussion document.

Dawson's study, for instance, found that, in industries characterized by high levels of subcontracting, accident rates were high and workforce involvement was 'almost completely absent'.[80] One key contributory factor the research identified was a failure to establish clear line management responsibility and accountability for health and safety, in the absence of which, 'the notion of self-regulation begins to break down'.[81] The emphasis accorded by Robens to self-regulation by industry, rather than external enforcement, has revealed its definite 'limits'. As Dawson points out, these limits to self-regulation are ultimately cost controlled:

> The costs to the businesses of meeting a particular safety provision, i.e. the 'sacrifice', will depend on solvency and market conditions. The very standard of 'reasonable practicability', if defined simply in terms of the employer's cost–benefit equation, is inevitably affected by the recession.[82]

Similar dislocation and fragmentation of established coherent safety procedures may well be accompanying the privatization process. Major public utilities such as gas, coal and rail transport are of particular concern. Though gas, for example, retains its own 'regulator', it is clear that the massive cutback in safety inspections (saving £8 million out of a total budget of £9 million) cannot be attributed solely to the sudden availability of 'maintenance free' pipes. New deregulated gas suppliers will enter the market in 1996. They will be obliged to produce safety cases detailing their safety management systems, but no new funds have been made available for their inspection and assessment by the HSE. By contrast, a new division has been created to oversee offshore safety cases. In rail transport, where, as in the offshore industry, safety cases specifying detailed risk assessment have been introduced, it is interesting that an early safety seminar organized by British Rail was not attended by a single potential rail franchisee. Apart from offshore safety, the attempt to preserve existing standards in the railways and the coal industry following privatization has been a major preoccupation of the HSE's legislative programme recently.[83]

Paradoxically, in some of the recently deregulated public utilities, newly appointed chairmen are currently complaining of increasing regulatory interference. Ian Vallance, the chairman of British Telecom, in his address to shareholders at the 1992 annual general meeting, commented on:

> the need for the regulator to stick to preserving the overall public interest, leaving management to decide on how the business is to be run, free from detailed regulatory interference.
>
> Regrettably, the trend in regulation in the UK – and not just telecommunications – appears to be towards greater intervention in management, without a clearly expressed vision or set of long term objectives.
>
> Regulators can be tempted to embark on a course of social engineering, or to tinker with operational matters in response to short term political and media pressures. Paradoxically, there is a real danger that regulated privatised businesses may be subject to more state interference than they were as nationalised industries.[84]

This suggests that the simple descending linear trajectory of the deregulation initiative, as envisaged by government, may actually result in a cycle of reregulation, albeit reregulation of a more general goal-setting character. Yet this process of reregulation is likely to be equally, if not more, vulnerable to economic pressures.

THE REAL COSTS OF COMPLIANCE

In the current period, the standard of 'reasonable practicability' has been forcefully circumscribed by the deregulation initiative. The DTI task forces' notion of compliance cost assessment expresses this unambiguously. Regulators should avoid making regulations that are 'out of proportion to the benefits obtained'.[85] Hitherto, reasonable practicability and its implicit cost–benefit equation had incorporated some element of wider societal interests to be weighed against the rather narrower interests of the individual employer. This was the positive element of social value judgement in cost–benefit analysis. The task forces' view of cost–benefit analysis reveals an interesting redefinition of the notion of 'reasonable practicability' at the heart of the Health and Safety at Work Act: 'HSE should assess regulations and requirements on the basis of professional, business-based costs and benefits, minimising the application of "the principle of extreme caution" and unsubstantiable benefits.'[86]

Michael Heseltine has claimed that the Deregulation Act would save industry 'hundreds of millions of pounds, at a very modest assumption'.[87] It is an assumption whose logic, however, even on its own restricted terms, is severely flawed. Dawson argues that:

> the costs of any compliance may be less than the costs of accidents experienced in the absence of inspection and enforcement, even where the calculation is focused on the cost to the employer rather than on the costs to society as a whole. This is because accidents and ill health do actually impose considerable costs upon employers. For example, there are the direct costs of stoppages of work, lost management and labour time and compensation payments, as well as the indirect costs of lowering morale and recruitment problems. These are important considerations quite apart from any fines or other penalties imposed by the courts or the enforcement officers. When the costs are considered from the point of view of the wider society, then one must also include health service costs, disability pensions and other benefits which may accrue to the victims.[88]

An attempt to quantify these costs had been made by the HSE itself based on case studies of the cost of accidents at work combined with data from the previously referred to 1990 Labour Force Survey.[89] These estimates revealed that workplace accidents and work-related ill-health cost individuals and their families around £1 billion a year (at

1990 prices) in reduced incomes and additional expenditures. The total cost, allowing for the further cost of pain, grief and suffering, was £4.3 billion a year, net of compensation. Workplace accidents and work-related ill-health cost employers between £4 billion and £9 billion a year in total, with about £900 million for injuries and £600 million for illness, equivalent to between 5 and 10 per cent of all UK industrial companies' gross trading profits or between £170 and £360 per person employed. The total cost to society as a whole was between £11 billion and £16 billion a year, equivalent to between 2 and 3 per cent of total gross domestic product. Work-related illness alone accounted for between £4 and £5 billion of this cost, and accidents between £6 and £11 billion.

These figures augment those produced in an earlier HSE study.[90] Rather than providing estimates of the cost of health and safety management failures at national level, the study examined costs at the level of individual workplaces through a series of case studies. Among the five organizations participating were a construction firm, a food manufacturer, a transport company, an NHS hospital and a North Sea oil production platform. The study included only those accidents which participating organizations agreed could have been prevented by the application of existing procedures or other cost-effective measures. All accidents were costed irrespective of whether they caused injuries or ill-health, and both direct costs and opportunity costs were taken account of, as well as whether the costs could be recovered from insurance. The results are summarized in Table 10.1.

Table 10.1   *The costs of workplace accidents*

	Total loss (£ thousand)	Annualized (£ thousand)	Loss representing
Construction site	245	700	8.5% tender price
Creamery	244	975	1.4% operating costs
Transport company	49	196	1.8% operating costs, 37% profits
Oil platform	941	3,764	14.2% potential output
Hospital	99	397	5% annual running costs

Figures quoted are actual at time of study; no adjustment has been made for inflation. Study 1 lasted 18 weeks; studies 2–5 for 13 weeks each.
Source: HSC (1993) (see note 90).

Table 10.1 shows that losses of a significant scale are incurred in all cases. Had the losses not been incurred, most of the money saved would have contributed to profits.[91] Le Guen, head of HSE's Risk Assessment Policy Unit, observes that the number of incidents is considerable; in most cases, the average cost of individual incidents is small; and the ratio of events resulting in injury or ill-health to those where only damage to property occurred is high (particularly so in oil production). Contrary to employers' popular beliefs, most of the costs could not be recovered from insurance.

Le Guen comments that these results, taken together with the costs derived from the wider Labour Force Survey study previously referred to, 'have added considerable weight to the arguments previously mooted by some leading industrialists and leading health and safety professionals that, for many firms in the UK, failure costs can be greater than the combined prevention and appraisal costs'.[92] As far as the offshore oil platform was concerned, the 262 preventable events in 13 weeks cost over £940,000. This was said to be equivalent (at a cost of around £3.75 million per year) to shutting the platform down for one day a week. Of these losses, only one part in twelve was insured. Thus, around 48 days a year of production were being totally lost.[93]

These figures do not simply provide cost–benefit arguments for good safety management. That the character of the incidents was generally small scale and preventable leads straight back to the argument for enhanced workforce participation as a key arena of accident prevention. As MacFarlane argues, 'It is, however, precisely those smaller less dramatic incidents causing the most loss which can be targeted by workforce participation.'[94] This is also, of course, where the currently fashionable human resources rhetoric of 'safety culture' and 'empowerment' meets the reality of a system of industrial relations in which the 'fear factor' often undermines employee attempts to voice everyday safety concerns.

A more speculative, but equally interesting, attempt to calculate the 'direct cost burden' of the HSE itself as a regulatory authority has been provided by IPMS (Institute of Professionals, Managers and Specialists), the trade union that organizes the HSE's inspectorates. The financial year 1992–93 was examined and a cost of £175 million estimated for the HSE. Accident rates overall are reducing at a rate of 5 per cent per year, more owing to the recession and labour market changes than anything else. However, if only 1 per cent of the reduction in accident rates (a saving of about £150 million a year) is attributed to improvements owing to heightened awareness and improved regulations directly resulting from HSE's operations, then HSE is 'an organisation that effectively operates at a zero cost (or very close to it) to the public purse'.[95] Such calculations, while not conclusive, are nevertheless authoritative and offer an alternative view of the 'regulatory burden' that can be directly weighed against compliance cost assessment.

The government's plan to eliminate the industrial injury compensation scheme creates a further incentive to employers to neglect workplace safety as, in future, employees can only recover damages by suing employers for negligence. The government's expectation of saving £600 million per annum has to be contrasted with the additional cost borne by individuals and society. Victims of industrial diseases such as asbestosis (whose numbers are expected to triple) have discovered that their compensation may be reduced via the Compensation Recovery Unit, which takes into account any income and disability support victims have received prior to court settlements. This move is in line with legislation that now requires employers to fund statutory sick pay without any government contribution, a move that is likely to create additional pressures on employees to ignore their illnesses. People who are seriously injured at work could be left without compensation, because companies with several subsidiaries are now allowed to take out a maximum insurance policy of £10 million in total, rather than £2 million per each subsidiary, as previous legislation required. And the Act which established employers' insurance liability, the 1969 Employers' Liability (Compulsory Insurance) Act, is now under review. The desocialization of the costs of illness and accidents, together with moves towards private medical insurance and health care provision, marks a significant departure from previous assumptions of social welfare and insurance.

In a hostile climate of deregulation, the growing tension in the emphasis on self-regulation as against enforcement is now being articulated at the highest level within the HSE. Rimington himself neatly summed up the dilemma now facing HSE: 'HSE often finds itself between a rock and a hard place, with criticism from some quarters of "over-zealous" behaviour by inspectors, and from other quarters of lack of "zeal", e.g. in pursuing individuals for health and safety offences.'[96] Squeezed between a public increasingly conscious of and concerned about the lack of individual and corporate account-ability, and a government dogmatically committed to removing any 'interference' with market forces, the uncomfortable position of the HSE can be sympathized with. The philosophical roots of the HSE as a regulatory authority lie in the consensus-seeking assumptions of the Robens Committee's pre-1979 political process and the assumption of equal partnership and responsibility. The mutual incompatibility of the HSE's different aims in the current period is starkly revealed. These are 'encouraging well-informed public discussion of the nature, scale and tolerability of risk' as part of 'the processes of democratic decision-making', and, at the same time, 'providing advice and information as required to Ministers'.[97]

Neil Hamilton MP, formerly Under Secretary of State for Corporate Affairs at the DTI, was the self-proclaimed 'deregulation minister' responsible for steering the Deregulation Bill through Parliament before he fell victim to allegations of sleaze and reluctantly tendered his resignation. In typically trenchant style, he had proclaimed the core of his government's view. Referring to the King's Cross fire, the *Marchioness* Thames pleasure boat sinking and other similar occurrences, he observed, 'Our response to recent large scale disasters has been out of all proportion to the disasters themselves.'[98] In a radio interview for the BBC *Opinion* programme, he had a chance to expound the deregulation equation with breathtaking frankness:

> The total amount of money which is generated by boats performing the kind of services which the *Marchioness* performed was £71 million per annum, and the costs of the regulations which are proposed are £27 million. Now, that is a very large figure for a very small market, and when you consider that although that was one dreadful accident with fifty-one deaths, for the whole of the rest of the century there were only twenty-nine deaths in similar circumstances, we have to ask ourselves whether the costs of regulation are proportionate to the risk. After all, risk is an essential part of life. [99]

It goes without saying that the relatives of the victims, who organized themselves and won a re-opening of the inquest (which returned a verdict of unlawful killing), have taken a rather different view. What was significant about the *Marchioness* disaster was not so much the failure to comply with regulations, but rather the absence of regulation. In that sense the tragedy was a necessary consequence of an unregulated environment.

THE EUROPEAN DIMENSION

The UK government has encouraged other member states of the European Union to embark upon a similar process of compliance cost assessment to that which it is conducting domestically. [100] The UK government is currently co-sponsoring what is known as the Anglo-German Deregulation Group, which was formed in 1994, when both governments agreed that a group of eight businessmen should be invited to review and eliminate unnecessary legislation. This highlights an important dimension of deregulation: the interaction between government, industry, the HSE and Europe. The government's reluctance to embrace the 'social dimension' of the European Union has previously been noted as a consistent theme. It was reiterated by Michael Heseltine, during the debate on the Deregulation Bill: 'That Social Chapter represents the greatest regulatory overload in history. It is the surest way to choke off the investment boom from overseas companies.'[101]

Under the heading 'Tackling European Regulation', the DTI's *Cutting Red Tape* document spoke of 'unnecessary and over-prescriptive EC legislation' and the need to alert the European Commission 'to any inconsistencies in the way member states implement and enforce European law'.[102] UK business leaders have voiced resentment, alleging that they enforce EU regulation more stringently than other Community members and that, in consequence, British business suffers from regulatory 'over-implementation'. [103] It is an attitude voiced by the CBI which has lobbied hard, and with some considerable success, to ensure that 'opt-outs' from European social legislation have been secured by the British government, most spectacularly from the Maastricht Treaty obligations.

While the Social Charter in itself creates no enforceable rights, the resulting Social Action Programme and the directives on worker protection which flow from it have the potential to do so. Under the Single European Act 1986, which introduced Article 118A into the Treaty of Rome, the Commission was given the authority to adopt directives laying down 'minimum requirements'. The system of qualified majority voting now applies to working environment issues. This prevents one single government, such as the current Conservative administration, from effectively blocking legislation by veto in respect of health and safety matters. This Act, and most of the European directives, applied to member governments by December 1992. However, the 'doctrine of subsidiarity' implies that individual national governments retain the power to enact 'strong' or 'weak' versions of EU proposals.

The European Framework Directive (89/391/EEC) adopted by the Council on 12 June 1989, and the various 'daughter' directives that have been promulgated, do impact on British domestic legislation, whatever the UK government might wish.[104] The framework directive seeks 'the introduction of measures to encourage improvements in the safety and health of workers'. It places broad general duties on employers and employees, but the primary responsibility for ensuring health and safety is put on employers. Employers are now obliged to assess the risks at work and take measures to prevent or reduce them. Yet, while the framework directive has strengthened existing UK regulations by enhancing employee information, consultation rights, training and job protection in respect of safety at work, James has argued that these reluctantly and unevenly applied advances should not be overestimated.[105]

As a direct result of European legislation, the Trade Union Reform and Employment Rights Act 1993 contains provisions which protect the right of employees not to suffer employment 'detriment' for health and safety reasons.[106] A worker may now remove himself or herself from hazard and cease work if it is anticipated that there is danger. Legislation against victimization arising out of health and safety issues has received a welcome impetus from Europe, although its efficacy has yet to be tested in the courts. The mere presence of a law on the statute book is insufficient to alter employer attitudes, unless it can be demonstrated that there is a real determination to secure compliance on the part of enforcement agencies. In any event, the remedy available to the individual worker remains after the fact and may not be sufficient (as with claims for unfair dismissal related reinstatement at industrial tribunals) to secure the individual's re-employment.

While EU legislation has resulted in marginally enhanced rights for British workers, the emphasis in European directives is upon participation in decision-making about safety, not through organized trade unions, but rather through the workforce in general. European law enhances the rights of the individual, rather than those of collectivities. In this respect it poses no real challenge to the philosophy of the current administration. The UK government, however, has rejected the corporatist–tripartite thrust of European legislation, with its emphasis on 'balanced participation' between industry's 'social partners'. Whether the corporatist thrust of European legislation can be effective is in itself questionable. The propositions of 'balanced participation' involving unions in lawmaking, and the focus on individual rather than collective rights in the workplace, are largely incompatible. This incompatibility quite possibly allows business to limit real safety involvement of unions as well as the enforcement of safety regulations at the firm level.

The UK government finds the broader scope of the new proposals brought forward since the adoption of Article 118A in 1988, which requires member states to cooperate in matters of accident prevention and occupational welfare, objectionable. The DTI has spoken of 'the potential for these Directives to go beyond pure health and safety considerations and to venture into industrial relations issues'.[107] The DTI has asserted that the HSE supported the government's opposition to qualified majority voting applying to Article 118A because of the fear 'that health and safety could be used as a Trojan horse by the European Commission to legislate on industrial issues'. The securing of assurances that health and safety legislation would not be so used was, in fact, the British government's sole success in its humiliating climbdown over the extension of qualified majority voting as a consequence of the enlargement of the Community.[108]

The ambivalent attitude of the HSE to European legislation is a matter of real concern. The leaking of an internal document of the HSE's management board suggested that it would do its best to secure a bare minimum of compliance and, on occasion, deliberately water down the objectives of the directives, where directives were deemed to go further than existing UK law.[109] This 'minimalist' approach, it should be said, was being floated during 1992, designated as the European Year of Safety, Hygiene at Work and Health Protection.

As far as the specific question of enforcement of EU legislation is concerned, member states are now required to ensure that the legal provisions necessary for implementation are put in place. Yet, as one commentator has warned, major difficulties confront any attempt to raise non-compliance by a government at a European level.[110] In fact, the European Court to date has made no significant rulings in the field of workplace safety and health, with the possible exception of a recent determination requiring UK public sector employers to consult with employees' representatives in non-union areas on health and safety matters.[111] While the UK record on enforcement may be open to major criticism, it nevertheless remains in advance of a number of other member states. Thus the government is not under any pressure from Europe to improve resources available to the HSE for enforcement.

While embarking on a programme of domestic deregulation, the British government used its time in the Presidency of the European Commission (in the second half of 1992) to encourage some form of initiative to improve enforcement in other member states as a means of ensuring that its own industry was not placed at a competitive disadvantage.[112] The European TUC has, since the early 1990s, begun to consider specific criteria for enforcement, but it faces strong employer opposition. A future directive on enforcement might be a step in the right direction but, as in the field of general employment rights, says James, 'improvements in occupational health and safety can only be secured where the financial interests of employers are adequately counterbalanced by pressures from their workforces and external enforcement agencies'. [113]

TRADE UNIONS AND HEALTH AND SAFETY

Since the mid-1970s, the trade union movement has played a pivotal role in health and safety at the workplace through the system of trade union appointed safety committees and safety representatives. Section 2(4) of the Health and Safety at Work Act, under which safety committees were established, provided for the appointment of safety representatives by 'recognized trade unions' (that is, by independent trade unions that the employer recognized for the purposes of collective bargaining on terms and conditions of employment). Section 2(5) of the Act required the election of safety representatives by the workforce instead of trade union appointment. This requirement was removed by the passage of the Employment Protection Act 1975. Thereafter, the Health and Safety at Work Act regulations became bound up with the legitimation of trade unions as the means of employee representation at the workplace on safety issues. The attempt to locate the role of the unions in safety representation within an orderly collective bargaining framework was part of the package of measures of the then Labour government's Social Contract of the mid-1970s, which promoted corporatist-style industrial relations.

The trade union movement itself had responded to the opportunities provided by the legislation to provide training and support for safety representatives on a nation-wide scale through TUC-sponsored and individual trade union shop stewards' health and safety training courses. Since the Safety Representatives and Safety Committees Regulations 1977 came into effect, over 200,000 safety representatives have been trained by the TUC. Many thousands more have attended individual union courses. It was this experience which led John Rimington of the HSE to comment, in his evidence to the Piper Alpha inquiry, on the valuable part played by safety representatives in the promotion of safety. For those who were appointed safety representatives, it was 'a very great strength' that they were appointed by the unions. As Rimington put it, 'The unions train them in quite a sophisticated way. They have the means of putting a great deal of power at the elbow of safety representatives where they care to do so.' [114]

As far as trade union training is concerned, however, the government grant which enabled the TUC to carry out its extensive programme was finally phased out in 1995. This is particularly alarming at a time when modern safety management requires that workforce representatives have more extensive and sophisticated training if they are to make a worthwhile contribution in the form of independent audit of increasingly complex safety assessments. Of even greater importance, as Rimington noted, is the 'power' that unions can give the individual representative. An accredited safety representative has traditionally enjoyed a measure of enhanced legal protection against victimization, which European legislation has now extended to all the workforce. Trade union backing has provided the confidence and authority for safety representatives to challenge management when necessary. By contrast, the individual safety representative (never mind the average employee), without the supportive context of a trade union constituency, will be to that degree more exposed to management pressure.

Many workplaces, particularly smaller establishments in which collective bargaining arrangements are absent, lack any form of safety committee. Nor do employees, in the absence of trade union recognition, have any statutory rights to safety representation. Where safety committees exist, they do so on an *ad hoc* voluntary basis. A possible future target for deregulation may be the Safety Representatives and Safety Committees Regulations 1977, which provide for the appointment of trade union-nominated safety representatives (the major basis for employee involvement in health and safety at the workplace for nearly 20 years). European legislation, in particular the framework directive (89/391/EEC), could provide a convenient rationale for dismantling the existing arrangements. The irony of the government being able to use European law to undermine workers' rights in this area should not be lost.

One very interesting finding from the third Workplace Industrial Relations Survey (WIRS3) of some 2000 establishments suggests 'an increasing reluctance of individual employees to put themselves forward for representative roles in the late 1980s'.[115] It would appear that a degree of apprehension about performing the role of safety representative has become a prominent feature of industry in the current period of recession and employment contraction. The individual reluctance to stand was most marked where no committee structure existed, itself perhaps an indication of employees' inhibition as a result of their potential exposure as isolated individuals. WIRS3 also found a rise in the proportion of workplaces where managers dealt with health and safety issues without consultation, particularly in the non-unionized private sector. This is despite 'consultation' and 'empowerment' being managerial human resource buzz words.

WIRS3 noted some quite surprising trends, however. Despite recession and a decrease in influence in other areas of industrial relations, trade unions in 1990 were, overall, as involved in health and safety representation as they had been in 1984. Establishment-level health and safety committees included trade union representatives in around three-quarters (77 per cent) of cases, with little variation by broad sector of employment. The proportion of workplaces where some representatives were chosen by unions actually increased from 27 to 36 per cent. By contrast, there was a slight drop, from 48 to 41 per cent, [116] in the proportion of all representatives chosen by trade unions. This continuing and positive role is a likely future target for attack.[117] It would appear that the government may be getting ready to launch a backdoor attack on the role of workers' health and safety protection, in much the same way that it has done in the case of the HSE as the regulatory agency.

The possible undermining of the system of health and safety representation, accompanied by declining union recognition, diminishing central government financial support for trade union training, reduced funding for the HSE itself, the emphasis in European legislation on an all-inclusive individualized system of employee representation and the more general climate of legislative deregulation, pose new threats to the continued existence and effectiveness of the union-appointed safety representatives and committees. Yet research has shown that it is precisely in those plants with established trade union based safety committees that the best safety records are to be found.[118]

But the outlook is not entirely bleak. Explicit individual trade union opposition to deregulation is now achieving much sharper focus on issues of health and safety. This was reflected in motions from a wide range of unions to 1994's TUC and Scottish TUC conferences, and the prioritization of safety as a campaigning issue.[119] A number of unions have issued considered statements or documents on the dangers posed by health and safety deregulation.[120] There are also ongoing trade union led campaigns, such as the Construction Safety Campaign in the building industry, important union-supported research and publications such as *Hazards*, and various trade union and unemployed workers' resource centres.[121] Both within the structure of the HSC as a tripartite body and from the grass roots of the trade union movement, there is now an opportunity to broaden the debate about the future of occupational health and safety in the UK. A united public campaign, led by the trade union movement, could not only make an informed contribution to the future shape of health and safety law, but in so doing crystallize much of the wider public unease about the supposed benefits of privatization and deregulation. Deregulation poses a challenge to the trade union movement which, while it cannot be ignored, may provide new opportunities to portray trade unionism in a positive light.

The HSC's internal review has not produced the *carte blanche* that the government sought to dispose of health and safety legislation. However, if the present government succeeds, Britain will enter the twenty-first century with a health and safety regime that owes more to *laissez-faire* nineteenth-century attitudes on the part of employers. Legislation on health and safety is now perversely seen as creating a power asymmetry that benefits labour at the expense of capital. Veljanovski, a right-wing economist, exemplifies this view:

> Typically they [regulations] impose technical and legalistic standards which the employer must observe and which focus on increasing safety inputs rather than deterring accidents. For example, they require the employer to make capital expenditures such as purchasing machines with guards. This has the effect of raising the costs of capital while leaving labour relatively unregulated despite the fact that most accidents are the result either of worker carelessness or a combination of employer and worker carelessness. This benefits labour – safety legislation of this type taxes capital and leaves labour relatively unconstrained.[122]

The passage of the Deregulation and Contracting Out Act in November 1994, taken together with such sentiments as expressed above, does not bode well for the future of health and safety law.

NOTES

1. L. Snider, The regulatory dance: understanding reform processes in corporate crime (1991) 19 *International Journal of the Sociology of Law* 209.
2. HSC, *Annual Report 1993/94* (London: HMSO, 1994).
3. Deregulation Task Forces, *Proposals for Reform* (London: Task Force Support Unit, 1994).
4. DTI, 1994.
5. 237 HC Debs 151 (8 February 1994).
6. K. Williams, Recent legislation: deregulating occupational health and safety (1995) 24 *Industrial Law Journal* 133, p.139.
7. *Financial Times*, 20 January 1994.
8. *Safety Management*, February 1994, p. 2.
9. Robens, *Safety and Health at Work, Report of the Committee 1970–72* (London: HMSO, 1972), Cmnd 5034, para. 138.
10. *Ibid.*, para. 28.

11. *Ibid.*, para. 41.

12. A.D. Woolf, Robens Report – the wrong approach (1973) 4 *Industrial Law Journal* 88, p. 90.

13. *Ibid.*

14. Robens, *op. cit.*, para. 2.

15. Woolf, *op. cit.*, p. 90.

16. *Ibid.*, p. 91.

17. *Ibid.*, p. 93.

18. Robens, *op. cit.*, para. 66.

19. T. Nichols and P. Armstrong, *Safety or Profit: Industrial Accidents and the Conventional Wisdom* (1973).

20. J. Phillips, Economic deterrence and the prevention of industrial accidents (1976) 7 *Industrial Law Journal* 148.

21. *Ibid.*, p. 148.

22. *Ibid.*

23. *Ibid.*, p. 149.

24. C. Codrington and J.S. Henly, The industrial relations of injury and death: safety representatives in the construction industry (1981) 19 *British Journal of Industrial Relations* 297.

25. *Ibid.*, p. 302.

26. Robens, *op. cit.*, para. 15.

27. S. Dawson, P. Willman, M. Bamford and A. Clinton, *Safety at Work: The Limits of Self-regulation* (1988), p. 210.

28. Robens, *op. cit.*, para. 265.

29. W.G. Carson, *The Other Price of Britain's Oil* (1982).

30. HSC, *op. cit.*, pp. 108–9.

31. *Ibid.*, p. 110.

32. *Hazards Bulletin* (1993) no. 42, p.12.

33. D. Bergman, *The Perfect Crime?* (Sheffield: West Midlands Health and Safety Advice Centre, 1994).

34. *Safety Management,* January 1995, p.19.

35. G. Stevens, Workplace injury: a view from the HSE's trailer to the 1990 Labour Force Survey, *Employment Gazette,* December 1992, 621.

36. *Ibid.*

37. *Safety Management,* November 1993, p. 3.

38. Law Commission, *Involuntary Manslaughter* (London: HMSO, 1994), Consultative Paper no. 135.

39. *Scotsman,* 9 December 1994.

40. *Scotsman,* 22 April 1994.

41. *Safety Management,* February 1994, p. 6.

42. *Financial Times,* 17 March 1995.

43. HSC, *Annual Report 1992/93* (London: HMSO, 1993), p. xiv.

44. IPMS (Institute of Professionals, Managers, and Specialists), *Health and Safety: Keep It Together* (December 1993); *Health and Safety at Work,* May 1995, p. 4.

45. National Audit Office, *Enforcing Health and Safety Legislation in the Workplace* (London: HMSO, 1994).

46. HSC (1994), *op. cit.*, p. 20.

47. *Health and Safety at Work Act Newsletter,* no. 24 (25 January 1994), p. 4.

48. Dawson *et al., op. cit.*, p. 233.

49. HSC (1994), *op. cit.*, p. 11.

50. DTI, *Working with Business – a Code for Enforcement Agencies* (DTI, 1993).

51. The risks of cutting red tape, *Labour Research,* October 1993.

52. HSC (1993), *op. cit.*, p. xiii.

53. IPMS, *op. cit.*

54. *Scotsman,* 4 April 1994.

55. CBI, *Update on the Government's Deregulation Initiative, Health and Safety Consultative Committee (Confidential),* 1994.

56. HSC, *Review of Regulation: Interim Report* (London, 1993), p. xii.

57. *Ibid.*, para. 5.

58. *Ibid.*
59. HSC, *News Release,* May 1993.
60. HSC (1993), *op. cit.,* note 58.
61. HSC, *Review of Regulation: Main Report* (London, 1994).
62. *Ibid.,* p. 7.
63. *Ibid.,* p. 1.
64. J. Bacon, Regulation in review, *Safety Management,* April 1994, pp. 48–51.
65. *Ibid.*
66. Carson, *op. cit.*
67. J. Hendy, International trade and international trade union and workers' rights (the first Jack Hendy Memorial Lecture, Thames Valley University, 1994).
68. Bacon, *op. cit.,* p. 49.
69. HSC (1993), *op. cit.,* note 58, para. 22 iv.
70. HSC (1994), *op. cit.,* note 4.
71. HSC, *Rationalisation of risk assessment and other common provisions in health and safety legislation* (HSE, 1994), Discussion Document DD194.
72. *Ibid.,* p. 1.
73. HSC, *The Role and Status of Approved Codes of Practice,* (London: HMSO, 1995), Consultative Document CD85.
74. DTI, *Deregulation – Cutting Red Tape* (DTI, 1994).
75. National Audit Office, *op. cit.*
76. DTI, *op. cit.,* p. 7.
77. *Safety Management,* April 1995.
78. Dawson, *op. cit.,* p. 248.
79. B. Barrett and P. James, Safe systems: past, present – and future? (1988) 17 *Industrial Law Journal* 26.
80. Dawson, *op. cit.,* p. 247.
81. *Ibid.,* p. 253.
82. *Ibid.*
83. HSC (1994), *op. cit.,* note 4.
84. Cited in C. Veljanovski, *The Future of Industry Regulation in the UK,* European Policy Forum, January 1993.
85. DTI (1994), *op. cit.,* p. 76.
86. *Ibid.*
87. *Financial Times,* 20 January 1994.
88. Dawson, *op. cit.,* pp. 256–7.
89. N. Davies and P. Teasdale, *The Costs to the British Economy of Work Accidents and Work-related Ill Health* (London: HSE, 1994).
90. HSC, *The Cost of Accidents at Work* (London: HMSO, 1993).
91. J. Le Guen, Reaping the rewards of risk assessment, *Safety Management,* March 1994, p. 32.
92. *Ibid.,* p. 93.
93. C. MacFarlane, Maximising safety through better project management: understanding the problems that projects leave behind (University of Strathclyde, unpublished paper, 8 July 1993).
94. C. MacFarlane, Participation: the lost strand in offshore safety (paper presented at STUC International Conference, 1993).
95. IPMS, *op. cit.,* p. 9.
96. HSC (1993), *op. cit.,* note 45, p. xiv.
97. HSC, *Future Plan of Work 1992/93* (London: HMSO, 1992).
98. General & Municipal Boilermakers, *Direct,* March 1993.
99. BBC, *Opinion* (Radio 4 broadcast, 23 September 1993).
100. *Safety Management,* July 1994, p. 54.
101. 237 HC Debs 154 (8 February 1994).
102. DTI (1994), *op. cit.,* p. 7.
103. DTI, *Review of the Implementation and Enforcement of EC Law in the UK* (DTI, July 1993).
104. *Ibid.*

105. P. James, The European Community: a way forward for worker health and safety? (paper presented at STUC International Conference, 1993).

106. K. Miller, Worker participation in health and safety matters offshore (paper presented at STUC International Conference, 1993).

107. DTI (1993), *op. cit.*, p. 88.

108. *Financial Times*, 17 March 1994.

109. James, *op. cit.*, p. 66.

110. *Ibid.*, p. 69.

111. *Safety Management*, April 1995.

112. James, *op. cit.*, p. 70.

113. P. James, *The European Community: a Positive Force for UK Health and Safety Law?* (London: Institute of Employment Rights, 1993).

114. Cited in Lord Cullen, *The Public Inquiry into the Piper Alpha Disaster* (London: HMSO, 1990).

115. N. Millward, M. Stevens, D. Smart and R.W. Hawes, *Workplace Industrial Relations in Transition* (1992).

116. *Ibid.*, p. 163.

117. C. Storey and R. Barker, The safety representative is an endangered species (parts 1 and 2), *Health and Safety at Work*, July/August 1994.

118. D. Walters, Employee representation on health and safety in Britain and Europe (paper presented at STUC international conference, Glasgow, 1993).

119. TUC, *Better Safety Standards at Work: Setting the Safety Agenda* (London: Trades Union Congress, 1994).

120. GMB, *Freedom to Kill? The Case against Deregulation* (London: GMB, 1994).

121. D. Bergman, *Deaths at Work: Accidents or Corporate Crime* (London: WEA, 1991).

122. C. Veljanovski, *The Economics of Law* (London: The Institute of Economics Affairs, 1991), Hobart Paper 114.

11

EU Labour Law and UK Workers

Damian Brown

It is important to assess EU labour law realistically, not least because of the grand claims made for it by many Labour Party and trade union figures. Ron Todd notably described Europe as 'the only game in town', and there is a certain tendency to look towards the EU as a guardian of workers' rights. It may be that this is a reflection of the maxim 'my enemy's enemy is my friend', emerging from the 17 years of legislation directed against working people. But how can this be reconciled with the fact that the UK, along with Portugal, has implemented 92 per cent of European employment and social policy directives? Surely this should afford sufficient safeguards and protection. In order to answer the claims it may be useful to address the following questions:

1 What areas does EU labour law cover?
2 What are the needs of UK workers?
3 To what extent are those needs addressed?
4 Will EU labour law be able to address those needs in future?

The third and fourth questions involve an examination of social policy to date, future EU proposals, the role of the ECJ and the views of the political actors in Europe as well as in the UK.

THE AREAS COVERED

EU labour law covers a variety of different working relationships and many different types of worker. In the former category there is legislation on health and safety as well as redundancies and transfers of undertakings. In the latter category there is legislation protecting pregnant workers, young workers and temporary workers. The needs of the workforce and its composition are changing and the recent EU labour law directives are at least intended to deal with the concept of the so-called atypical worker and the needs of the increasing numbers of women at the workplace.

It is accepted that some of the areas covered by EU labour law therefore mark important advances in protection of employees. However, when we examine the directives that have received the most scrutiny, so far, in the ECJ and domestic courts, a clearer picture emerges of the protection afforded. While there are great expectations for the newer directives, their impact remains to be seen as there is no domestic or European case law. To that extent, any analysis of those directives is premature. While I accept that the analysis in the section below is partial, it is none the less necessary – these are the directives most people are familiar with and about which claims are made. If they are found to be wanting then the new directives may need to be treated with caution.

The Collective Redundancies Directive (75/129)

On the whole the directive offers workers mild consultation rights in the face of closures. There are no co-determination rights in this or any other directive. Davies[1] has pointed to the differences between the draft directive, which allowed local authorities to exercise a veto over redundancies, and that adopted, which merely provided for consultation. Whether a local authority or some other body chooses to exercise the veto in any particular case would involve a degree of public scrutiny and accountability in a reorganization. That should encourage management to act in a more rational and humane way than might otherwise be the case. This is not a very ambitious goal, it must be admitted, but it is difficult to disagree with Wedderburn's conclusion that the directive is designed not to protect workers but to protect business by ensuring that all employers have the same consultation obligations.[2] Perhaps the best illustration of the limitations of the directive in action is the pit closures of 1992. Although the government's action was delayed, rights of consultation – as Wedderburn ruefully remarks – 'rarely stop closures'.[3]

Equal Pay Directive (75/117), Equal Treatment Directive (76/207) and Article 119

The increased employment of women in the labour market and the new and diversified forms of employment have brought new problems for women employees. The directives clearly mark an important step forward in terms of individual rights and combating cases of individual discrimination. But their impact on the sex-segregated labour market has been much less significant, although there has been some narrowing of the gap between men and women's earnings.[4] Davies points out that the impact of the equality legislation in the UK was 'relatively slight' because domestic labour law was to some extent ahead of Community labour law and it was not until 1982 that the ECJ decided that the directive and Article 119 required states to have laws ensuring equal pay for work of equal value.[5] It is also important to remember that many of the developments in equality have been as a result of ECJ decisions in developing the very concept of 'equality'[6] and in establishing procedural safeguards and direct effect.[7]

It has been suggested that a major flaw in the equality directives is that they empower only the individual worker and there is no attempt to secure group justice. A different approach to the problem of inequality might address the institutional problems and could include an obligation on employers to eliminate discrimination in their pay structures, involving trade unions at all levels.[8] This is not, however, a model that appeals to the EU.

The Acquired Rights Directive (77/187)

Much of the litigation on the acquired rights directive so far has concerned its applicability to the various forms of privatization. The ECJ has taken a bold stance and extended the directive to contracting out of services in both public and private sectors. While the directive gives some protection to workers in a transfer situation, and again stresses consultation, the remedies for breach of the consultation provisions and any dismissals are left to the individual state to determine.

Business transfers and reorganizations tend to involve the fragmentation of the labour force and usually reduced terms and conditions. Time and again domestic courts have refused to intervene and have given effect to the managerial prerogative at the expense of the workers' need to resist cuts in their terms and conditions. So, although the directive proclaims that 'it is necessary to provide for the protection of employees in the event of a change of employer, in particular to ensure that their rights are safeguarded', at the end of the day we are left with the protection in domestic law that, as we will see, is of little use at all. In addition, if an employee refuses to transfer, his or her only remedy is the perilous course of claiming constructive dismissal (if there are changes in terms). If he or she simply objects to the change in employer there is not even a dismissal.[9]

The Insolvency Directive (80/987)

The insolvency directive is largely implemented by EP(C)A ss. 122–128,[10] and it sets out to protect some of an employee's claims during insolvency. The protection is of a limited nature, with a ceiling on the amounts preserved and, while one cannot argue with the accordance of preference to employees, one can ask (as Davies has[11]) whether the application of the acquired rights directive would better protect such rights. An obligation on a receiver to consult with employees would be of some use, since it would provide employees in the undertaking with some influence over decisions concerning their future. Sadly, the directive does not attempt to provide any such right.

WHAT ARE THE NEEDS OF UK WORKERS?

In 1993, NACAB conducted a survey of CAB clients and their employment-related problems and found that these were the third largest subject of enquiries after consumer debt and social security.[12] The report pointed out that the main complaints included unilateral changes to terms and conditions and systematic exploitation of the qualifying periods for various statutory rights. The problem of changes to terms and conditions is a common one in times of recession. When a business is restructured, labour costs are often the first that are cut and the individual employee has little in the legal armoury to help her resist. If the employer breaches the contract the employee can claim damages at common law or underpayments pursuant to the Wages Act 1986. The clever employer knows that it does not need to breach the contract, however. It can instead terminate with notice and offer new terms and conditions. The employee who signs, no matter how reluctantly, will be surprised that legally he or she has not done so under duress – the ready availability of social security provides an alternative to agreement.[13] What of statute, one might wonder. The employee can claim unfair dismissal even if he or she accepts the new terms. But the employer can simply point to s. 57(1)(b) of the EP(C)A, and utter the mantra-like phrase of 'some other substantial reason' or perhaps 'redundancy' under s. 57(2)(c) as the reason for the dismissal.

The burden on the employer in proving the reason is slight and challenges based on alternatives to cuts in labour costs will not succeed. Once the reason is proved, the focus of an industrial tribunal's enquiry will pass on to the reasonableness of the decision to dismiss. The reasonableness of the employer's decision to dismiss is judged at the time of the dismissal, and if most of the workforce has accepted the new terms this is a factor that weighs against any refuseniks.[14] In the circumstances the individual worker is entirely justified in worrying about such situations.

The concerns revealed by the NACAB's report are echoed in Waddington and Whitston's survey[15] of union members, which shows that a main concern of active union members at their workplace is the introduction of human resource management (HRM) techniques. Concerns relate, in particular, to 'commitment strategies' (e.g. team briefings and quality circles), measures to increase flexibility and approaches intended to individualize aspects of the employment relationship. These are often (although not necessarily) attempts to communicate direct with the workforce and to by-pass unions or, at the very least, to operate in tandem with existing collective structures and practices. A further concern was the interpretation of collective agreements, something that may lead one to conclude that the active representation of members by shop stewards was something implicitly accepted as a benefit by those surveyed. Workplace health and safety, as one might expect, also had some prominence, but by far the biggest concern was management attitudes and styles. This is supported by the MSF *Quarterly Survey of Workplace Opinion*, which has consistently reported that fears about job security, health and safety and management attitudes are the issues that figure most in members' responses.

It may be felt, at first glance, that to empower workers against management attitudes is a surreal exercise. However, if we ask ourselves what function labour law should perform, the answer ought to be clear.[16] Labour law should support and extend the concepts of democracy and social justice in employer/employee relations. Democracy is not just a right to vote in elections but is a means of empowering the members of our society. It can be reflected in provisions respecting the worker's right to choose to have representation, or by a right to participation and even access to effective sanctions to promote workers' economic and social well-being. Social justice demands that, in an unequal relationship, the unequal partner is empowered, thus assisting in both democracy and the achievement of another of the aims of social justice.

In concrete terms, the shaping of labour law to fulfil these goals demands a wide-ranging review to open management decisions on

recruitment, discipline during employment and termination of employment to effective democratic scrutiny and accountability. It includes
giving workers rights to participation and consultation and to take
effective action when consultation breaks down – this includes access to
effective judicial remedies as well as industrial action. It includes
requiring the courts to judge the actions of an employer not against that
of the 'reasonable employer', but against broader standards of
individual rights and civil liberties. An individual rights culture will
probably only flourish with collective support. Where the individual
feels isolated in exercising rights, the law will not be used. The law must
engender a confidence among workers and a further task of labour law
must be to promote union membership – the only guarantee of
effective day-to-day policing of management.

We can sum up the concerns articulated above as being about job
security and terms and conditions, and about having the right to object,
mainly through representation by independent trade unions. To what
extent, then, do the European rights outlined above address this
agenda?

TO WHAT EXTENT ARE THE NEEDS OF UK WORKERS ADDRESSED?

While some directives address the issues that arise from a changing
labour market (e.g. the working time directive and other measures
dealing with 'atypical' workers) and provide a measure of protection for
workers, they do not address the questions of job security, trade unions
and the other concerns of UK workers. As seen above, the idea of a
veto on redundancy closures by the workforce or local authorities was
dropped at an early stage. The most that the collective redundancies
and acquired rights directives do is provide for consultation. Neither
strengthens the position of unions, and both may weaken union
presence. Indeed, the absence of any concrete programme of labour
rights has been described by Wedderburn as 'a hole in the heart of
Community labour law'.[17] Similarly, the lack of support for freedom of
association and collective bargaining threatens to undermine whatever
prospects there are for social dialogue, as we shall see below.

As far as democracy is concerned, although the Commission
proceedings on the failure of the UK government to enact any
machinery to ensure worker consultation in the collective redundancy

and acquired rights directives were successful, the Advocate General took the view that legislation providing for a temporary committee of workers might be enough to fulfil the requirements of the directive.[18] The ECJ was silent on this aspect and there are strong arguments against the Advocate General's position, but one can see the obvious attraction to the government and employers of legislation providing for consultation with workers on an *ad hoc* basis if and when redundancies and transfers take place.[19] Such legislation would contain the usual 'special circumstances' exclusion for the lawyers to fight over. As John Kelly argues,[20] it is highly unlikely that a system of works councils will promote any resurgence in trade unionism, as they form an easy rival organization for employers to support.

The existing directives have been disappointing at best. The ECJ has been left to expand the protection of workers by developing the concepts of direct and indirect effect (they are found nowhere in the Treaty or directives), and to develop enforcement principles (such as the liability of the state for non-implementation of directives) and procedures. Nearly all directives, although establishing principles, leave the precise nature of the remedy to the state. This has left UK workers exposed owing to the inadequacy of common law and statutory remedies.

Examining just why the directives have had such a limited effect is useful, since this might help us in our prognosis for the future. The blame for most of the current failings in domestic labour law can be levelled quite properly at the post-1979 governments. But, as far as the EU is concerned, Davies [21] and Wedderburn have consistently identified as the chief obstacle to the development of social policy the fact that it is wedded so firmly to economic integration.

One of the first steps towards the foundation of the EU was in 1951 with the Schuman Plan, which resulted in the European Coal and Steel Community. This was not simply a trade agreement – it was felt that greater cooperation between nation states in economic areas would lead to greater cooperation and unity at the political level and avoid a repetition of the war from which Europe was still emerging. Trade liberalization, however, was the primary aim of the Treaty of Rome and, although it contained a number of articles dealing with the social dimension (e.g. see Articles 48–51, 117–21 and arguably 54(3)(g)), it concentrated mainly on trade issues (the customs-free zone, common external tariff and the Common Agricultural Policy). Social issues were only a concern where they interfered with the goal of market integration, so that even an enthusiast for the potential of European labour law like Bercusson freely admits that 'labour, and even more so, social matters, were relatively marginal to the original objectives of the EEC'.[22]

The view of the secondary nature of social policy was not confined to the founders of the EU. Even the ILO report, commissioned by the member states shortly after the Treaty of Rome, referred to social legislation as a necessary step to deal with the consequent problems emerging from the economic measures.[23] This view becomes even more striking when one considers the ILO arguments against labour market regulation. The committee of experts asserted that general differences in labour costs between countries did not impede fair competition between member states where the higher labour cost merely reflected greater productivity. The ILO concluded that member states need not harmonize labour standards in general, but only in certain specific instances, most notably gender discrimination. The argument for regulation in this area was that inequality of pay might distort competition by reducing a member state's labour costs in a particular industry below the general level. So the protection afforded is aimed at the market as opposed to the individual worker. As Davies puts it, 'Legislation could be justified only where necessary to remove obstacles to the proper functioning of the market, and it was anticipated that such occasions for legislating would be few.'[24] This rationale for intervention against gender discrimination makes the lack of any corresponding protection for ethnic minority workers, save in the freedom of movement provision, even more lamentable.

The end of the 1960s marked the end of the boom for many of Europe's economies and some of the above labour law directives were brought in to protect workers against the inevitable restructuring of national and international economies. The political impetus behind the Social Action Programme was the fact that the benefits of economic growth had not been evenly spread throughout member states and the EU. A social policy might just, in the words of Michael Shanks (a former Director General for Social Affairs), ensure that the benefits of growth were evenly dispersed and defuse the criticism of the common market as simply a device for business to exploit the benefits of integration. The Social Action Programme was an attempt to create greater social cohesion by forging a European identity for the citizens of the Community, thereby furthering the economic project, which was coming under attack. It was accepted that economic progress would lead to redundancies and closures and there should be rights for employees in such a situation.

In 1985, when Jacques Delors became President of the Commission, the internal market received a kick-start with a completion date of 1992. Allied to this project were Economic and Monetary Union, a European central bank and a single currency. The new lease of life required amendment to the Treaty partly as a way of getting around the

intransigent stance of the UK government, and the new Article 118A
allowed majority (as opposed to unanimous) voting on 'improvements,
especially in the working environment, as regards the health and safety
of workers'. The UK government was content to vote in favour of this
measure at the time. Health and safety was one of the first areas in
which the state had intervened and high sickness/absentee rates affect
productivity. One wonders, however, with the Deregulation and
Contracting Out Act 1995 and the current interest in deregulation of
health and safety, whether it now regrets its decision.

The Social Charter emerged from the report of the Commission
working party, *The Social Dimension of the Internal Market*. Adopted
by all the member states except the UK, it proclaimed in its preamble
that social policy has a role equal to economic policy in achieving a
unified market. The protocol was qualified, however, by the concept of
subsidiarity – that legislation at Community level may not necessarily
be the best way to implement the proposals in the charter. A second
qualification was the 'social dialogue' (the achievement of goals through
collective bargaining), to which we return below. A third emerged from
Article 2(2) of the protocol, which stated that any new social directive
should avoid 'imposing administrative, financial and legal constraints in
a way which would hold back the creation and development of small
and medium-sized undertakings'.

The Commission's Action Programme, designed to implement the
charter, drew back from some of the original proposals. Of 21
proposals for directives, 15 have been implemented to date, including
91/533 (proof of employment relationship enacted in TURERA 1993),
91/383 on health and safety (and the six pack regulations on specific
health and safety hazards), 92/85 (providing greater maternity
protection), 93/104 (on working time) and 92/56 (amending the
collective redundancies directive). The Action Programme proposed
that there would be some method of implementing a European works
council.

But collective bargaining and freedom of association are all matters
that are ruled out of the protocol (Article 2(6)). As stated earlier, a
commitment to collective rights enhances the rights of individuals and,
some would say, is indivisible from them. Attempts to make good this
gap by the social dialogue (a relationship somewhere between
consultation and collective bargaining) are, as Wedderburn points
out, inadequate, not least because collective bargaining can be
conflictual rather than consensual (something the dialogue does not
seem able to accommodate). What happens when the dialogue breaks
down? The Commission seems unable to envisage such a situation.
The social dialogue cannot replace collective bargaining and does not

necessarily encompass it. In any event both are arguably underpinned by the need for strong independent trade unions.

No one would suggest that it is an easy task to harmonize EU labour laws. After all, we must all bear in mind Kahn-Freund's warning about simply grafting legislation from one society on to another. Besides the problems outlined above, the spoiling action by the UK and other neo-liberal governments has meant that a number of directives were simply not implemented or were diluted.

FUTURE DEVELOPMENTS

There are three areas to which we should look when attempting to star-gaze and assess future prospects. The first concerns Commission proposals: if the Commission is following the same policies hopes ought not to be raised too high. The second concerns the composition and actions of the ECJ: this is relevant given the important role it has played in the implementation of labour policy. The third relates to the political will or political composition of the member states.

The Commission

In 1993 the Commission published the consultative Green Paper, *Options for the Union*,[25] followed in July 1994 by the White Paper, *European Social Policy – A Way Forward for the Union*.[26] The Green Paper trotted out the familiar view that economic progress and social progress are similar goals and advanced the proposition that EU integration is perceived as resulting in an improvement in social and living standards. 'There can be no social progress without wealth creation', it proclaimed, and went on to stress, not unreasonably perhaps, that the focus on labour law would shift to the rights of citizens in general.

The White Paper repeats these themes. Again, labour law has a diminished role. The Commission believes that 'Jobs must continue to come top of the agenda and the proposals on employment and training in this White Paper are an integral part of the process initiated by the White Paper on growth, competitiveness and employment.'

Let us put to one side any disagreements we might have about the strategies that are proposed to achieve better employment levels. Others must deal with those arguments,[27] although we may agree with the European TUC General Secretary's recent comments that trade unionists are fed up with the gulf between EU politicians' concern at mass unemployment and the absence of any policies to tackle the problem.[28] We must also set aside any disagreements we have on whether labour rights result in less productivity. But we may find ourselves in agreement with Szyszczak,[29] who sees in the White Paper an 'underlying tension of *how* to regulate the labour market', resulting in a compromise between those who believe that labour rights result in higher costs and loss of competitiveness and those who believe that competitiveness is the key and that labour rights have always played an integral part of such a labour market. Any future legislation, she points out, will be closely scrutinized to assess the extent to which it affects efficiency and competitiveness. The rights of 'citizens' are stressed, but is this new social policy to receive a separate lease of life and not to remain shackled to economic integration? Of course not – the Commission tells us that the values of the European social model (i.e. democracy and individual rights, free collective bargaining, the market economy, equality of opportunity for all and social welfare and solidarity) are held together 'by the conviction that economic and social progress must go hand in hand'.[30] In case we are in any doubt about this we find under the heading 'Competitiveness and social progress: two sides of the same coin', statements such as 'Continuing social progress can be built only on economic prosperity, and therefore on the competitiveness of the European economy.'[31] But this is what we have been told in the past, and we have been disappointed. When we turn to the specific proposals on labour law, the view of the Commission is that there are three principal components: the Commission intends to complete the Social Action Programme, to consolidate existing labour law standards and to promote health and safety. New legislation will only be introduced where 'strictly necessary'. The White Paper is explicit in its emphasis on 'soft law', not legislation, and proclaims that there is 'no need for a wide ranging programme of new legislative proposals in the coming period'.

It is not hard to foresee reversals of the limited successes of the past. The proposed revisions to the acquired rights directive would exclude transfers of activities and once again remove transfers of services and parts of undertakings from the protection of the directive and regulations. Elsewhere, the Administrative and Legislative Simplification Committee is exploring the ways in which the burdens on business caused by legislation can be eased.

The ECJ

As we have seen, the ECJ can bear responsibility for a number of daring initiatives in ensuring that individuals benefit from directives. This has made it some enemies and some member states are openly critical of this interventionist role. The court's reinvention of itself can be seen in the recent spate of pensions cases,[32] where, among other things, the use of discriminatory actuarial figures in pensions was allowed. One of the leading discrimination lawyers in the country recently noted that member states are likely to appoint conservative judges in the future and the court is likely to adopt 'a less radical posture' in sex cases in future.[33]

The Member States

The recent French elections have returned a right-wing government committed to a different approach to the EU to that adopted by M. Delors. Reports have also surfaced recently concerning the Anglo-German Deregulation Group's proposal to deregulate health and safety law.[34] The recent utterances of Mr Major leave us in no doubt that he will fight any labour law directives tooth and nail and, as noted above, the UK government is currently challenging the introduction of the working time directive on the ground that it has no Treaty base.[35]

Of course, we may have a change of government so it is useful to look to the proposals of the Labour Party. In *Jobs and Social Justice Labour's Response to the Green Paper on European Social Policy: Options for the Union*, there is an impressive commitment to full employment and to the right to belong (and not to belong) to a trade union. Labour intends to ratify the Social Chapter and a *Charter of Rights for People at Work* is proposed, with a basic set of legal rights for every worker, including:

- the right of all workers to be covered by a basic contract of employment regardless of hours, length of service or size of company;

- a national minimum wage;

- strengthened health and safety protection to include a way of ensuring that employees do not face dismissal if they refuse to do dangerous work that is a genuine health and safety hazard;

- measures strengthening and extending the discrimination legislation;

- new rights in relation to maternity, paternity and parental leave;
- abolition of unfair dismissal qualifying periods;
- discrimination on the grounds of trade union membership or activities to be made unlawful.

However, we also find the following statement:

> Economic and social policies are inextricably linked as two sides of the same coin. Social progress is only possible through economic success, and an active open democracy of citizens with rights and high social standards is a vital part of a competitive economy.[36]

Note not only that this view is similar to that of the Commission, but that even the metaphor is the same. This similarity is not isolated – we also find the beliefs that

> Europe collectively should set the framework of economic and social objectives of full employment, social justice and basic civil and political rights, but each nation must have the independence to strive for these goals within their own context, within their own cultures and according to their own priorities;[37] [and] while the role for the European political structure is to set the broad framework for goals, it is the responsibility of national governments to work independently towards these goals in their own way.[38]

The views coincide with those of the Commission in a remarkable way. Labour's Shadow Employment Secretary has recently expanded upon this in a speech to the Fabian Society, where she stated that any further EU directives on labour law, and any domestic legislation, must be 'necessary' and must not interfere with the flexibility of the domestic labour market.[39] As Mr Blair said, in a little-noticed speech two weeks earlier, while Labour would sign the Social Chapter 'that does not mean agreeing to any and all social costs which other European countries have'.[40] If this simply means that Labour believes that some forms of intervention are called for on a national level, while other forms are more appropriate on an international level, then there is little to disagree with here. However, Mr Blair went on to say that Labour does not even view the function of labour law as redressing power between one side of industry or another, but as providing 'a fair framework of law based on the rights of the individual at work'. Read together these statements appear to reject social justice (in redressing imbalances of power) and to accept the argument that labour rights lead to reduced competitiveness and efficiency, rather than showing a willingness to enter into a debate about the form of such regulation. The choice that we are seemingly presented with is one between jobs and rights. As can be seen in the USA, the sort of jobs that can emerge from a flexible labour market are low paid with high levels of exploitation. This is a false choice and it should be rejected, but how?

We are constantly told that the nation state has very little relevance in today's world.[41] The challenges thrown up by globalism require a response from unions and the left, and while an international strategy is necessary in many ways, that response can only start at the level of the nation state – that is the only sphere in which there is any democratic input at present. Unions, and their allies, must adopt a twin-track approach in lobbying for better labour laws. While debate about the level of international regulation and the role of international union bodies is essential, to abandon pressing for better laws on a national level would be foolish given the previous record of EU social policy and bleak prospects for the future.

NOTES

1. P.L. Davies, *The Emergence of European Labour Law in Legal Intervention in Industrial Relations* (1992).

2. Lord Wedderburn, *Labour Law and Freedom* (1995), Chapter 10.

3. *Ibid.*

4. See *Labour Research*, November 1994.

5. *Commission* v *UK* [1982] ICR 578.

6. See S. Fredman, European Community discrimination law: a critique (1992) 21 *Industrial Law Journal* 119.

7. See especially *Defrenne* v *Belgian State* [1976] ECR 455.

8. See A. McColgan, *Pay Equity – Just Wages for Women* (London: Institute of Employment Rights, 1994), for a critique.

9. Transfer of Undertakings Protection of Employment Regulations 1981, reg. 5.

10. Although there is a discrepancy between the directive and the EP(C)A in the definition of insolvency.

11. P.L. Davies, Acquired rights, creditor's rights, freedom of contract and industrial democracy (1989) *Yearbook of European Law* 21.

12. *Job Insecurity* (London: NACAB, 1993) – CAB evidence on employment problems in the recession.

13. See *Hennessy* v *Craigmyle & Co. Ltd* [1986] ICR 461.

14. See *St John of God (Care Services) Ltd* v *Brooks* [1992] ICR 715.

15. *New Forms of Bargaining and Participation: the Perspectives of Active Union Members* (1994).

16. See K.D. Ewing, Democratic socialism and labour law (1995) 24 *Industrial Law Journal* 103.

17. Wedderburn, *op. cit.*

18. *Commission* v *United Kingdom* [1994] IRLR 392 at para. 14.

19. See the Collective Redundancies and Transfer of Undertakings (Protection of Employment) (Amendment) Regulations which came into force in October 1995.

20. See Chapter 4, this volume.

21. Davies, *op. cit.*, note 2.

22. B. Bercusson, The conceptualization of European labour law (1995) 24 *Industrial Law Journal* 3.

23. (1956) 74 *International Labour Review* 99.

24. Davies, *op. cit.*, note 2.

25. Luxembourg: Office for Official Publications of the European Communities, 1993, COM(93)551.

26. Luxembourg: Office for Official Publications of the European Communities, 1994, COM(94)333.

27. See Chapter 9, this volume.

28. *Guardian*, 13 May 1995.

29. E. Szyszczak, Future directions in European Union social policy law (1995) 24 *Industrial Law Journal* 19.

30. *European Social Policy – A Way Forward for the Union, op. cit.*, p. 9.

31. *Ibid.*, p.12.

32. See *Ten Oever* v *Stichting Bedrijfspensioenfonds voor het Glazenwassersen Schoonmaakbedfijf* (Case C-109/91) [1993] IRLR 601; *Neath* v *Hugh Steeper Ltd* (Case C-152/91) [1994] IRLR 91); *Coloroll Pension Trustees Ltd* v *Russell and others* (Case C-200/91) [1994] IRLR 586.

33. M. Rubenstein (1994) 2(1) *Employment Law Briefing* 8 (Financial Times, Law and Tax).

34. *Labour Research*, June 1995.

35. The EU cannot legislate unless it has a legal base in the Treaty. Article 119 gives it authority to legislate on equality and Article 118 gives it authority to legislate on health and safety. See Q. Mirza, *Race Relations in the Workplace* (London: Institute of Employment Rights, 1995), for a summary of the arguments concerning the Treaty base for a race directive.

36. Labour Party, *Charter of Rights for People at Work*, p. 5.

37. Labour Party, *Jobs and Social Justice: Labour's Response to the Green Paper on European Social Policy: Options for the Union* (London: Labour Party, 1994), p. 5.

38. *Ibid.*, p. 19.

39. Harriet Harman MP, 21 June 1995.

40. Tony Blair MP, addressing a GMB conference on 7 June 1995.

41. For strong arguments to the contrary see *Socialist Register: Globalism and Nationalism* (1994) especially Panitch, Globalization and the state.

12

Disability Rights
Sue Maynard Campbell

The law relating to the employment of disabled people is going through a very interesting time, but one of great uncertainty. It is impossible to understand my view of the future without looking at the past, and giving some thought to the position of disabled people in society today.

HISTORIC BACKGROUND

Disability was the first equal opportunities issue to hit the statute books, with the Disabled Persons (Employment) Act 1944. But disabled people still do not have the sort of comprehensive anti-discrimination legislation that ethnic minorities and women 'enjoy'.

The 1944 Act has, for years, determined thinking on disabled people and employment. It introduced registration for disabled people who were *capable of working* (in the view of a professional, rather than that of the disabled person). And from this followed the quota, which required employers of 20 people or more to employ at least 3 per cent registered disabled people. Unfortunately, there have only been ten prosecutions in the 52 years of its existence (none since 1975) – despite the fact that a majority of those who ought to comply do not. The maximum fine still stands at £100, and disabled people have no right of enforcement. The decision about when to prosecute belongs to the Secretary of State, via a convoluted chain of recommendations.

In a move towards positive discrimination, the 1944 Act introduced the concept of designated employment – certain jobs *could* be reserved for disabled people only. Only two jobs have ever been reserved and these are car-park attendant and electric lift attendant. The Act also provided for the setting-up and financing of sheltered workshops. Such workshops segregate disabled people from their peers, and provide dead-end work at low wages.

It is only relatively recently that the Conservative government has accepted publicly that disabled people face significant discrimination. Nicholas Scott, Minister for Disabled People, declared in December 1991 that 'We all know that there is too much unjustifiable discrimination against disabled people.'[1] The government has consistently ignored the recommendations of the Committee on Restrictions against Disabled People (CORAD), which recommended, in 1982, that

> There should be legislation to make discrimination on the grounds of disability illegal ... The law should cover all areas where discrimination occurs, and particularly employment, education, the provision of goods, facilities and services, insurance, transport, property rights, occupational pension schemes, membership of associations and clubs, and civic duties and functions.[2]

Lack of action on these recommendations might be explained by the fact that the committee was set up by Alf Morris, the minister under the previous Labour administration, after the Silver Jubilee Committee on Improving Access for Disabled People formally identified discrimination as a major issue in relation to disabled people.

In January 1995, the government (in the eyes of many on the right wing) bowed to pressure from the disability lobby, and introduced its Disability Discrimination Bill.[3] This Bill promised to bring in, for the first time, rights for disabled people not to be unreasonably discriminated against in employment and in the provision of goods and services. It requires employers to make reasonable adjustments to accommodate the needs of disabled people. It was heralded by the government as a great step forward for disabled people. However, those of us who are active within the disability movement, and many of those who have supported us, knew that the Bill's proposals were disgracefully inadequate. The definition of who qualifies as a disabled person is so steeped in traditional medical definition that many people who patently are discriminated against on the ground solely of disability will be denied redress because they do not appear sufficiently disabled from a medical viewpoint. Large areas of disabled people's lives, such as education, were virtually ignored, and vital parts of the picture, like transport, were dealt with in a piecemeal way and only as a result of major pressure during the Commons stages of the Bill's passage through Parliament. Unlike with the race and gender legislation, the government did not give disabled people a commission to assist them in enforcing their rights; it merely proposed a National Disability

Council with an advisory role only. A great deal of pressure built up, and it was hoped that the government would relent (or be defeated) in the Lords. But the Bill, which received Royal Assent on 8 November 1995, was little changed by its passage through the Lords (though not for want of trying). There are those who argue, very cogently, that disabled people will in fact be in a worse position when the Act comes into force, a process which will start late in 1996 but may not be completed until 2005! Certainly, without a commission, this seems more and more likely for a large section of the disabled community, particularly as – without waiting to prove the effectiveness of the new measures – the legislation will remove the quota. The disability movement sees the backbench Civil Rights (Disabled Persons) Bill, introduced in the same session by Harry Barnes MP, as the type of Bill that would give us the power to ensure that discrimination is effectively tackled. Sadly, like its predecessors, the Barnes Bill has been prevented from receiving due consideration by both Houses as a result of dubious use of parliamentary procedure by its opponents. In order to understand the arguments and to see how we view the way forward for employment law relating to disability (and laws relating to disability in general), it is essential to have some understanding of the way we look at disability.

MODELS OF DISABILITY

The traditional method of viewing disability, and that which still prevails among professional people whose job it is to make provision for disabled people, is the medical model. This determines what disabled people can and, more importantly, cannot do by referring to their medical diagnoses. The medical model dictates that disabled people cannot operate or participate in mainstream society by reason of their impairment or condition (i.e. their medical condition and its physical implications) alone. This locates the problem within the disabled person, and has led to the cure or care agenda for 'dealing with' disabled people. In contrast, the social model, espoused by the disability movement, defines disability as the disadvantage or restriction of activity caused by contemporary social organization. This organization takes little or no account of people who have impairments, and thus excludes them from mainstream activities.

As a wheelchair user, I can function without difficulty within my own home environment. There my needs as an individual (for turning space, low-level cupboards and raised-level electric sockets) have been taken into account. I run into problems that disable me when I move out into an environment constructed by a society which has not taken into account my needs as a member of that society. I find inaccessible 'public' transport, 'public' toilets with no room for a wheelchair, heavy doors that prevent independent access to 'public' buildings and so on, almost *ad infinitum*. There are also job descriptions that exclude me by including tasks which are not essential to the job I would be employed for, and which I *physically* cannot do. There are the people who arrange a meeting in an upstairs room without a lift and then say, 'Oh dear, what a pity your chair is too heavy for us to get you up there' – not that I would want the indignity and possible dangers involved in being carried. After all, how many others at the meeting have to go through that in order to attend? They are the ones who have excluded me by their arrangements. But they are steeped in the medical model, and put the blame for my exclusion on me.

I have used the impairment I am most familiar with, but the model applies to every impairment. Deaf people are excluded not because they cannot hear. They are disabled by a society which does not bother to take the time to understand the language they use (British Sign Language) or provide the interpreters necessary or invest in text telephones – all of which would enable access and inclusion through communication. Blind people are disabled by the lack of tactile signs, which would enable them to move safely around unfamiliar environments, and by the fact that so few organizations provide information, or try to communicate, in anything other than the written word.

The social model means that we do not have to be pigeon-holed by medical diagnosis. Without laying individual *blame* for abnormality, it can define the problems faced by anyone who does not fit neatly into 'a nation (designed) for the average, normal, able-bodied majority'[4] – for example, people substantially taller than the norm.

AN INTEGRATED VIEW OF LIFE

If you move, on the strength of the social model, to look at employment in relation to a disabled person, you should see that employment legislation alone could never be an option. Take me as a wheelchair user. In order to obtain work I need to be educated, but very few schools are accessible. I then move on to higher education, where the same picture exists. In order to find a university or college offering the course I want, I may well need to move. I then need transport that is accessible, a viable personal care network (I would be out of my own local authority area), accessible living accommodation and so on.

When my peers and I begin to think about employment, we have a considerable number of barriers to face in addition to finding employers who think us right for their jobs. The employer must be in accessible premises, and be prepared to take the radical view that people with my degree of impairment are capable of doing a valuable job. When I started out, it took me six months to persuade the disablement resettlement officer that I could work at all. He was the disability professional in the Department of Employment whose job it was to help me in finding employment *and* to assess me for a Green Card (registration under the 1944 Act, which is not available to those being assessed as incapable of work). Since then I have never been out of work!

The preconceived notions of those in a position to acquire or provide employment for disabled people (employment agencies, employers, the Employment Service), are only the first hurdle. I have to find or acquire accessible transport – I can't take a minicab if the car is in for a service. I have to find an accessible house, something my family never managed when my father's job moved. We have always had to buy and then adapt – often a long and expensive business. And bridging finance is certainly not available to a disabled person on the lower rungs of the promotion ladder, where most will stay. Care networks also have to be built up. Professional carers are costly if you can't get statutory funding, or if it is delayed owing to red tape. Employers will not generally hold a job open while such niceties are resolved.

I hope it is now clear why, for disabled people, employment legislation alone is not sufficient.

THE DISABILITY DISCRIMINATION ACT: WHY IT IS NOT ENOUGH

The government's Disability Discrimination Act approaches legislation to prevent discrimination against disabled people in an incomplete way. Early in summer 1994 there was an outcry over the government's wrecking of the thirteenth attempt to pass a backbench Bill: Roger

Berry's Civil Rights (Disabled Persons) Bill. The Bill would, if passed, have introduced comprehensive anti-discrimination legislation. In response to the outcry late in July 1994, *Disability – on the Agenda* appeared, 'a consultation on Government measures to tackle discrimination against disabled people'. Responses were required by 7 October 1994. Disabled people and their organizations were posed a major problem in consulting widely before responding (although I also believe that at least one major employers' organization asked for an extension of time). This was especially true in view of the holiday period and the fact that, although the consultation document was published in late July, it took some considerable time to disseminate through the organizations. Some parts of the taped versions did not even arrive from the distributors within the consultation period. Self-advocacy groups of people with learning difficulties had particular problems, as government documentation was not produced in an accessible form for them.

After all the effort put into responding within the time-limit, it is difficult to reconcile the claim that the government listened to those responses with the resulting Disability Discrimination Bill, published in mid-January 1995. Time and time again the Bill proposed what we knew to be directly contrary to the majority of responses.

The Bill was not comprehensive. As originally presented to Parliament, it covered a very limited number of specific areas of life and gave rights to some disabled people. Some amendments have been accepted but it is so set about with provisos that it will take some considerable time before it becomes clear how strong its interpretation is in the courts, and disabled people are understandably sceptical. The accepted amendments widened the Bill's terms slightly. Each one resulted from a great deal of lobbying up to and during its passage through the Commons. For instance, provision is now included relating to the sale and letting of property, and also to access to, and use of, communication and information services. Some concessions were also made in relation to transport, although it is unclear how these will take shape in practice. The employment rights are limited in that firms employing fewer than 20 people are (currently) exempt. This effectively excludes nearly 20 per cent of jobs. The Bill was explicitly linked to the White Paper *Ending Discrimination Against Disabled People*, which 'explains' how the government saw some at least of the areas not covered by the Bill being tackled.

Transport vehicles were originally specifically excluded from the Bill (but not train stations and the like!). Anything new in transport was covered in the White Paper, which said that the government was committed to ensuring that all new buses are of low floor construction, 'as far as that is technically feasible'.[5] However, as I have indicated above, they have bowed, to some extent, to pressure. This was a major thrust of lobbying in the Commons because accessible transport (particularly drawing on the lessons of the USA) is a vital prerequisite of true integration. Education was also specifically excluded, and still is by the Act, despite a little tinkering with the edges. So it will still be entirely legal for professionals to make judgements based on irrelevant assumptions about ability when disabled students apply for further and higher education places. When I applied for a university place, the English department apparently said that I wouldn't be able to cope. It did so without even interviewing me, so I never had a chance to counter it face to face. I had a much better A level grade in English than in the subject I actually got a place to read. Universities will be able to continue excluding disabled people in this fashion.

Civic rights and duties is another area not addressed by the Disability Discrimination Act. Provision at polling stations during the last election has been researched, and only 12 per cent were found to be accessible to all disabled voters.[6] Disabled people are frequently excluded from jury service, and service as magistrates, as a result of selectors' prejudice. Very often, disabled people find themselves in a situation where they have no right to challenge the assumptions obviously being made by those who make decisions that affect their lives.

The definition of disability is another area where the Disability Discrimination Act is downright divisive. If you are a disabled person there is no guarantee that you will be able to benefit from the Act. You may just not be considered, in the eyes of the government, as disabled. For example, people who are HIV-positive but who have yet to show any symptoms which affect their daily living, will still face the prejudice unsupported. The position is also unclear with many others, like people with mild epilepsy not controlled by drugs. All these people face direct discrimination in very many areas of life, not least employment, yet they were drafted out of the government's Act.

As I have indicated, some things were changed during the Bill's passage through the Lords, but now the Disability Discrimination Act is on the statute books, and it looks little different from the Bill I have described. The major amendments to the original drafting were thanks to the concerted efforts of disabled people, their organizations and those who support their arguments for a comprehensive approach (especially the voluntary sector consortium, Rights Now!). Any failure of the government to grasp the issues and produce effective legislation to tackle discrimination was not for want of trying on our part.

THE IMAGE OF DISABILITY

Attitudes cannot be legislated away. Nevertheless, comprehensive anti-discrimination legislation that covered all areas of our lives would give disabled people a means to challenge those things which reinforce negative attitudes: charity advertisements, media features, etc. There would be a legal basis for challenging organizational issues, such as the lack of equality training. This could combat the ignorance that fuels prejudice.

Few people appreciate the factors that influence their view of disabled people unless these are specifically brought to their attention. Children are raised on literature in which disabled characters are either baddies (*Treasure Island*), or to be pitied and then, at the end of the book, cured (*Heidi* and *The Secret Garden*). Adults do not fare much better – James Bond's villains are often disabled. There are so many myths about disabled people that still pervade, such as blind people having a sixth sense. Generally, moral attitudes still tell us that disabled people should not contemplate having children (and how do they have sex anyway?). Charities, wanting to raise money, often portray disabled people as tragic and helpless. Their advertising penetrates into every household through the media – newspapers, television advertisements, radio appeals, the list is endless. It is very unusual these days for an individual to remain untouched by the influence of the media.

The legal profession and the judiciary are no exception. The case of the girl with cerebral palsy who took her education authority to court over bullying showed the discrimination we all face as disabled people. She had suffered teasing and taunts in relation to her disability, during her time with the school band, which her teachers apparently knew about but failed to tackle. The judge's comment that she had 'reacted over-sensitively'[7] indicates that he had never been in a similar situation in his life, and had no idea of the position the plaintiff was in.

But there is also a conflict: the conflict over damages. Personal injury lawyers need to get the best deal for their injured clients. It is advantageous to play upon the helpless, tragic image society has of the disabled person. Consider the £3.5 million damages awarded to a postgraduate MBA student seen as being condemned to a useless life, unable to work again.[8] This case highlighted the dilemma within the law. As a lawyer, I understood the issues considered by the court. As a disabled person, I understood other issues that the court probably did not even know existed, let alone considered: the influence of the images being used, the fact that severely disabled people can and do work very successfully with the right support, and so on.

The image of disability within the law, and its influence on the judicial process, is an area where much work needs to be done. It would be a good start if disability were addressed within the legal training process.

SO WHAT IS 'THE WAY FORWARD'?

Comprehensive anti-discrimination legislation along the lines proposed by the most recent Civil Rights (Disabled Persons) Bill is, in my view and that of the vast majority of disabled people, the only way. This is also the view of those who do not face the same discrimination that we do, day in day out, but who understand the issues. Between the CORAD report's publication, in 1982, and the introduction of the government's Bill, there were no fewer than 14 unsuccessful attempts to bring in anti-discrimination legislation through a backbench Bill. The Civil Rights Bill, introduced by Harry Barnes (MP for North Derbyshire), was the fifteenth attempt. The Barnes Bill was based on a draft which, with minor amendments, has been the form of the last few attempts. This had solid support from the disability movement and the increasing number of organizations, not always directly involved in disability issues, who have come to see the logic of the 'comprehensive' argument.

The Barnes Bill would have provided a remedy for anyone who suffers discrimination as the result of disability. Its definitions are not tied to medical diagnoses. If a person is facing discrimination because of someone else's prejudices about disability, it does not matter that he or she is not (in a medical sense) disabled. Thus, the Barnes Bill covers not only persons with '(a) a physical, sensory or mental impairment the consequence of which substantially limits one or more of the major life activities of that person': it also covers people with '(b) a history of having had such an impairment; or (c) a reputation as a person who has or had such an impairment'.[9] In the employment section, protection from exclusion from employment or other limiting of opportunity, status or benefits as an employee is extended to a person who is discriminated against 'because of the disability of a person with whom he is known or believed to have a relationship or association'.[10] Thus the partner of someone with AIDS would be protected from prejudice based on the fear that so often arises from ignorance in such cases.

Unlike the government's Act, the Barnes Bill did not give exemption to firms of fewer than 20 employees, believing that the provisos, that any adjustment (physical or organizational changes) needed should be reasonable, would include a consideration of the size of the firm or company concerned and the extent of the adjustments needed. The White Paper associated with the 1995 Act explains it may be more difficult and burdensome for smaller firms without specialist personnel to get to grips with the new right, and obtain the advice they need in particular cases.[11]

Transport and education are fully included in the provisions of the Barnes Bill. Additional areas, such as new constructions and private property, are covered and discrimination is outlawed in the field of lettings (now an accepted amendment incorporated into the Act). Access to polling stations is also specifically covered.

Perhaps one of the most important differences between the Barnes Bill and the Disability Discrimination Act is the enforcement provision. The Act introduces a National Disability Council with an advisory role. Disabled people know that such bodies, of which we have fair experience in specific areas, have no teeth and are not what we need to assist us to combat the discrimination we face. Unsupported by a commission with at least the powers of those for race and gender, we do not stand a chance of enforcing our rights under the legislation. Individual disabled people will be more disempowered in a 'difficult and burdensome' task (the government's own words when explaining, in its White Paper, why it proposed to exempt firms employing fewer than 20 people) than even those small firms the government showed such concern for. Harry Barnes's Bill would have given us a commission that would comprise a majority of people with direct experience of discrimination and the issues a disabled person faces. In short, we needed the Civil Rights (Disabled Persons) Bill and will, I believe, continue to do so despite the Disability Discrimination Act now being law. Nothing less will, again in the government's own words in describing its proposals, have a chance of 'ending discrimination against disabled people', whatever it argues. Disabled people are the experts when it comes to disability, but many people, including legislators, are unwilling to acknowledge it.

DISABILITY LEAVE

The only other item on my disability agenda for future specific legislation is disability leave.[12] Maternity leave, and with enlightened employers paternity leave, is now a common feature of working life.

When a person becomes disabled during his or her working life, whether through a long-term illness or through impairment (perhaps an industrial injury or a sudden loss of sight), major adjustments are often needed. Disability leave would provide a period during which people could come to terms with their new situation without the pressures of keeping up with a job. Some employers have given such a scheme favourable consideration. Until it is enshrined in legislation, however, there will be an uneven playing field for fair-minded employers and for employees of those who do not value the experience and abilities of someone they see as having become useless. Accepted amendments to the Disability Discrimination Act have included 'rehabilitation leave' as something that could be a 'reasonable adjustment' an employer might make. So perhaps we are part way there, but only the future implementation of the legislation will show.

A FINAL HOPE

In view of the current position on disability legislation, I trust you will forgive me for dwelling almost exclusively upon anti-discrimination legislation. However, I do firmly believe that *comprehensive* anti-discrimination legislation is *essential* to put disabled people on a level playing field. Once there, we will be able to take advantage of mainstream protection, such as that against unfair dismissal, and of health and safety initiatives. Disabled people do not belong in a separate group, seen as flawed, as abnormal, and 'treated' to segregated provision. Unfortunately, mainly because of its heavy reliance on the medical model of disability, the Disability Discrimination Act will not have the impact that it should. Disabled people belong in the mainstream, as part of an effective, diverse workforce.

NOTES

1. 4 December 1991. Cited at the Second Reading of Civil Rights (Disabled Persons) Bill, 202 HC Debs 1251 (31 January 1992).

2. *Report by the Committee on Restrictions against Disabled People* (1982, reprinted by RADAR 1994), recommendations 1 and 3.

3. The Act will, when implemented, repeal the mandatory provisions of the Disabled Persons (Employment) Act 1944.

4. F. Bowie, *Handicapping America*, quoted in C. Gooding, *Disabling Laws, Enabling Acts* (1994).

5. *Ending Discrimination against Disabled People*, Cm 2729, Chapter 5.8.

6. The Spastics Society, *Polls Apart* (1992).

7. *Guardian*, 16 July 1994, 'Judge takes "bullied" girl's father to task'.

8. *Guardian*, 15 March 1994, 'Crash victim settles for record £3.4m'.

9. Civil Rights (Disabled Persons) Bill, Clause 1.

10. *Ibid.*, Clause 4(2)(d).

11. *Ending Discrimination ...*, *op. cit.*, Chapter 3.10.

12. RNIB, *Disability Leave – a Guide for Employers* (1993).

13

Equal Pay: A New Approach

Aileen McColgan

INTRODUCTION: HOW BRITISH WOMEN FARE

The European Commission recently published its *Memorandum on Equal Pay For Work of Equal Value*.[1] The memorandum, which forms part of the European Union's Programme for Equal Opportunities, has been long in the writing. Many hoped that it would include radical proposals for improving women's wages. In the event, it contains little of substance. Insiders suggest that its teeth were pulled in order to placate governments concerned with the cost of challenging women's exploitation in the labour market. So much for action.

What the document does contain, however, is the news that British women workers are among the lowest paid, relative to men, in Europe. Manual women workers earn less than 70 per cent of manual men's hourly rate, while non-manual women workers take home just over half their male colleagues' monthly wage. The only women who fare (marginally) worse are manual workers in Ireland and Luxembourg, while Danish non-manual women workers earn 85 per cent and Italian manual women workers 83 per cent of their male colleagues' monthly and hourly rates.[2]

Why are British women's earnings so low? Many factors influence the gender pay gap. Wherever women work, they tend to be clustered at the bottom of the average earnings ladder. Where the overall spread of wages is narrow, women's structural position will result in smaller average pay differentials than where, as in the UK, the spread of wages is wide. The earnings spectrum is influenced by the existence or otherwise of a minimum wage (whether sectoral or national, legislated or fixed by the extension of collective agreements). The UK and Ireland are the only member states that have neither national minimum wages (as do France, Greece, the Netherlands, Belgium, Luxembourg, Portugal and Spain) nor sectoral collective agreements covering practically all workers (as do Germany, Italy and Denmark). Until the end of 1993, Ireland and the UK both had systems which mixed collective bargaining and industry-based minimum wages.[3] In both countries, however, many workers were excluded entirely from the scope of minimum wages.

The overall spread of earnings is also affected by the return of wages to perceived skills. Where the cost of perceived 'skills' is high, differentials will be more substantial than is otherwise the case. This can impact on women's wages in two ways:

1   Where women are in fact relatively underskilled, they will bear the cost of this underskilling to a greater degree according to the premia paid for skill.
2   The actual measurement of 'skill', and the perception of what counts as a rewardable 'skill', may disadvantage women individually and as the main incumbents of stereotypically female jobs. In such a case, the disadvantage is double, as the skills involved in female work are first undervalued, and then men are paid significant premia in respect of their perceived skills.

The overall level of pay inequality in the UK has actually widened over the past decade, in contrast with its reduction during the 1970s. A greater proportion of workers in the UK than in any other member state (20 per cent) receive less than two-thirds of the median wage. The same is true of workers receiving less than 80 per cent of the median wage (35 per cent). In Denmark, in contrast, no worker receives less than two-thirds of the median wage, and a mere 1 per cent of workers receive less than 80 per cent of the median. The other countries in which relatively low-paid workers fare worst are Ireland, Portugal and Spain (with 30, 31 and 32 per cent of workers respectively earning less than 80 per cent of the median wage).[4] The gender pay gaps in manual earnings in these countries are among the widest in the European Union.[5] The widening wage spectrum in the UK during the 1980s had the effect that part-time women's hourly earnings actually fell, relative to those of full-time women (and hence to those of men), from 81 per cent to 75 per cent between 1981 and 1989.[6]

THE FUTURE

The level of pay inequality, and hence the extent of the gender pay gap, is set to widen in the UK. Part of the reason lies in the abolition, in late

1993, of the remaining Wages Councils, with the effect that the workers previously covered by them (80 per cent of whom were women) have been deprived of the right even to the minimal proscribed rates of pay. Studies carried out since have shown that wage rates in those industries previously covered by them have fallen.[7] Other pressures, too, are at work. Among the factors which, worldwide, influence the extent of pay inequality are the extent to which pay is centrally determined, the proportion of women working in the public sector, the relative rates of pay in that sector and the level of union density (which in turn influences the central determination of pay).[8]

The ever-increasing UK drive towards deregulation (save of the internal affairs of trade unions), the decline in union density and the dismantlement of the public sector and of the national pay bargaining associated with it all conspire to drive an even greater wedge between the well paid and those at the bottom of the pay ladder. For all the promises of the Transfer of Undertakings (Protection of Employment) Regulations and the Acquired Rights Directive, the protection of the pay and conditions of contracted-out workers applies, at best, only to workers employed at the time of the transfer and, even then, does not apply indefinitely. The scope for contractors to drive down pay over the duration of the contract is wide, and any attempts by local authorities to prevent such practices is vulnerable to challenge under the Local Government Act 1988, s. 17(5)(a) of which precludes consideration of workers' terms and conditions in the allocation of contracts.

The House of Lords' decision in *Ratcliffe & others* v *North Yorkshire County Council*[9] may be expected to deter public employers from cutting wages in predominantly female jobs in order to compete with prospective tenderers (unless wages in comparable male jobs are also cut). But it will not assist public employers to retain work in-house, and it does not apply to cases where incoming employers reduce wages in predominantly female jobs (whether gradually over time or for employees taken on subsequent to the transfer) to below the rate of comparable men still employed in the public sector – the Equal Pay Act 1970 only applies to those employed by the same or associated employers.

EQUAL PAY LAWS

What of the role of the legislation specifically aimed at the gender pay gap? The UK has had in place, since 1975, legislation which requires that women receive equal pay for work which is either substantially the same as that done by male colleagues, or which has been rated by the employer as of equal value to male work.[10] Since 1984, women have been entitled to receive equal pay for work which is of equal value to that done by men within the same establishment.[11] In that time, full-time women's relative hourly earnings rose by just over 5 per cent (from 74.2 per cent in 1983 to 79.5 per cent in 1994).[12] The general rise masks some downward fluctuations between 1983 and 1987.

In contrast, many member states have seen little or no specific legal intervention in the field of equal pay. Despite European legislation that requires equal pay for work of equal value,[13] equal pay legislation in Luxembourg, Italy, Spain, Greece and Portugal does not define the concept of equal value, and neither France, Luxembourg, Greece nor Italy have seen any litigation in the equal value arena. The gender pay disparity is similar in Luxembourg to that in the UK and in Ireland (both of which have explicit legislative commitments to equal pay for work of equal value); while Greek manual women workers, Spanish and Portuguese non-manual women workers and all Italian women workers fare considerably better than their UK counterparts.[14]

What does this tell us about equal pay legislation's potential to change the gender pay gap? First impressions would suggest that it is next to useless, and that attention would be more profitably paid to the pursuit of other strategies designed to improve the wages of low-paid workers generally. If the gender pay gap results, to a large extent, from the wider pay disparity between low and highly paid workers, a strategy of reducing the earnings disparity will have a profound impact on women's relative underpayment, as well as on poverty pay more generally.

Such a conclusion would, however, be hasty. While overall pay inequalities determine the absolute financial penalties on workers clustered at the bottom of the pay hierarchy, strategies aimed exclusively at the overall level of pay inequality do little to challenge women's position within the hierarchy. The fact that women's wages have increased, albeit very gradually, relative to those of men since 1983, while the overall levels of pay inequality have widened during that time, suggests that the existence of equal pay legislation has had some impact on the relative payment levels of men and women within the hierarchy. To remove the commitment to legislation specifically directed at the gender pay gap would remove the potential for further change, quite apart from contravening the UK's obligations under EC and international law.[15]

'DISCRIMINATION' AND THE GENDER PAY GAP

Why are women clustered at the bottom of the pay hierarchy? Economists provide different explanations according to their political persuasion.

First, there are *'compensating differentials'* theories – the idea that women's work is rewarded *differently*, rather than *less*, than that done by men. So, for example, while 'men put more emphasis on wages and leadership opportunities ... women ... are more apt to stress non-monetary benefits, such as good physical conditions, convenient hours, or rewarding interpersonal aspects of the job – relations with co-workers and supervisors, the opportunity to help others, and the like.'[16] Women, it seems, have the luxury of being able to pick and choose between jobs on the basis of curtain patterns, while men have to sacrifice such frivolities in order to fulfil their manly obligations.

Second, there are *'human capital'* theories[17] – the idea that women are paid less because they are less skilled, less qualified, less committed to the labour market. Women, apparently, choose jobs on the basis of immediate gratification (high starting salaries) while men choose jobs that will give them training and skills and pay more in the future. Women choose instant gratification because they know that their labour market experience will be less than men's, with the effect that they will have less opportunity to recoup the immediate losses suffered by taking high-training, low-paid jobs. Further, women's skills, such as they are, depreciate during periods out of the labour market and in part-time work, with the effect that the gender wage gap increases over time. Finally, even when women do have the same qualifications, skills and training as men, those who are married (or, presumably, mothers and/or cohabitees) have less 'effort' to expend on paid work.[18] Hence they are less valuable, as employees, than are men.

Third, there are *'crowding'* theories. Women are segregated into a small range of occupations, which are flooded with an excess of low-skilled workers and, as a result, pay low wages.[19]

Some answers to these assertions are necessary. As far as the first is concerned, there is little to support any claim that women's jobs are more 'pleasant', more 'rewarding', 'safer' and more 'convenient' than are those done by men. Women are concentrated in the lowest-paid jobs. These jobs included, in 1990, those of nursing auxiliaries and assistants, shop assistants, security guards, bar staff, hospital ward orderlies, road sweepers, sewing machinists, footwear workers and repetitive assemblers.[20] Not all of these jobs are performed solely or mainly by women, and not only women are low paid. Few of them could be described in the terms set out above – many are arduous, dangerous, stressful and performed in circumstances of serious physical discomfort.

It is the case that women tend to work in jobs whose hours could be considered 'convenient' – if 'convenient' is taken to mean 'part-time'. Almost 50 per cent of working women work part-time. But women's 'choice' to work part-time is frequently a chimera. The expense of good quality childcare, coupled with the inadequacy of its provision, means that one or other parent must take a substantial role in looking after children, during the day, in all but the richest households. Women are likely to be paid less than men in the first place: even if they weren't, societal expectations about childcare responsibility mean that women are more likely to be able to do part-time work than are men. So women 'choose' to work part-time, and the employers who are willing to give them part-time work effectively have them over a barrel. Part-time workers are usually in a weaker bargaining position: because they cannot compromise to a significant extent on hours and so on, few are in a position to make significant demands about money. Employers are well placed to make the most of this, and they do: *Pay and Gender in Britain (2)* reported that employers tend to take the view that the availability of part-time work is itself a sufficient incentive for women (with the effect that pay incentives were necessary for part-timers to a lesser extent than for full-time workers). In addition, Blanchflower and Corry's study of part-time employees found that:

> a higher proportion of the workforce tended to be part-time in establishments where unions were not recognised ... in establishments which did *not* have formal procedures for dealing with pay and conditions, dismissals or individual grievances, part-timers constituted nearly twice as high a proportion of the labour force than [sic] they did in establishments with formal procedures.[21]

It is unlikely that employment in such establishments is all that the 'compensating differentials' theorists assume it to be. As for 'human capital' theories, they stand up poorly to empirical testing. Detailed discussion of this is beyond the scope of this chapter but, briefly: even where education levels are held constant women earn considerably less;[22] women do not start work in higher-paying jobs than do men;[23] although women do lose position as a result of absences from the labour market, these losses (at least in the USA) tend to be short-term, as within a few years the initial salary loss has been regained;[24] such evidence as there is suggests that women are likely to invest *more*, rather than less, effort in their jobs.[25] In addition, human capital theories significantly fail to explain why, even when skills, education, training, labour market, etc. are held constant, men *still* earn more than women.[26] Recent estimates of the relationship between 'human capital' and the gender wage gap in Britain suggest that 'The primary reason for women's lower pay is smaller remuneration for human capital attributes in their jobs: if women's human capital was remunerated at the same rate as men's, their hourly pay would be substantially – of the order of one fifth – higher.'[27] If full-time women's hourly remuneration was one-fifth higher than at present (80 per cent), the gender pay gap would virtually disappear.

Equally important is the point that human capital theorists assume that women's enforced time away from paid work (if they are to assist in society's reproduction of itself) is value-neutral to society and should, therefore, be at the risk of the individual women. Were men to play a greater role in undertaking domestic tasks, the burden would not fall on women alone. And whether or not such a redistribution were to occur, society has an interest in child production. The UK's population is falling, with the effect that the average age and the proportion of pensioners is increasing. This in turn has serious repercussions on the cost of social security, as well as on the ability of the state to meet those costs (there being proportionately fewer people of working age). Given the unlikelihood of any abandonment of immigration controls, the apparent solution lies in people being encouraged to have children, rather than women being penalized for so doing.

Finally, 'human capital' arguments presuppose that women's contribution to the labour market is in fact rendered less valuable by time spent away from it. This may be far from true: many women take relatively short career breaks which do not significantly affect their work-specific skills on return. (In 1991, for example, McRae and Daniels reported a 'striking increase [1979 to 1988] in the rates at which mothers have been returning to paid work within a few months of having a baby. By the end of the 1980s, about two-thirds of mothers who were in work when they became pregnant were economically active within nine months of having their babies.'[28]) In any case, the provision of skills-updating courses prior to return from a prolonged absence would solve any problem and prevent the wastage of highly skilled and educated women to relatively menial jobs after childbirth. Further, coping, caring and educational skills associated with child-rearing are likely to be useful in the performance of many stereotypically female jobs, such as teaching, childcare and nursing. And any argument that women part-time workers are less valuable than those with a full-time commitment to paid work simply does not stand up to scrutiny. For women, part-time work tends to be poorly valued and poorly paid. Men who work part-time, by contrast, frequently do so in the capacity of director, advisor or consultant. It is bizarre that the men who are so highly paid for managing health trusts or advising banks are, in many cases, the same men who claim that part-time workers lack the commitment to the labour force that full-time workers display.

'Crowding' theories are also open to challenge to the extent that they depend upon the assumption that the poorly paid work which women perform is poorly paid precisely because it is low-skilled. Studies in the USA, Canada and the UK illustrate that this is frequently not the case. In one study of workers in Northampton, for example, researchers found that paying men and women the same for jobs of similar content would reduce the gender wage gap by *three times* as much as would redistributing the skill content of jobs between them.[29] Research into the Northern Irish clothing industry found both extremely high levels of sex segregation and different pay structures for men's and women's jobs.[30] Men's jobs were rated as more highly skilled, with no account being taken of the pre-factory skills possessed by women. And female jobs had a flat pay structure, which, unlike male jobs, did not reward increasing skill. The study concluded that women were being paid a 'female rate' regardless of actual work.

In *Why Britain Needs a Minimum Wage*, Frank Wilkinson declared the claim that low pay results from low skill

> an argument of impregnable circularity in which the outcome – low pay – is used as evidence for the alleged cause: low skill and personal inefficiency. . . . Years of formal education and training may help to explain the relative high pay and job attainment amongst white males but the returns to human capital investment are much lower for women and racial minorities and, in the lower strata of the labour market, the wage benefits from education and training are very small.[31]

The evidence points to a modified version of the third explanation, above. Women's payment is indeed linked to their labour-market segregation, but the connection does not lie in their lower levels of skill or education. Women are underpaid because they are women. Women's position within the labour hierarchy can be explained in the following terms.

JOB (HORIZONTAL) SEGREGATION

Women are segregated into a narrow range of occupations and workplaces. The reasons for this segregation lie partly in socialization: women are expected to be nurses, men engineers. They also lie in employer and employee discrimination: employers typically select men for particular types of job, women for others, and male domination of occupations and workplaces can be maintained by sexual harassment. It is not only the fact that this happens which encourages sex segregation – equally important is that women expect it to happen and tend to steer away from occupations and workplaces that are seen as the preserve of men.[32] In addition, men are typically deterred from entering female occupations and workplaces by the lower pay associated with them and, at least as far as occupations are concerned, because of the stigma attached to 'women's' jobs.[33]

Segregation, in turn, is associated with lower levels of pay for women. This results from a number of factors, among them different levels of unionization and bargaining power and the undervaluation of 'women's' work.

Unionization

Women workers are less likely to be unionized than men. Their relative lack of organization results in part from: their fragmented labour market experience; their tendency to work part-time, which renders union dues less affordable in many cases; their perception of trade unions as uninterested in the 'minority' issues that affect women at work; and the tendency of women to work in small organizations, where union membership is seen as evidence of disloyalty to employers. Women who work in female-dominated workplaces and occupations (and many women do) are, therefore, less likely to benefit from the 'union premia' which frequently attach to male wages.[34]

Bargaining Power

Women have less power to demand higher wages than do men. The many women who cohabit with men are not entitled to social security payments, with the effect that there is no wage that is lower than the money they would otherwise receive. This effect is mitigated to a certain extent in full-time employment, as women with (at least preschool) children may have to earn enough to pay for childcare. On the other hand, women often rely on informal arrangements and many work part-time in order to fit themselves around such arrangements. They are further constrained in terms of travel-to-work time and, for them, the choice is between a low wage and no wage at all. The availability of part-timers in turn impacts downwardly on full-time women's wages: since full- and part-time women workers tend to be concentrated in the same occupations and workplaces, employers who pay too little to retain full-time workers can replace them with part-time workers whose bargaining position is weaker.[35]

Undervaluation

Women's work is, because it is performed by women, seen as being less valuable than that performed by men. The skill, effort, responsibility and working conditions associated with women's work are rendered invisible because the work is performed by women. Thus, for example, while the (male) job of garbage disposal is seen as dirty and potentially hazardous to health (and, therefore, typically attracts a premium on these grounds), nurses are seen as performing a pleasant, caring, clean job. Further, the skills of 'caring' associated with stereotypically female jobs such as nursing, teaching and childcare are seen as natural attributes of women rather than as rewardable skills.

Studies have shown that the rates of pay within any given occupation, even where other factors are held constant, decline in inverse proportion to the number of women in the workforce. One US study found that 15 factors explained 90 per cent of the variation in wages between different jobs. *Independently of these factors*, wages were inversely proportional to the number of women in any particular job.[36] The Ontarian Public Service Employees Union (OPSEU) applied the method in Ontario, and found that weekly wages decreased by $1.15 for every 1 per cent increase of women in a job.

VERTICAL SEGREGATION

Women fail to progress within their jobs to the same extent as men. Women solicitors and doctors, for example, earn substantially less than their male colleagues. This results to a large extent from barriers to women's progression, which include the penalties imposed on women who take time out to have children and male refusal to see that women are equally talented as their male colleagues. In 1994, for example, women accounted for 44 per cent of personnel managers, but fewer than 10 per cent of personnel directors.[37] Eighty-one per cent of primary and 49 per cent of secondary schoolteachers were women, but only 57 and 30 per cent respectively of headteachers.[38] In the NHS, too, 'the higher the level of management, the lower the proportion of women'.[39] And women accountants are only half as likely to become company directors or partners in large firms as are men.[40] Women are also often excluded from the highest-paying specialisms (such as corporate law and surgery) and pushed into subject areas (family law and general practice) that are seen as 'suitable' for women and that, invariably, attract lower rates of pay.

INCREASING WOMEN'S PAY

Although policies aimed at reducing the overall extent of pay inequality are absolutely essential, and should form a major part of any assault on the gender pay gap, they will do little to challenge women's relative position *within* the labour market hierarchy. Nor is it sufficient simply to adopt an 'equal opportunities' approach aimed at enabling women workers to move into traditional male jobs.

In the first place, while desegregation of the labour market is an important aim, it is too long-term a project to assist women who currently work in female-dominated occupations. To state, as Mr Justice Wood did in *Enderby* v *Frenchay Health Authority*,[41] that the way in which a senior speech therapist could improve her pay is to requalify as a senior clinical psychologist or hospital pharmacist is, to say the least, unhelpful.

There is also substantial evidence (above) that the movement of women into previously male-dominated jobs actually serves to reduce the rates of pay in those jobs. Jobs become 'feminized', and even where occupations are predominantly male, pockets of (lower-paid and less prestigious) 'women's work' are formed. The widespread movement of women into previously male jobs will not therefore, suffice to do away with the gender pay gap.

Finally, it is politically unacceptable (and economically absurd) to insist that women improve their rates of pay by avoiding female jobs. In the first place, teachers, health workers and clerical workers are as necessary to the economy as are workers in stereotypically male jobs.

And the dynamics of a sudden move to sex integration are mind boggling: in 1981 in the USA, where sex segregation is less extreme than in the UK,[42] over *60 per cent* of either men or women would have had to move into jobs usually performed by the opposite sex in order to achieve a sex-integrated workforce.[43] The probability of this (or anything close to it) happening in the relatively short term must be zero.

Some mechanism aimed at equalizing women's position within the hierarchy is, therefore, necessary. Equal pay legislation is not of itself sufficient to tackle the gender pay gap for the reason, explained above, that this gap is strongly associated with the general levels of pay inequality within an economy. Nevertheless, it is necessary to target specifically the position of women within the existing pay hierarchy if they are to be paid on the basis of something other than their sex. That legislation can have some impact is evidenced not only by the gradual reduction of the pay gap (in the face of countervailing pressures) that has occurred over the past few years, but also by the staggering 12.4 per cent improvement in women's pay associated with the implementation of the Equal Pay Act between 1970 and 1975.[44]

What can be done? The Equal Pay Act 1970 simply required that women be paid equally with men when they performed (broadly) the same jobs, and where the employer had allocated their jobs equal value in a (voluntarily undertaken) job evaluation scheme. The effect was to render overtly discriminatory male and female pay scales unlawful, but many employers were able simply to retain discriminatory pay practices by renaming male and female jobs, differentiating payment on the basis of job titles and allocating all female workers to the bottom rung of the pre-existing pay scale.[45] While the Central Arbitration Committee (CAC) was empowered to amend overtly discriminatory provisions of collective agreements and pay structures, its attempts to look behind the titles and require real equality of treatment were impeded by procedural obstacles[46] and by the Divisional Court,[47] and the amending power of the CAC was abolished entirely by the Sex Discrimination Act 1986. Countless thousands of collective agreements and pay structures were never scrutinized for evidence of discrimination, at least in the absence of overtly discriminatory provisions.

There is no doubt that pre-1975 pay structures did operate to the disadvantage of women. Men have traditionally been paid on the basis of a 'family wage', while women's wages were calculated, at best, on the assumption that they were responsible only for themselves. Trade unions embraced the notion of the 'family wage' at the same time that they pressed for men to be rewarded on the basis of effort.[48] Even those economists who embraced the 'marginal productivity' theory of wage setting, claiming that wages were dependent on the worker's utility to the employer, abandoned this theory when it came to explaining women's lower wages. To the extent that they were unable to explain women's lower wages in terms of their lower productivity (the result of their lack of employment opportunity and training), they justified them in terms of subsistence theory.[49] Whatever the ideology surrounding men's wages, women's salaries were depressed by virtue of the assumption that they were not responsible for others; that, indeed, they were subsidized by male family members and so did not even have to receive subsistence wages.

Just as many employers effected little real change in their pay structures in response to the passage of the Equal Pay Act, there is scant evidence that they embraced the spirit of the equal value amendments. Even in those organizations which do job evaluation, a 1991 study commissioned by the Equal Opportunities Commission (EOC) found that little attention was paid to the equal value implications of pay structures:[50]

> Many of the personnel specialists interviewed told us that pay equality was 'not a live issue in our organisation', sometimes in spite of factual evidence that their pay systems might not pass muster if challenged on the equal pay principle ... many union officials seem to share this view.[51]

Although most organizations surveyed had reviewed their use of job evaluation schemes in the five years preceding the survey, few did so with equal value considerations in mind. The schemes frequently retained different pay structures themselves, reflecting continuing job segregation, or marginalized women in unsegregated pay structures into lower grades than men. Bonuses and premium payments were in practice often restricted to those in male-dominated jobs (labourers earning £2000 less in basic wages than word processor operators in one organization took home £1200 more as a result of overtime payments), as women were frequently unable to work overtime because of family commitments, or were denied access to premium payments as part-timers unless they worked more than normal full-time hours. Nor did merit payments do anything to equalize men and women's pay, being in general restricted to male-dominated managerial grades and, even where available to both men and women, allocated largely on the basis of stereotypically male characteristics.[52]

The elimination of women's underpayment requires a radical re-ordering of the wage hierarchy. Existing equal pay legislation, with its staggering complexity, cumbersome procedures and, above all, its individual focus, is incapable of performing such a feat. Equal pay comparisons are limited to workers employed by the same employer (and, in practice, often workers in the same workplace[53]). Absolute parity of value is required between applicant and comparator in order for the applicant to win – it is not sufficient, in other words, that the tribunal finds disproportionate rewards to 'skill' between applicant and comparator. Even if a woman manages to jump all the hurdles and win an equal pay claim, her employer is free to refuse the increase to other women in the workplace, so the costs of legal action are rarely justified. Women's underpayment is a structural issue, and any attempt to solve it by individual means is doomed to failure.

The tendency for many is to look towards Europe, whose intervention has been responsible for the benefits, such as they are, of having equal pay legislation at all. The EOC initiated action against the UK government in late 1993 as a result of the abolition of the last Wages Councils (in whose sphere of influence the gender pay gap was narrower than elsewhere) and the government's rejection of the bulk of the EOC's proposals for change to the equal value legislation. Given the generally toothless nature of the Commission's memorandum, however, a pessimist might hold out little hope for improvement from that front. And the ECJ appears recently to have adopted a rather more conservative approach to equal pay than before: in pension cases, in particular, it has allowed direct discrimination on the basis of sex.[54] In any event, fine as European equal pay legislation is in theory, at the level of practice its impact has been much less apparent.

It is clear that there will be no improvement on this front under the present government: the most recent of its displays of indifference (if not hostility) towards discrimination issues was its response to the recommendations of the House of Commons' all-party Select Committee on Employment: *Mothers in Employment*. It was 'unnecessary and inappropriate', according to the government, 'to legislate for a minimum right [five days] to family leave for all employees'. Even if paternity leave was to be unpaid it would constitute a 'burden', which would increase unemployment. 'How parents combine their domestic responsibilities with their wish or the need to work is essentially a matter for them to decide in the light of their own particular circumstances.'[55]

To this small example might be added the government's 'justification' for the abolition of the Wages Councils – that 80 per cent of the workers covered by them were 'secondary earners' (read women)[56] – and recent suggestions that equal value applicants be restricted to naming a single comparator and that the appointment of an independent expert be at the discretion of the tribunal.[57] Nevertheless, it begins to appear that this government may not be with us forever. How should a Labour government address the problem of unequal pay?[58]

COLLECTIVE APPROACHES TO EQUAL PAY

In 1987, the provincial government of Ontario, passed the Pay Equity Act. The Act, which took a collective approach to pay inequality, required that employers examine the pay structures within their organizations and eliminate from them any pay discrimination. It placed an obligation upon employers to cooperate with recognized trade unions (compulsory recognition procedures operate), and to peg the wages in predominantly female jobs to those in comparably valuable male jobs. Recent amendments also allowed for comparison with more 'valuable' jobs where no comparably valuable male jobs existed for particular female jobs, and for the proportional adjustment of the female wage. Pay disparities may continue to exist where they are the result of one of a number of permissible factors.

Ironically, the Pay Equity Act's continued existence is under threat even as it is being widely considered as a model for legislative reform elsewhere. The collective bottoms of the newly elected Conservative government had scarcely touched their seats when they set about slashing public spending. This included setting a cap on the pay equity adjustments that can be made by public employers and announcing plans to stop funding the free legal service currently available to women seeking 'pay equity'.[59] Despite this, and despite the Pay Equity Act's many shortcomings (discussed in detail elsewhere[60]), the legislation still illustrates some of the potential (as well as the pitfalls) of a collective approach to the problem of unequal pay.

Taking the pitfalls first, the implementation of the Pay Equity Act has demonstrated the following.

- 'Value' is a slippery concept – where employers have control over the assessment of jobs' relative values, women can expect to gain relatively little from any requirement of 'equal pay for work of equal value'.

- More generally, employers cannot be trusted with the task of reducing the sex wage gap. The workplaces in which the Act has brought results are those in which (committed) unions have been able to do battle with employers' natural desire to limit the cost of 'pay equity'.

● Any requirement for exact parity between applicant and comparator is problematic. It leaves many women whose jobs pay less for reasons connected with their being 'women's jobs' without any recourse.

● The restriction of wage comparisons within pay bargaining units, workplaces and/or employing organizations serves to limit the possibilities of equal pay legislation. Workers within pay bargaining units workplaces and/or employing organizations tend to receive similar levels of pay, with the effect that the wages of the lowest will not be substantially improved by intra-organization comparisons. Equally, the exemption of small organizations from the demands of 'pay equity' legislation denies wage increases to those women at the very bottom of the pile.

● 'Technicalities' such as the definition of 'employer' are of paramount importance. Problems can arise where employers are able to contract out work in order to circumvent the equal pay requirements, and where public sector employers are allowed to regard themselves as separate entities for the purpose of comparisons.

● Given that 'pay equity' will, of necessity, require a rolling implementation programme, it is essential to ensure that employers do comply with pre-set targets. Currently in Ontario, the Pay Equity Commission (which is responsible for implementing the legislation) is confronted with many small defaulting employers who have made no efforts to increase female wages in the seven years since the implementation of the Act, who have been in breach since their (1 January 1995) deadline and who can either 'do' pay equity or stay in business. Had the costs been spread over the seven-year period this would not have occurred.

But perhaps the most intractable problem with the whole approach lies in the fundamental issue of the 'valuation' of work upon which wage adjustments depend. 'Value' is so relative a concept that it can be utilized to serve any particular end. Further, since the assessment of 'value' is influenced by evaluators' experience of a world in which work done primarily by women is under-rewarded, job evaluation tends to be supportive of existing hierarchies.

Even if value is to be assessed under the categories of skill, effort, responsibility and working conditions (as in Ontario), this does not determine the ratings to be given to any particular job under each heading. Is value to be assessed in terms of what the market will pay? Any such measure will result merely in the entrenchment of women's underpayment. In terms of workers' marginal productivity? How is the marginal productivity of a nurse or a cleaner to be assessed? The Pay Equity Commission in Ontario advises that care must be taken, in determining value, not to unduly favour jobs dominated by employees of either sex. But what does 'unduly' mean? The Commission also advocates that value should be assessed in accordance with the 'relative importance [of jobs] to the organization',[61] or to the 'nature' and 'goals' of the organization.[62] Such an approach can favour female job classes where, as in *ONA* v *Women's College Hospital*,[63] the tribunal responsible for enforcing the Pay Equity Act found that the hospital's job evaluation system failed to reward aspects of nurses' jobs which were central to the hospital's own declared aims (or 'mission statements'). But employers are free to define the goals of their organizations in a manner inimical to the interests of women workers. This can be done not only by emphasizing production over clerical work in, for example, a factory situation, but also by laying stress on any factor indirectly disadvantaging women. The most obvious such factor is status itself: where 'responsibility' as defined by a job evaluation system depends on the position of the job within the organization, the tendency for women to be clustered at the bottom of the ladder will frequently result in low scores on this factor.

The Pay Equity Commission and, in the UK, the EOC suggest that care should be taken, in designing a job evaluation scheme, to ensure that the skills, etc., in men's and women's jobs are equally recognized. The EOC went further, in its publication *Job Evaluation Schemes Free of Sex Bias*, and stated: 'it is important to check the factor scores of the jobs performed predominantly by female employees and if there are a lot of low scores ... then the set of factors is discriminatory and should be changed.'[64] Michael Rubenstein declared the suggestion 'wrong under any conceivable standard of discrimination'. In one sense he is right: by determining in advance that men's and women's jobs should be valued equally (in terms of *results*, rather than in the sense that both types of jobs are valued with equal *respect*), the job valuer would be 'jumping the gun' in terms of the job evaluation procedure. But the EOC's suggestion could be read as pointing to the vacuity of approaching the issue of underpayment in terms of job 'value' at all. One proponent of pay equity made the following statement in evidence to the Pay Equity Hearings Tribunal:

> The goal of pay equity is to achieve non-discriminatory wage rates.
> The tool that has been used to achieve these goals is job
> evaluation ... To achieve this goal requires a recognition that
> systems of job evaluation have been socially constructed and that
> they must be *socially reconstructed* to achieve gender neutrality.
> Specifically, this goal requires the design or redesign, where
> appropriate, of systems of job evaluation to reflect and value
> positively the range of content found in *both* male-dominated and
> female-dominated jobs.[65]

Steinberg recognizes that the assessment of value will depend, in
essence, on the purpose in respect of which evaluation is being
undertaken. Where the proposed aim is the elimination of discrimination in pay it is not sufficient that predetermined value criteria are
applied in a gender-blind manner to jobs done by men and women. It
is necessary, rather, that the very criteria upon which value is
determined are themselves scrutinized for evidence of discrimination
– that their impact upon the evaluation of men's and women's jobs is
examined.

Traditional job evaluation relies upon the drawing-up of a list of
factors on the basis of which 'value' is assigned to jobs. The next step is
to examine either all or a selection of jobs in the light of these factors
and to assign each job a particular 'value' under each heading. Values
may be assigned either by way of points which are then added up to
find the total 'value' of each job or, more simply, on the basis of paired
comparisons whereby each job is slotted into its 'proper' place in the
hierarchy. Many job evaluation techniques then allow for a re-ordering
of the hierarchy on a 'felt-fair' basis, before wage rates are established
in line with the 'value' hierarchy.

The difficulty with this approach is that, as explained above, it does
little to challenge the basis on which particular factors are deemed as
'value-adding', or the weights that are assigned to particular jobs under
these headings. If, for example, an employer wishes to reward seniority
by paying increments dependent upon length of service, such a practice
can be incorporated in the job evaluation method. Equally, if an
employer wishes to reward financial responsibility over and above
responsibility for people, then nothing in job evaluation methodology
operates to prevent this practice. Both of these factors, however, would
operate to the disadvantage of women workers.

In order to eliminate discriminatory payment practices, employers
must be forced to re-think the concept of value. One possibility is
suggested by European Community case law. Cases decided by the ECJ
under Article 119 of the Treaty of Rome and the Equal Pay Directive

(which require equal pay for work of equal value) require that job-related factors are rewarded only where their reward impacts equally upon men and women, or where any disparate impact is nevertheless objectively justified.[66] Thus, to take the example of 'flexibility', this factor can only influence pay (if this has the effect of increasing men's pay over that of women) to the extent that the 'flexibility' in question is actually practically important to the performance of the particular job.[67] Equally, 'seniority' can only be rewarded (assuming this impacts unfavourably on women's relative rates of pay) if the time spent in the job actually renders the employee a more effective worker. [68] Further, the ECJ has ruled that it is for employers to make transparent the basis on which wages are paid if they are to avoid a finding of discrimination based on average pay differentials.[69]

The radical revision of pay structures requires the factors upon which pay depends to be made transparent, examined in terms of their impact on the average pay of men and women within the organization, and retained only where they can be justified. Only then can a genuinely non-discriminatory pay-setting mechanism be designed. The identification of wage-setting factors could be accomplished either by wage regression analysis (in which a computer program analyses the wages within an organization to determine what factors actually influence pay), or by requiring the employer to articulate the basis upon which relative wages are determined. However the current pay-setting factors are identified, the crucial step involves the analysis of the gender-related impact of these factors and the determination of their justifiability in the light of any disparate impact they have on women's wages.[70]

Pay structures could then be renegotiated expressly, with the aim of allowing male–female wage disparities only where the factors which create them have been passed as crucial to the performance of the jobs themselves. Nor need such a re-ordering depend upon the management-centred tool of job evaluation. Equally possible is a practice of equalizing base rates for male and female jobs at entry level and by ensuring that the pay structure of employees in female-dominated jobs mirrors that in male-dominated jobs (e.g. in the Northern Irish clothing industry, by setting women's entry rates to reflect their pre-factory skills and by rewarding increasing skill levels in female as well as male jobs).

But even these solutions fail to address one of the most significant factors associated with women's low pay. While 'pay equity' (in common with 'equal pay') challenges pay gaps across occupational barriers *within* workplaces, neither challenges pay disparities that arise *between* workplaces. The significance of these gaps should not be underestimated. In 1983 Millward and Daniels reported that:

The higher was the female proportion of the manual workforce the lower was the level of pay for semi-skilled and skilled workers. The trend was marked and consistent. *In cases where all manual workers were women, pay levels were only just over half of those in cases where hardly any or no manual workers were women.*[71] [Emphasis added.]

In 1995, Millward and Woodland confirmed that: 'Where the establishment's workforce is 60 per cent or more female, semi-skilled workers' pay is approximately 30 per cent lower than in an establishment with at least 80 per cent males.'[72] And in the same year, Millward's report for the EOC, *Targeting Potential Discrimination*, claimed that, where workplaces were at least 70 per cent female, they were almost three times as likely to employ low-paid workers as where they were predominantly male.[73]

Some mechanism is necessary whereby women's wages can be increased in line with the wages of those who work in male-dominated workplaces, as well as male-dominated occupations. In this, again, the role of trade unions is vital. The importance of trade union involvement has already been mentioned. But trade union involvement can go much further than is the case under Ontario's model. More useful than workplace bargaining over relative male and female wages is likely to be an approach that takes place on a sectoral level.[74] There is much cheering precedent in this regard from the Nordic countries, where strong emphasis on the role of collective bargaining in pay determination has been coupled with very high levels of female labour-force participation and comparatively small gender wage gaps.[75] In Australia too, where pay determination is centralized, women earned 84 per cent of men's *weekly* wages in 1993 (the figure for the UK was a mere 71 per cent).

Significant advances have been made in Australia despite levels of sex segregation comparable to those in the UK. But what is perhaps most impressive in the Australian experience is that such progress has been made in the absence of specific equal value legislation and without any real attempts being made to address the issue of 'value'. The 1972 decision of the national wage-setting body that required equal pay for work of equal value was explicit in holding that 'the value of the work refers to worth in terms of award wage or salary fixation, not value to the employer'. In other words, the 'value' to which pay had to be accorded equally was the value already established in existing job relativities. According to one commentator,

the improvements that occurred were based on conventional 'rule of thumb' views about the value of different sorts of work rather than on any systematic or analytical method of comparing male occupations with female occupations ... women's jobs were slotted into existing classifications without any real attempt to assess their value. Typing, for example, was simply placed at the bottom of the clerical range since it was assumed to be inferior to other, male-defined clerical tasks.[76]

The major strides towards equal pay that have taken place in Australia have been achieved even in the absence of any requirement that male and female jobs be compared in terms of skill, effort, responsibility, etc., and paid equally on the basis of these features. In other words, it appears that the strength of centralized pay determination, coupled with equal minimum wages for men and women, has been more effective than any attempt to compare male and female jobs and to determine their pay accordingly. The strides that have taken place in Australia appear now to be under threat in the move away from centralized pay determination, but the Australian experience points to the potential associated with centralized pay determination. If such centralized pay determination were coupled with an attempt to rationalize the pay differentials between male and female jobs (in terms of the work 'value', however determined, rather than in terms of *traditional* 'value' hierarchies), the potential would be enormous indeed.[77]

CONCLUSION

If pay discrimination is to be eliminated, it is necessary to extend the benefits of collective bargaining at the sectoral level, as well as establishing recognition procedures at the workplace level.[78] An explicit commitment must be made to tackle the gender pay gap at this level, and consideration must be given to the way in which the relative wages in particular jobs are established. Job evaluation methodology is probably at its weakest in this type of exercise: 'pay equity' advocates, in particular, emphasize that its potential lies in its ability to rank the particular jobs carried out in particular workplaces, rather than the relative worth of 'sewing machinists', 'dyers' and 'finishers' within the textile industry as a whole. But, on the other hand, the very strength of a centralized system of pay determination in this context would be to ensure that the jobs performed by women are not allowed, for that reason, to fall behind those of men within individual organizations or throughout industrial sectors more generally. The advantage of bringing some aspects of 'job evaluation' to bear on the ranking of jobs is that the methodology at least allows for the examination of what particular jobs (or job families) actually entail, rather than allowing ranking decisions to be made on traditional, sex-stereotypical and predominantly masculine assumptions about what secretaries, nurses and sewing machinists do, what skills these jobs require, what responsibilities they encompass and what working conditions they are performed in.

This issue of how, if at all, job evaluation should play a role in the renegotiation of pay structures, and of the relationship between workplace and sectoral bargaining as means of eliminating pay discrimination, are complex. Simpler, and of tremendous importance, is the matter of a national minimum wage. In 1991, Frank Wilkinson estimated that 20 per cent of female full-time and 50 per cent of female part-time workers (but only 7 per cent of full-time male workers) would benefit from a national minimum wage pitched at £3.40 per hour.[79] The most recently suggested figure is in the range of £4 an hour:[80] if this is applied to 1994 wage statistics, it is clear that the situation has not changed much in the intervening years. Taking full-time workers first, 24.4 per cent of manual and 4.1 per cent of non-manual women workers would see their wages rise by at least 50 pence per hour if the minimum wage was implemented at this level; 42.9 per cent of manual and 9.2 per cent of non-manual workers would receive some increase, as would 10 and 3.7 per cent respectively of male manual and non-manual workers. The improvements for part-time workers would be even more dramatic: in 1994, 25 per cent of all women who worked part-time received less than £3.50 per hour, and half of those who worked in manual jobs earned less than £3.63 per hour.

Although the implementation of a national minimum wage would not itself solve the gender pay gap, it would be a valuable first step. The higher the level at which such a wage is set, the greater would be its impact on the gender pay gap. For example, the Low Pay Unit classifies pay that is below two-thirds of the weekly male median as 'low'. This translates as roughly £5.40 per hour. Currently, while none of the nine major occupational groups has average male wages lower than this figure,[81] all but three of these groups (managerial and administrative, professional and associated professional and technical) pay part-time women less than £5.40 per hour and only those three, together with clerical and secretarial occupations, pay full-time women workers more than £5.40. Those occupations with average pay levels below £5.40 per hour employ 80 per cent of part-time and 44 per cent of full-time women workers.

There is little chance of a minimum wage being set at anywhere near the £5.40 level: the TUC appears content to settle for £4 or thereabouts;[82] the Labour Party is still resisting all calls to name a figure before the next election; and even the Low Pay Unit has declared itself willing to settle for around half the median (just over £4 per hour) for the moment.[83] While the election of a Labour government is almost certain to result in the implementation of a national minimum wage, it is vital that the potential benefits, in terms of the gender wage gap, are not frittered away – one way in which this might occur would be if the minimum was not applied to the million or so homeworkers in the UK.[84] In 1991, a national survey of homeworkers found that they earned, on average, £1.28 per hour for a 36-hour week.[85] This rate was 29 per cent of the average earned by full-time women employees in that year, and 23 per cent of the average hourly rate for full-time men. Women were working for as little as 20 pence per hour.[86]

Just as the national minimum wage must be *made* to work, so the pressure must be kept up for the reform of legislation addressed specifically at the equal pay issue. Prior to its defeat in 1992, the Labour Party promised to amend equal pay legislation so as to oblige employers to review pay structures, to make available both proportional and cross-establishment wage comparisons, to allow collective tribunal actions and to expand the EOC's investigative and enforcement powers. There has been scant mention of any of this in the years since: 'New Labour' seems as wary of committing to anything that might prove unpopular with employers as it is of appearing to favour trade unions. But if changes are to be made they must not consist of cosmetic tinkering with the existing legislation. Nor should momentum be wasted on a copy of Ontario's Pay Equity Act, with all its potential for avoidance. If 'New Labour' is committed to the elimination of discrimination in pay, it must be prepared to grasp the nettle and:

- implement at the national level a minimum wage which is adequate (both in terms of level and of coverage) to eliminate poverty pay;

- require the revision of pay structures in order to eliminate existing discrimination;

- ensure that this is done in such a way as to prevent employer manipulation (this requires trade union involvement at the workplace level);

- ensure that women who work in predominantly female workplaces are not denied the benefits of any legislation (this requires, in essence, the application of wages collectively agreed at a sectoral level with specific regard to the issue of sex discrimination).

NOTES

1. Luxembourg: Office for Official Publications of the European Communities, 1994, COM (94)6.

2. *Ibid.*, p. 5.

3. In both countries, collective bargaining affected the wages of fewer than 60 per cent of workers and minimum wage levels a further 6 and 12 per cent respectively. See S. Brazen and G. Benhayoun, Low pay and wage regulation in the European Community (1992) 30 *British Journal of Industrial Relations* 623, p. 629.

4. *Ibid.*, p. 625.

5. *Memorandum, op. cit.*

6. J. Rubery, Pay, gender and the social dimension to Europe (1992) 30 *British Journal of Industrial Relations* 605, p. 609.

7. Low Pay Network, *Priced into Poverty*, reported in the *Independent*, 30 August 1995. See also the *Scotsman*, 31 August 1995, on research published by the Scottish Low Pay Unit. The studies found that, in Great Britain and Scotland respectively, 37 and 47 per cent of employers were paying less than the (updated) Wage Council rates which previously applied. In the retail sector (throughout Great Britain), this figure was 60 per cent.

8. See J. Fletcher and S. Gill, Union density and women's relative wage gains. In N. Folbre *et al.* (eds), *Issues in Contemporary Economics Volume 4: Women's Work in the World Economy* (New York: New York University Press, 1992).

9. *Times, Independent*, 7 July 1995.

10. Equal Pay Act 1970, implemented in 1975.

11. Equal Pay (Amendment) Regulations 1983, SI no. 1794.

12. These figures, which are taken from the *New Earnings Surveys* of the relevant years, appear higher than the EC statistics as they exclude part-time workers who earned (in 1993) only 58.6 per cent of the full-time men's hourly rate. They also exclude the 25 per cent (2.6 million of 10.28 million) of women workers whose earnings fall below the PAYE threshold.

13. Article 119 of the Treaty of Rome requires member states to 'ensure and subsequently maintain the application of the principle that men and women should receive equal pay for equal work'. Article 1 of Council Directive 75/117 (the Equal Pay Directive) made it clear that 'equal work' covered not only like work, but also 'work to which equal value is attributed'.

14. *Memorandum, op. cit.*

15. See note 12. See also ILO Equal Remuneration Convention, no. 100 (1951).

16. S. Rhodes, *Incomparable Worth: Pay Equity Meets the Market* (1993), p. 14.

17. See generally G. Becker, Investment in human capital: a theoretical analysis (1962) 70(5)(II) *Journal of Political Economy* 9; S. Polachek, Sex differences in college majors (1978) 31 *Industrial Labour Relations Review* 498; S. Polachek, Occupational self-selection: a human capital approach to sex differences in occupational structure (1981) 63 *Review of Economic Statistics* 60; J. Mincer and S. Polachek, Women's earnings re-examined (1978) 13 *Journal of Human Resources* 118.

18. G. Becker, Human capital, effort, and the sexual division of labour (1985) 3(I)(2) *Journal of Political Economy* S33, p. S35.

19. See, for example, B. Bergmann, Occupational segregation: wages and profits when employers discriminate by race or sex (1974) 1 *Eastern Economic Journal* 103.

20. F. Wilkinson, *Why Britain Needs a Minimum Wage* (London: Institute for Public Policy Research, 1992), Table 1. Figures taken from the *New Earnings Survey* 1990.

21. D. Blanchflower and B. Corry, *Part-time Employment in Great Britain: an Analysis Using Establishment Data* (London: Department of Employment, 1987), Research Paper no. 57, pp. 58–9.

22. See, for example, D. Blanchflower and P. Elias, *The Occupations, Earnings and Work Histories of Young Adults – Who Gets the Good Jobs?* (Department of Employment, 1989) Research Paper no. 68; P. Dolton, G. Makepeace and G. Inchley, *The Early Careers of 1980 Graduates* (Department of Employment, 1990), Research Paper no. 78.

23. This is demonstrated for the USA by M. Marini, Sex differences in earnings in the US, (1989) 15 *Annual Review of Sociology* 343, p. 351. In the UK it is clear from the *New Earnings Survey* statistics, which list (Tables 10 and 11) wages for men and women workers according to age.

24. See M. Corcoran, G. Duncan and M. Ponza, Work experience, job segregation and wages. In B. Reskin (ed.), *Sex Segregation in the Workplace: Trends, Explanations, Remedies* (Washington, DC: National Academy Press, 1984), p. 15.

25. Marini, *op. cit.*

26. See, for example, R. Wood, M. Corcoran and P. Courant, Pay differences among the highly paid: the male and female earnings gap in lawyers' salaries (1993) 11 (3) *Journal of Labor Economics* 417.

27. J. Ermisch and R. Wright, Differential returns to human capital in full-time and part-time employment. In Folbre *et al., op. cit.*, p. 208.

28. S. McRae and W. Daniels, *Maternity Rights in Britain: First Findings* (London: Policy Studies Institute, 1991). Half of the total were already in paid employment, twice as many as a decade before. Mothers in the labour market, *Employment Gazette*, November 1994, p. 403, also reports that, whereas in 1984 only 37 per cent of women with children under five participated in the labour market, 52 per cent did so in the winter of 1993–4.

29. S. Horrell, J. Rubery and B. Burchell, Unequal jobs or unequal pay? (1990) 20 (3) *Industrial Relations Journal* 176. Redistribution of skill content would remove 26 per cent of the gap; paying equally for job content would remove 71 per cent.

30. E. McLaughlin and K. Ingram, *All Stitched Up: Sex Segregation in the Northern Ireland Clothing Industry* (Belfast: Northern Ireland Equal Opportunities Commission, 1990).

31. Wilkinson, *op. cit.*, pp. 7–8.

32. See D. Black, Discrimination in an equilibrium search model (1995) 13 (2) *Journal of Labor Economics* 309.

33. See generally M. Strober, Towards a general theory of occupational sex segregation: the case of public school teaching. In Reskin, *op. cit.*

34. Even in those organizations in which unions are recognized, as B. Casey, J. Lakey and M. White, *Pay Systems: a Look at Current Practice* (Employment Department, 1992) Research Series no. 5, p. 16 illustrates, collective bargaining is more likely to take place in respect of predominantly male occupational groups. See also N. Millward and S. Woodland, *Gender Segregation and Male/Female Wage Differences* (London: London School of Economics, 1995), Centre for Economic Performance, Discussion Paper no. 220, p. 18. A study of WIRS data suggested that 'collective bargaining only has a beneficial effect upon the pay of male-dominated groups of workers'.

35. See generally Blanchflower and Corry, *op. cit.*; Casey, Lakey and White, *ibid.*

36. R. Steinberg *et al., The New York Pay Equity Study: a Research Report* (New York: State University of New York at Albany, 1986).

37. Survey of 407 companies carried out by Sedgwick Noble Lowndes, reported in the *Equal Opportunities Review*, no. 57 (September/October 1994).

38. Great Britain: Central Statistical Office, *Social Focus on Women* (HMSO, 1995).

39. IHSM Consultants, *Creative Career Paths in the NHS. Report No. 3: Managers in 15 NHS Organizations* (NHS Women's Unit, 1994).

40. *Equal Opportunities Review*, no. 60, pp. 5–6. Report of CIMA publication, *The Balance on Trial: Women's Careers in Accountancy.*

41. [1991] IRLR 44.

42. A. Dale and J. Glover, *An Analysis of Women's Employment Patterns in the UK, France and the USA* (Department of Employment, 1990), Research Paper no. 75, pp. 15–16; M. David and C. Starzec, Women and part-time work: France and GB compared. In Folbre *et al., op. cit.*

43. A. Beller, Trends in occupational segregation by sex and race, 1960–1981. In Reskin, *op. cit.*, 11, p. 15.

44. In 1970, full-time women workers earned 63.1 per cent of men's hourly rate. By 1975, this proportion had increased to 75.5 per cent. Part of this improvement was most probably owing to incomes policies.

45. See, for example, the facts in *Hobson* v *Rowntree Mackintosh Ltd* (cited in J. Coussins, The Equality Report (London: NCCL, 1976)); *Graviner Ltd* v *Hughes* (1978) EAT 46/78 (cited in Incomes Data Services, *Equal Pay, Sex Discrimination, Maternity Rights* (London: IDS, 1979), p. 41); and *Electrolux Ltd* v *Hutchinson & others* [1976] IRLR 410.

46. The committee was dependent upon references by the Secretary of State or one of the parties to the disputed collective agreement, and made only about 50 awards in connection with equal pay between 1976 and 1979 (its period of activism).

47. *R* v *Central Arbitration Committee, ex parte Hy-Mac Ltd* [1979] IRLR 461. For a full discussion of this see P. Davies, The Central Arbitration Committee and equal pay (1980) *Current Legal Problems* 165.

48. The TUC retained the policy of bargaining in respect of a 'family wage' until 1960 and, even more recently, the 'family wage' argument has resurfaced in the government's purported justifications for the abolition of the minimum wage. See, for example, 215 HC Debs 139 (3 December 1992): '80 per cent of wages councils workers are in households with two or more wage earners. The biggest source of poverty is not low pay'. For critiques of this approach, see R. Dickens *et al.*, Wages Councils: was there a case for abolition? (1993) 31 *British Journal of Industrial Relations* 515.

49. F. Edgeworth, Equal pay to men and women for equal work (1922) 32 *Economic Journal* 431; Women's wages in relation to economic welfare (1923) 33 *Economic Journal* 487.

50. Industrial Relations Services, *Pay and Gender in Britain* (Equal Opportunities Commission, 1991).

51. IRS, *Pay and Gender in Britain: 2* (Equal Opportunities Commission, 1992), p. 40.

52. See S. Bevan and M. Thompson, *Merit Pay Performance Appraisal and Attitudes to Women's Work* (Brighton: University of Sussex, 1992), Institute of Manpower Studies Report no. 234.

53. While the Equal Pay Act allows comparisons between workers in the same 'establishment', and defines establishment somewhat more widely than 'workplace', see the decision of the Court of Appeal in *British Coal Corporation* v *Smith* [1994] IRLR 342 for an indication of how narrow the provision is.

54. See *Neath* v *Hugh Steeper Ltd* (Case C-152/91) [1994] IRLR 91. In addition, the ECJ has allowed levelling down in relation to pension ages (i.e. allowed women's pensionable ages to be raised, rather than insisting on men's being lowered) in *Coloroll Pension Trustees Ltd* v *Russell and others* (Case C-200/91) [1994] IRLR 586 and *Smith and others* v *Avdel Systems Ltd* (Case C-408/92) [1994] IRLR 602.

55. *Mothers in Employment – Government Reply to the First Report of the Committee in Session 1994–95* (HMSO, 1995), reported in *Equal Opportunities Review*, no. 62, p. 4.

56. *Ibid.*

57. Green Paper, *Resolving Employment Rights Disputes: Options for Reform* (HMSO, 1994), Cm 2707. The problem with the independent expert provision is that a tribunal, armed only with the reports of expert witnesses for the parties (in turn involving expense for the applicant) or with the members' knowledge of industrial relations, is potentially more likely to reach its decision on value on the basis of traditional views on the nature of 'men's' and 'women's' work than on hard data relating to what the applicant and her comparator actually do. The only equal value claim of which the author is aware that was decided without an independent expert's report was dismissed (*Cato* v *West Midlands Regional Health Authority*, see Equal value update, *Equal Opportunities Review*, no. 51, 11, pp. 28–9).

58. In 1992, the Labour Party promised to amend equal pay legislation so as to oblige employers to review pay structures, to make available both proportional and cross-establishment wage comparisons, to allow collective tribunal actions and to expand the EOC's investigative and enforcement powers.

59. *Ottawa Citizen*, 22 July 1995.

60. See A. McColgan, *Pay Equity: Just Wages for Women?* (London: Institute of Employment Rights, 1994).

61. Pay Equity Commission, *Pay Equity Implementation Series No. 9, Gender-Neutral Job Comparison* (Ontario: Pay Equity Commission, 1989), p. 9:4.

62. Pay Equity Commission, *Step by Step to Pay Equity: a Guide for Small Business*, Volume 1, *The Workbook* (Ontario: Pay Equity Commission), p. 28.

63. *Women's College Hospital No. 4*, (1992) 3 *Pay Equity Reports* 61.

64. Cited by M. Rubenstein, Discriminatory job evaluation and the law (1985–6) 7 *Comparative Labor Law* 172, p. 187.

65. R. Steinberg, *Report Concerning the Proposed Testimony of Dr Ronnie Steinberg, PhD. Concerning the Appropriateness of the Respondent Hospitals' Proposed Comparison System*, p. 11, cited by Pay Equity Hearings Tribunal in *Women's College Hospital No. 4, op. cit.*, p. 109.

66. *Bilka-Kaufhaus GmbH* v *Weber von Hartz* [1987] ICR 110.

67. *Handels-Og Kontorfunktionaererues Forbund i Danmark* v *Dansk Arbejdagiverforening (acting for Danfoss)* [1991] ICR 74.

68. *Nimz* v *Freie und Hausestadt Hamburg* [1991] IRLR 222.

69. *Danfoss, op. cit.*

70. McColgan, *op. cit.*

71. W. Daniel and N. Millward, *Workplace Industrial Relations in Britain: the ED/PSI/ERSC Survey* (1983).

72. Millward and Woodland, *op. cit.*, p. 16.

73. N. Millward, *Targeting Potential Discrimination* (EOC, 1994).

74. Equalizing within sectors is more important than equalizing between them – women are actually concentrated in higher-paying industrial sectors (banking, insurance, finance, public administration, health, education, etc.) than are men. While women are also concentrated in very low paying sectors such as hotels and restaurants, the implementation of an appropriately pitched national minimum wage would do much to benefit men and women in these sectors.

75. See G. Whitehouse, Legislation and labour market gender inequality: an analysis of OECD countries (1992) 6 *Work, Employment and Society* 65.

76. M. Thornton, Equal pay in Australia. In F. Eyraud *et al., Equal Pay Protection in Industrialised Market Economies* (ILO: Geneva, 1993), 23, pp. 27 and 33.

77. For the economic repercussions of Australia's system, see L. Hunter and S. Rimmer, An economic exploration of the UK and Australian experiences (1995) 2 *Gender, Work and Organization* 140. For a traditional economist's view of centralized pay determination, see Rhoads, *op. cit.*

78. The Labour Party committed itself, prior to election defeat in 1992, to introducing a right to recognition: *Looking to the Future* (London: Labour Party, 1990). See K.D. Ewing, Trade union recognition – a framework for discussion (1990) 19 *Industrial Law Journal* 209. Trade union representation at the workplace is still very important from the point of view, *inter alia*, of enforcement.

79. *Op. cit.*, p. 6.

80. *Times*, 2 September 1995. This is reported as having been adopted by the TGWU and the GMB.

81. The major occupational categories are managerial and administrative, professional, associated professional and technical, clerical and secretarial, personal and protective services, sales, craft and related, plant and machine operatives, and other occupations.

82. *Ibid.* The £4.15 figure has also been widely mentioned: *Herald* (Glasgow), *Daily Mail, Scotsman*, 24 August 1995.

83. *Times*, 5 January 1995.

84. U. Huws, *Home Truths: Key Results from a National Survey of Homeworkers* (National Group on Homeworking, 1991), report no. 2, p. 2.

85. *Ibid.*, p. 15.

86. *Ibid.*, p. 20.

14

Remedying Dismissal Law
Michael Ford and Steve Gibbons

This chapter discusses proposals to improve the remedies for employees who are dismissed or threatened with dismissal. It is increasingly clear that neither contract law nor its statutory successor, the unfair dismissal legislation, has been very effective in deterring employers from dismissing or in returning dismissed workers to their jobs.

We consider, first, the existing, weak protections for employees dismissed in breach of contract[1] before going on, second, to consider the current and potential scope of statutory remedies. As far as the contractual position is concerned, even if we accept the justifications that underpin the law it is not clear why employees should have such short notice periods as they in fact do, nor why an employer who dismisses in breach of contract should be entitled to limit damages by reference to the notice period. But probably of more importance is reform of the statutory remedies. The chapter considers the reasons why tribunals so rarely grant the remedy of reinstatement or re-engagement. Reforms are suggested that might make return to work the primary remedy rather than an exceptional order.

EXISTING CONTRACTUAL REMEDIES

The law regarding master and servant is not in doubt. There cannot be specific performance of a contract of service, and the master can terminate the contract with his servant at any time and for any reason or for none. But if he does so in a manner not warranted by the contract he must pay damages for breach of contract.[2]

Some fuss has been made, mostly by lawyers, of improvements in the contractual rights and remedies of employees.[3] These developments, it applicants before an industrial tribunal are re-employed after the conclusion of their legal action for unfair dismissal.

As is to be expected, however, merely looking at the results of cases determined by tribunals does not give a wholly satisfactory answer to the question of how many unfairly dismissed employees actually end up with their job back. Tremlett and Banerji also considered a number of scenarios other than the simple consideration of tribunal awards and orders. It is of particular interest to consider their analysis of the results of conciliation.[33] The data provided to the survey by employers who had made an offer during the conciliation stage show that 9 per cent of these were offers either to give the applicant his or her old job back or to re-employ the worker in a different job in the organization. In data supplied by applicants, 14 per cent of offers were for re-engagement or reinstatement. These figures may not, however, be totally representative, as ACAS reports that in 1994, of 19,111 cases that were settled, settlements were reached on the basis of re-employment in 309 cases, which amounts to a figure of only 1.6 per cent.[34]

Why is there such a discrepancy between the voluntary offers of employers at the conciliation stage and the awards actually made by industrial tribunals? The answer may simply lie in the unacceptable length of time it takes to complete a tribunal case and the hardening of attitudes that occurs during the course of this procedure. The simplest way to establish the right of workers to be re-employed following an unfair dismissal may therefore lie not in legal change, but in structural changes to the system of adjudication that speed up the procedure and, perhaps, rely more heavily on arbitration.

International Comparisons

It is well beyond the scope of this chapter to carry out an exhaustive analysis of the law and practice relating to re-employment following unjustified dismissals in other member states of the European Union. However, it is clear that there is far from uniformity in the provisions which apply in this regard.[35] While some states' legal systems do not appear to envisage re-employment at all, others give re-employment a high priority. In Italy, for example, the legal provisions effectively mean that the remedy available to an employee depends on the size of the employer. In the case of an employer who employs more than 60 workers, when an employee is found to have been unfairly dismissed the magistrate (*pretore*) must order reinstatement of the employee and payment of damages equal to a minimum of five months' pay, unless the employee refuses reinstatement and requests damages (which must be equal to 15 months' pay) instead. Where reinstatement is ordered, employers who refuse to comply can be required to continue to pay the employee at the full rate until they do comply. Where an employer who employs fewer than 60 workers in total is found to have unfairly dismissed an employee, the employer must either reinstate the employee within three days or pay damages.

Before the Italian reinstatement remedy was strengthened in 1990,[36] Roccella found that the majority of employers complied with the reinstatement requirements.[37] Of some 300 reinstatement orders it was found that reinstatement had actually been implemented in 58 per cent of all cases. The percentage was impressive even in small enterprises, with 16 to 50 employees, where 43 per cent of employees were actually reinstated. In general, however, Roccella found that older workers were more likely to be re-employed than younger workers and men more likely than women, and that larger firms were more likely to comply with reinstatement orders than smaller firms. Hepple suggests that this overall high success rate 'may be due in part to the absence of virtually any other remedy in Italy and the active role of *pretore* and the unions'.[38] Wedderburn notes that reforms carried out to the Italian system 'provided procedures in a one-judge labour court which are informal and speedy (hearings take place inside the workplace itself) and – a major change in this jurisdiction – are mainly oral, in addition to a variety of conciliation methods including tripartite or "joint" commissions of employers and unions'.[39]

In reviewing the question of reinstatement from a comparative international perspective, Hepple states that the 'continuation of the employment relationship' is the principal remedy for unjustified dismissal in an increasing number of countries. He classifies the means by which this process is carried out under three heads:

1   An order annulling the dismissal.
2   An order for reinstatement in the same job as if the worker had not been dismissed.
3   An order for re-engagement in a different job, or with an associated employer, on such terms as the competent body directs.

The second and third categories are in effect found in UK labour law, so it is the first that is of particular interest. In commenting on the first category, Hepple states that it is

> facilitated by legal provisions which suspend the effects of dismissal until the competent body has reached a decision. The suspension may be automatic (e.g. for dismissals with advance

notice in Germany, Norway and Sweden) or by order of the court or tribunal (as in several Arab countries). This approach has the advantage of overcoming the psychological barrier which may be caused by the rupture of the relationship by dismissal and encourag[ing] the worker to await the decision of the court or tribunal instead of seeking alternative employment. However, it can only work in practice if cases are quickly determined. One may compare in this respect, the relative success of the remedy in Sweden where cases are dealt with in about 6 months, with the situation in Germany where it is estimated that only about 5% of employees whose cases go to the Labour Court are reinstated, partly because cases take 3 or 4 years to reach a decision and so workers do not await the outcome.[40]

With regard to international standards on the question of reinstatement following unfair dismissal, the most important is probably the ILO Termination of Employment Convention, 1982.[41] Article 10 of the Convention provides that if a dismissal is found to be unjustified by the relevant adjudicatory body, 'if they are not empowered or do not find it practicable, in accordance with national law and practice, to declare the termination invalid and/or order or propose reinstatement of the worker, they shall be empowered to order payment of adequate compensation or such other relief as may be deemed appropriate'. Thus, the Convention, while envisaging the possibility of reinstatement or the nullifying of dismissals, does not require it, provided that compensation or other remedies are available in the alternative.

The UK Law Relating to Reinstatement and Re-engagement

At first view, the law relating to reinstatement and re-engagement in the UK is such that one would expect the figures for orders made by tribunals to be a much higher percentage than actually prevails. Essentially, reinstatement and re-engagement are the 'primary remedy' for an unfairly dismissed employee. The first relevant statutory provisions are those that state that an industrial tribunal which finds that an employee has been unfairly dismissed 'shall explain to the complainant what orders for reinstatement or re-engagement may be made ... and in what circumstances they may be made, and shall ask him whether he wishes the tribunal to make such an order'.[42]

In *Pirelli General Cable Works Ltd* v *Murray*,[43] the EAT stressed that these requirements are mandatory and held that a failure of a tribunal to carry out the proscribed statutory explanation amounted to an error of law. This strict approach to the provisions has subsequently been relaxed. In *Cowley* v *Manson Timber Ltd*,[44] the Court of Appeal rejected an argument that a tribunal's failure to explain re-engagement and reinstatement rendered the compensation award it made a nullity, stating instead that the failure may make the proceedings voidable where it can be shown that the failure has caused the applicant some degree of injustice. However, Neill LJ went on to consider the fact that orders for re-engagement or reinstatement were only made in around 1 per cent of cases, and that the questions of reinstatement or re-engagement were not being addressed by tribunals as they should be. He expressed the view that this was 'a matter of regret and a matter which ought to be remedied. Indeed ... the Employment Appeal Tribunal ought in appropriate cases to be very ready to send a case back for further hearing on remedies.' It is too early to judge whether Neill LJ's statement will have any effect on the approach of the courts and tribunals.

When an applicant does ask a tribunal to make an order for reinstatement or re-engagement, the key issue to be determined is whether compliance with the order is practicable. This question arises at two stages: first, the tribunal must consider the question at the time it determines whether to make the order; second, it must be considered again should the employer fail to comply with the order. Where an employer resolutely refuses to re-engage, a tribunal is faced with a difficult situation. On the one hand, reinstatement or re-engagement is supposed to be the primary remedy open to the tribunal. On the other, how can it be practicable to make such an order when the employer is standing firm and saying 'no way will I have this employee back'?

A perfect example of the 'difficult case' lies in the litigation arising out of the Port of London Authority's (PLA's) dismissal of 18 shop stewards at Tilbury docks following the abolition of the National Dock Labour Scheme in 1989. The tribunal found that all of their dismissals were unfair on the grounds of trade union membership and ordered that 12 of the applicants should be re-engaged. At a second hearing to consider the PLA's failure to comply with the re-engagement order, the tribunal decided that the authority had not demonstrated that it was not reasonably practicable to re-engage the 12. The tribunal's decision was overturned by the EAT,[45] and the EAT's decision on this question was subsequently upheld by the Court of Appeal.[46] The court stated that the assessment of the practicability issue at the first hearing was a provisional one that did not create any estoppel with regard to the second hearing. Further, authority makes it clear that it is not necessary for the tribunal to be convinced of practicability at the first stage, but merely to have regard to practicability as an issue.[47]

In setting out the correct approach for tribunals to take when determining whether re-employment is practicable at the second hearing, Neill LJ in the PLA case stated that:

> the test is practicability not possibility. The tribunal, though it should carefully scrutinise the reasons advanced by an employer, should give due weight to the commercial judgment of the management unless, of course, the witnesses are disbelieved. The standard must not be set too high. The employer cannot be expected to explore every possible avenue which ingenuity might suggest. The employer does not have to show that reinstatement or re-engagement was impossible. It is a matter of what is practicable in the circumstances of the employer's business at the relevant time.

The result of the guidance from the Court of Appeal is that an employee's right to have his or her job back in accordance with a tribunal order for reinstatement can effectively be defeated at a second hearing by reasons put forward by the employer based on business convenience.

Why Doesn't the Reinstatement Remedy Appear to Work?

It must therefore be asked why more employees do not get re-employed when they have been unfairly dismissed. First, it should be acknowledged that often employees simply will not want to go back to work for employers who have treated them badly. As one Mexican commentator has put it, 'One thing is certain: unpleasant though it is for the employers to reinstate someone they – advisedly or ill-advisedly – dismissed, it is even more unpleasant for workers to return to a place where they are clearly not wanted.'[48] It is clearly wrong, however, to dismiss the low percentage of employees who are re-employed as a product of an allegedly high percentage of employees who do not want to be re-employed. Any suggestion that, in the context of apparently institutionalized high levels of unemployment, the vast majority (99.5 per cent) of employees do not want their jobs back simply cannot be empirically sustainable.

There has been some discussion over the role of ACAS conciliation officers in the question of re-employment. Conciliation officers are under a statutory duty to promote a settlement of a dispute, and 'in particular seek to promote the reinstatement or re-engagement of the complainant by the employer, or by a successor of the employer, or by an associated employer'. [49] ACAS stressed in its 1994 annual report that the circumstances of many cases often cause the parties to feel that such a remedy is inappropriate. In ACAS's view, however,

> where parties are willing to settle their dispute in this way there can be mutual benefits. The employee does not have to face the possibility of unemployment and retains, with the job, continuity of employment, and occupational benefits and statutory employment protection rights. To the employer, re-employment may provide a more cost-effective remedy than a tribunal hearing and an adverse award with attendant publicity. In addition, recruitment and training costs can be saved. [50]

ACAS goes on to stress that 're-employment is more likely to be a possibility if talks can commence with the parties soon after the dismissal has occurred', giving the example of a case where two employees of a subcontractor were summarily dismissed for allegedly breaching company rules while on a customer's site. Following immediate ACAS conciliation, the matter was resolved before claims were submitted to an industrial tribunal and the employees were reinstated.

There have been a number of criticisms of ACAS and the tribunal system in the context of the low level of re-employment following unfair dismissal claims. The most comprehensive analysis of the issue was that carried out in the 1980s by Dickens *et al.*,[51] who demonstrated that there did appear to be a higher level of desire among applicants for reinstatement (24 per cent requested reinstatement as a remedy on their IT1 form) than was borne out by the percentage of applicants who were actually reinstated. They also demonstrated that the proportion of conciliated settlements that involve reinstatement has declined – and there has been a further decline since the survey that formed the basis of the study conducted by Dickens *et al.* was carried out. Dickens *et al.* suggest that the priority given by conciliation officers to reinstatement may be lower than it should be. The study also revealed that over a quarter of employers who made a settlement did so because they admitted the dismissal was unfair, thought their case was weak or admitted that they had not followed the correct procedure. Dickens *et al.* thus suggest that there are strong arguments, on the basis of such statistics, that there should be more orders of reinstatement or re-engagement.

A number of the common rejoinders to charges such as those levelled by Dickens *et al.* appear insufficient.[52] The question is quite simple: if the law provides for reinstatement, why is the level of reinstatement and re-engagement so pitifully low unless the tribunals and others in the system are failing to take it seriously enough, or the law is not strong enough, or a combination of the two? It is not enough to point to (perhaps the majority of) cases that are pursued to a tribunal determination and state that it is difficult practically to bring about re-employment, given the parties' attitudes, the likely breakdown in trust and confidence, etc. The question that needs to be addressed is why the level of re-employment is so low, on the assumption that a sizeable minority of unfairly dismissed employees would like their jobs back.

FRAMEWORK FOR DISCUSSION

Practice and Institutions

The key issue in relation to bringing about re-employment, it is suggested, is one of speed and time. The quicker an application comes before the tribunal or other adjudicatory body, the easier it will be for an employee to be re-employed. The reasons for this almost go without saying, but include the following: the quicker the application is determined the less likely it is that the employee will be looking for alternative work;[53] the less the employee's skills and job familiarity will have diminished; and the less likely it is that the employer will have replaced the dismissed employee.

Statistically, it would appear to be the case from both national and international figures that an employee is more likely to be back at work in his or her old job following an unfair dismissal where there has been a voluntary agreement for re-employment or where the case has been determined through a fast, relatively informal process, than when he or she has to wait a number of years to have the case determined in a formalistic court or tribunal. In this light it would appear to be desirable fundamentally to reassess the means by which employment disputes are resolved.

The fact that the government is currently looking at the nature of the tribunal system is therefore to be welcomed, although not all of the proposals contained in the Green Paper on industrial tribunals are appropriate, and much of the Green Paper appears to be motivated by the desire to reduce the cost of the tribunal system to the tax-payer rather than by a commitment to achieving industrial justice.[54] One key change that could be brought about with regard to the mechanism of dispute resolution is the introduction of arbitration as an alternative to cases being determined by industrial tribunals.[55] Where cases are still heard by tribunals it is essential that the procedure should be carried out more quickly.

There are also strong arguments for a form of labour inspectorate or other such body or official which would have authority to determine some disputes in a speedy manner. For example, where an employee claims that he or she has been dismissed without the appropriate procedure being carried out, the labour inspectorate or an official of a tribunal or labour court could determine cases that are lodged quickly. Should it be clear that the procedure has not been complied with, the official could so declare, with the effect that the dismissal is void. The practical consequence of this would be that the employer would simply have to continue to pay the employee until the correct procedure had been carried out.

Law

One avenue of reform that could change the way in which reinstatement operates would be to reconsider the legal result that stems from a finding of unfair dismissal. As was pointed out above, an international comparison of the remedies available to employees who have been found to have been unfairly dismissed demonstrates a third category of remedy that is not found in UK law – namely, that the effect of a finding of unfair dismissal is to invalidate or nullify the dismissal. If such a concept were introduced in UK law, it would mean that, where a tribunal decided that an employee had been unfairly dismissed, it would simply declare that the employer's dismissal had not effectively terminated the contract of employment and the contract was still in existence. This would have the effect that the employee was contractually entitled to pay from the date the employer sought to terminate the worker's employment until such future time as the employment was lawfully terminated. The introduction of the concept of a void dismissal would have major consequences for the whole of employment law.

If such a concept were to be introduced, an employer who unfairly dismissed an employee would be faced with the prospect of having an industrial tribunal declaring that the dismissal was ineffective and having to treat the employee as if he or she had never been dismissed. In general terms it can be argued that the void dismissal is no different from reinstatement, but this is not the case. To provide for an automatic finding that a dismissal is void would deny a tribunal discretion on the question of whether to grant reinstatement. The 'removal' of the dismissal and the requirement upon the employer to continue to honour contractual obligations (including, of course, the obligation to pay wages) would be an automatic consequence of an unfair dismissal finding.

As Hepple has pointed out,[56] one means by which the concept of a void dismissal is facilitated is by providing that, where an employee claims that his or her dismissal is unfair, the effect of that dismissal is essentially suspended until the relevant adjudicatory body has determined its legality. It is perhaps instructive in this context to consider the procedures that are already available in interim relief cases. In trade union dismissal cases an employee who wishes to avail himself or herself of the interim relief provisions must lodge an IT1 within seven days of dismissal. This must be accompanied by a certificate from an authorized union official, stating that there appear to be grounds to suggest that the employee's dismissal is on the grounds of trade union activity or membership. The tribunal then holds a hearing, as soon as is practicable, to determine whether it is likely that the employee's claim will succeed at a full hearing on the merits.[57] If it is so decided, the tribunal then asks the employer whether it is prepared to re-employ the applicant and, if it is, makes the appropriate order. If it is not prepared to re-employ, the tribunal must make an order for the continuation of the employee's contract of employment until the matter is determined or settled.

It is probably impracticable, for a number of reasons, to implement the concept of a void dismissal – or any form of 'holding order' akin to interim relief or an injunction – in all dismissal cases. However, there are arguments that it should be available in certain circumstances. It is suggested that, in order to be able to claim that a dismissal is void, certain criteria must be satisfied by applicants. These should bear in mind the fact that it is only where the procedure moves reasonably quickly that employees can be placed back into their jobs without major problems. In determination of the model to be proposed in this context a number of distinctions could be drawn. First, breaches of procedure could be treated in a different manner from other issues. Second, what may be generally termed 'civil liberties' dismissals – namely, dismissals that are based on, among other things, sex or race discrimination, trade union activities or assertion of a statutory right – could be treated slightly differently from 'industrial' dismissals, such as redundancy selection cases, sickness, conduct, etc.

Under such a scheme – which we shall call the 'fast track' claim – an employee could be required to lodge an application with the tribunal or adjudicatory body within a specified period of time in order to be availed of the right to argue that the dismissal was void. The relevant time period could be as short as a week or as long as a month – no firm suggestion as to the appropriate period is made here. Once it is lodged, the claim could be assessed quickly by a member of the tribunal staff, some other form of labour official or the tribunal itself, who could clarify the facts and give a preliminary view on the strength of the employee's case. The case could then proceed either by way of a continuation of contract order through to a full hearing, at which the tribunal could declare the dismissal void if the case was made out on the merits, or by way of the tribunal or official declaring in certain circumstances that the dismissal was void at an early stage in the procedure.

To take an example, which was explained above, in cases where it is alleged that an employee has been dismissed without the proper procedure being carried out, arguably the best way to deal with the matter is for an official or tribunal to determine whether the procedure has been carried out and, if it has not, to declare the dismissal void. The reason why this could work in such circumstances is mainly that quite a straightforward question is being raised: has the procedure that an employee is entitled to been carried out or has it not? This could be easily determined and all that would be required of an employer is to carry on paying the employees and to carry out the correct procedure. The introduction of the possibility of dismissals being declared void where certain procedural safeguards are not complied with is envisaged by the TUC in the context of a failure to allow an employee to be represented by a union official.[58]

While procedural shortcomings may be relatively easily dealt with by making any offending dismissals void, the situation is slightly more complicated where the dismissal is alleged to be substantively unfair. One means of distinguishing cases would be to say that only certain types of claim could be automatically void. They could be restricted to cases that fell into what are automatically unfair dismissals under the EP(C)A – which include trade union activities and membership cases, pregnancy dismissals, health and safety dismissals, dismissals for asserting a statutory right and dismissals in connection with a transfer – and discriminatory dismissals.

The logic behind such a proposal is that, in these cases, the legal argument being put forward is that the reason behind the dismissal itself makes the dismissal unfair or unlawful, compared with other unfair dismissal cases where it is a matter of judging whether the employer's decision to dismiss on the basis of the stated reason is within the band of reasonable responses. On this argument, the dismissal should have no validity in those cases where an employer could never lawfully dismiss for the reason it did, in contrast with other cases where the employer could potentially dismiss for the chosen reason.

One obvious problem of introducing a procedure whereby an employee has to make an application quickly to a tribunal in order to gain a particular remedy is that it disadvantages certain categories of worker. Those particularly disadvantaged in this context are workers without ready access to legal or trade union advice and assistance, and employees who are purporting to remedy the matter through in-house appeals procedures. With regard to the former, such worries may to a degree be addressed by making it a statutory obligation on employers to issue all employees who are dismissed with a (perhaps government-prepared) leaflet that explains the employee's rights on dismissal, sets out the basic procedural requirements for lodging a claim, gives details of where help can be obtained and provides the address of the local tribunal office. It could be provided that the time for lodging the initial 'fast track' claim did not run until the employer had complied with these formalities, rather than from the date of dismissal. Similarly, in respect of the employee who is pursuing his or her grievances in-house, it could be provided that the time for lodging a 'fast track' claim did not begin to run until internal procedures were completed.

In some cases, even where a continuation of contract order was made and the dismissal declared void by a tribunal, an employer might still refuse to allow the employee to recommence his or her work. It is suggested that in such cases, as in trade union dismissals at present, the employer should incur substantial financial penalties. It should not, however, be open to the employer to argue that re-engagement was not practicable – the dismissal would simply be declared void and the employee's employment deemed to have continued. The pressure would be essentially on an employer either to re-employ or to pay such a sum in compensation that the employee was prepared to accept that his or her employment had come to an end and settle the case accordingly.

What is set out above is merely a brief sketch of the kinds of questions that would need to be addressed in order to reinvigorate what has been termed the 'lost remedy' of re-employment. As has been mentioned on a number of occasions, the legal mechanisms available should not be considered in isolation from other institutional and industrial matters. A recent case involving the dismissal of two guards on London Underground's Central Line on the basis of their trade union activities only serves to illustrate this point. Interim relief was obtained for both men and they were re-employed within weeks following voluntary arbitration. However, there was a further factor in this case, the effect of which should not be underestimated. The workers on the Central Line had voted for and commenced a campaign of industrial action to pressurize management to reinstate the two men.

NOTES

1. We do not consider the position of office holders who may have the benefit of judicial review protections. That category is, in any event, increasingly marginal. On this, see H. Carty, Public sector workers and Judicial Review (1991) 54 *Modern Law Review* 129.

2. *Per* Lord Reid in *Ridge* v *Baldwin* (1964) AC 40, p. 65.

3. See, for example, H. Carty, *Dismissed Employees: the Search for a More Effective Range of Remedies* (1989) 52 MLR 449; A. McColgan, Remedies for breach of employment contracts (1992) 21 *Industrial Law Journal* 58.

4. See, for example, *Imperial Group Pension Trust* v *Imperial Tobacco Ltd* [1991] IRLR 66.

5. See *Scally* v *Southern Health Board* [1992] AC 294.

6. See, for example, *Powell* v *London Borough of Brent* [1987] IRLR 466; *Robb* v *London Borough of Hammersmith* [1991] IRLR 72; *Jones* v *Gwent CC* [1992] IRLR 521; *Newns* v *British Airways* [1992] IRLR 575.

7. We are not aware of empirical evidence on the number of, say, contractual injunction cases brought each year. We would imagine it is very low.

8. Cf. *Jones* v *Lee* [1980] ICR 310, (CA); *Jones* v *Gwent CC, op. cit.*

9. See *Lavarack* v *Woods* [1967] 2 QB 278. This principle was recently reaffirmed in *Boyo* v *Lambeth LBC* [1994] ICR 727, (CA): although a repudiatory breach of contract did not of itself terminate a contract of employment, liability was restricted to the period during which the employer could lawfully have terminated the contract. A court may, exceptionally, add on the time it would have taken to go through a disciplinary procedure in the context of disciplinary dismissals, as was done in *Gunton* v *Richmond London Borough Council* [1980] ICR 755, (CA).

10. See s. 49 Employment Protection (Consolidation) Act 1978.

11. See *Lavarack, op. cit.,* per Diplock LJ at 292. Contrast the position in tort.

12. See *Addis* v *Gramophone Co. Ltd* [1909] AC 483.

13. See *Malik* v *BCCI* [1995] IRLR 375, (CA).

14. See, for example, S. Deakin and F. Wilkinson, Rights v efficiency? The economic case for transnational labour standards (1994) 23 *Industrial Law Journal* 1.

15. Given that the constraints on corporate management are often minimal – the product market, the market in corporate control and shareholder power may not be real constraints – the space for such irrationality is obvious. See generally J. Parkinson, *Corporate Power and Responsibility* (1993).

16. It is odd how much these two models of management continue to exist together. Managers are supposed either to act from hunch, charismatically, or attempt carefully to manipulate the environment around them, purposive-rationally. For criticisms of the second, see A. Macintyre, *After Virtue* (1985), Chapter 6: comparing management 'success' to priests who happen to pray just before rain falls, he writes that 'the levers of power – one of managerial expertise's own key metaphors – produce effects unsystematically and too often only coincidentally related to the effects of which their users boast'.

17. Of course, some contend that any kind of rationality is contingent and therefore should be rejected. Ignoring the philosophical difficulties in sustaining that position, it may well be that there is a greater empirical consensus on standards of procedural fairness.

18. Cf. *McClory* v *Post Office* [1993] IRLR 159.

19. See P.S. Atiyah, *The Liberal Theory of Contract* and *Essays on Contract* (1988).

20. Why else were minimum periods of notice introduced? A rational employer might otherwise introduce a notice period of five minutes.

21. See C. Offe, *Disorganised Capitalism* (1985), Chapter 1.

22. At present, the courts imply a reasonable notice period, which merely reflects the existing market position of employees. Giving reasonableness, some cutting force would base this period on the reasonable needs of the employee.

23. See *Gunton, op. cit.* This would apply just as much if the employer dismissed ostensibly on notice when the real reason was suspected misconduct.

24. In the USA, the courts have implied terms that employees cannot be dismissed for arbitrary reasons: see G. Pitt, Dismissal at common law: the relevance in Britain of American developments (1989) 52 *Modern Law Review* 22. It should not be difficult to imply similar terms in English law, even on the ostensibly strict test of necessity.

25. See note 8 above. The Court of Appeal in *Boyo* was reluctant to follow *Gunton* on this point: see Ralph Gibson LJ at pp. 745-5 and Staunton LJ at p. 748.

26. *Op. cit.*

27. Alternatively, it may be viewed as unfair to permit a party that has breached the agreement to limit its liability by reference to another term of that contract. The courts have, for example, debarred parties in breach of contract from relying on restrictive covenants.

28. Consider *Blackpool and Flyde Aero Club* v *Blackpool BC* [1990] 3 All ER 25.

29. See also the contract case of *Chaplin* v *Hicks* [1911] 2 KB 786. Alternatively, and more radically, the very decision could be treated as being void.

30. *Per* Kilner Brown J in *Merridan Ltd* v *Gomersall & another* [1977] ICR 597, p. 603.

31. *Employment Gazette*, October 1994.

32. Tremlett and Banerji, *The 1992 Survey of Industrial Tribunal Applications* (London: Employment Department, 1994), Employment Department Research Series no. 22.

33. *Ibid.*, Chapter 5.

34. ACAS, *Annual Report 1994.*

35. For a brief overview, see C. Barnard, J. Clark and R. Lewis, *The Exercise of Individual Employment Rights in the Member States of the European Community* (London: Employment Department, 1995), Employment Department Research Series No. 49.

36. Article 1, Law 108 of 11 May 1990.

37. M. Roccella, The reinstatement of dismissed employees in Italy: an empirical analysis (1989) 10 *Comparative Labor Law Journal* 166.

38. B. Hepple, Flexibility and security of employment. In R. Blanpain and C. Engels (eds), *Comparative Labour Law and Industrial Relations in Industrialized Market Economies* (Dordrecht: Kluwer, 1993).

39. Lord Wedderburn, The Social Charter in Britain: labour law and labour courts? In Wedderburn, *Employment Rights in Britain and Europe, Selected Papers in Labour Law* (1991).

40. Hepple, *op. cit.*, pp. 278-9.

41. Convention no. 158, adopted on 2 June 1982, coming into force on 23 November 1985.

42. S. 68(1) EP(C)A 1978.

43. [1979] IRLR 190.

44. [1995] IRLR 153.

45. *Port of London Authority* v *Payne* [1993] ICR 30

46. [1994] ICR 555.

47. See *Timex Corporation* v *Thomson* [1991] IRLR 522.

48. N. De Buen Lazano, La extinción de la relación de trabajo en México. In *La Extinción de la Relación Laboral: Perspectiva Iberoamericana* (Lima: AELE Editorial, 1987).

49. S. 134(2)(a) EP(C)A 1978.

50. ACAS *Annual Report 1994*, p. 52.

51. L. Dickens *et al.*, *Dismissed* (1985).

52. See, for example, P. Lowry, *Employment Disputes and the Third Party* (1990).

53. It should be noted that changes to social security law, particularly the introduction of the Job Seekers' Allowance, may have a severely detrimental effect on the employee who genuinely wants his or her job back by forcing the employee to look for and obtain alternative work at an early stage following his or her dismissal.

54. The Green Paper, *Resolving Employment Rights Disputes - Options for Reform* (HMSO, 1994) Cm 2707, was published by the government in December 1994. At the time of writing, final proposals arising from it had not been made public.

55. For a discussion on the case in favour of arbitration, see J. Clark and R. Lewis, *Employment*

Rights, Industrial Tribunals and Arbitration; the Case for Alternative Dispute Resolution (London: Institute of Employment Rights, 1994).

56. *Op. cit.*

57. This has been interpreted as meaning that the employee has a 'pretty good chance of success', *per* Slynn J in *Taplin* v *C. Shippam Ltd* [1978] ICR 1068.

58. See *Your Voice at Work, TUC Proposals for Rights to Representation at Work* (London: Trades Union Congress, 1995).

Index